Perspectives on the Mistreatment of American Educators

Throwing Water on a Drowning Man

Norman Dale Norris

A SCARECROWEDUCATION BOOK

The Scarecrow Press, Inc.
Lanham, Maryland, and London
2002

A SCARECROWEDUCATION BOOK

Published in the United States of America
by Scarecrow Press, Inc.
A Member of the Rowman & Littlefield Publishing Group
4720 Boston Way, Lanham, Maryland 20706
www.scarecroweducation.com

4 Pleydell Gardens, Folkestone
Kent CT20 2DN, England

British Library Cataloguing in Publication Information Available

Library of Congress Cataloging-in-Publication Data Available

ISBN 0-8108-4216-5

∞ ™ The paper used in this publication meets the minimum requirements of American National Standard for Information Sciences—Permanence of Paper for Printed Library Materials, ANSI/NISO Z39.48–1992.
Manufactured in the United States of America.

To my daughter, Sarah

Contents

Foreword

There is a wonderful story in this passionate and eloquent book that illustrates the thoughtful and independent-minded character of its author. A statewide checklist had been instituted for observing and evaluating teachers. The author, as a young and vulnerable teacher, was being observed by an outside observer. The young teacher knew well that both the checklist and the observer were unreliable, so much to the annoyance of the observer, he decided to tape-record the lesson as a check against the checker. This caused a bureaucratic furor, but it also brilliantly (and courageously) exposed the shortcomings of the system.

No group in American society is more idealistic, dedicated, and deserving of public support than our public schoolteachers. Yet no profession is more victimized by our anti-intellectual traditions. This passionate book defends teachers and deplores the false creeds they are taught in education schools. At the same time it defends the ideal of a truly professional education school that could, if reformed, help teachers and administrators become better at their work.

One does not have to agree with every conclusion in this thoughtful book to agree that Norris is a refreshing voice from the trenches—a learned foot soldier in the education wars who is in an excellent position to criticize the generals, having taught in the inner city, the country, and in the suburbs. Now a professor of education, he is a soldier's soldier in those wars. He knows from the field what the teacher is up against. He wants our teachers to be given the sound education they deserve. Above all, he wants our society to show more understanding and offer more respect to those on whom its future so profoundly depends.

E. D. Hirsch Jr.
August 27, 2001

Acknowledgments

This is my first book and writing it has been a journey and learning experience unlike any other. Many of the arguments and perspectives I have presented are often discussed among those who work in public education. I have long believed these arguments and perspectives needed to be written and presented in a scholarly format rather than the ordinary "gripe" format. Many of the problems in our schools are not new and likewise many of the ways in which educators are mistreated have been around for a while. While I have taken the time to research and write about my experiences, they are hardly atypical. When recalling and writing about experiences that were particularly painful, the feelings of anger that had long subsided found their way to the surface.

This book could not have been written without the guidance and assistance of many colleagues, friends, and family. Thanks are due to Michael Cornell McCoy for his enduring support and encouragement; Thomas W. Seale for the hours of thought-provoking conversations that helped me to gain perspective; Claudia J. D'Aquin for her expertise, encouragement, and always clever advice; Dr. Barry W. Birnbaum for his advice and encouragement.

I extend appreciation to Dr. Susan W. Roark and Dr. J. Lavone Rodrique-Landry for their encouragement and belief in me as a scholar of teaching and learning; Dr. James A. Taylor for his assistance, support, and insight; Dr. Michael H. McCoy for his input and assistance. I must thank the untold numbers of coworkers and school administrators who answered difficult questions as I sought to clarify my perspectives. Thanks are due also to Cindy Tursman, acquisitions editor for Scarecrow Education.

I must offer deepest appreciation to my parents, Arnold C. and Mary Norris. Their contribution to this book, in addition to support and some editing consideration, is to have set an indelible example by demonstrating the importance of learning and the pursuit of higher education. It is a fortunate child who sees his parents earn graduate degrees and knows the pride and increased quality of life that such an accomplishment brings.

Introduction

. . . about as helpful as throwing water on a drowning man . . .

Southern colloquialism

The reader has probably picked up this book mostly out of curiosity. One is likely wondering how a book with this subtitle could possibly relate to the field of public education, the real problems in our public school systems, and how it could ever be perceived that our educators are mistreated.

Throughout this book will be a recurring theme of "polite conversation"—that level of conversation that happens among casual friends over dinner or other intimate gatherings that is well intentioned but often ill informed. The reader will surely deduce from this book that polite conversation can be a very dangerous and destructive thing. It is often discussed in polite company that our schools are failing miserably and that practically all graduates of the public school system are functionally illiterate upon exiting the system (Berliner, 1993). Further discussion in polite company will indicate that no one knows what's going on; there is no leadership, teachers are not truly scholars in their field, and the whole system is a sham. Some polite conversation laments the deplorable status of schools "in other places" while affirming that "my child is exceptional." Most polite conversation will likely determine that if everyone who is employed at any level of public education would simply do the job they were hired to do, listen to the experts, and get back to basics, most of the problems would correct themselves. If these solutions are so simple, why have they not worked by now?

I have chosen the subtitle of this book by virtue of an old Southern figure of speech. Much of what happens in the name of reform in our schools, as well as what is discussed in polite conversation, has the same effect as throwing water on someone who is drowning. While the analogy, on the surface, might seem trite, it would seem appropriate that polite conversation tends to offer more criticism than real suggestions for problem resolution relative to our schools. Many of the efforts/suggestions to isolate problems and improve our schools, most of which are probably sincere and well intended, do the same additional damage as throwing water on the drowning victim. It does not take a team of scholars to recognize that if a man is drowning, more water is not going to cause the existing water to go away, lose any of its inherent liquid properties, or do less damage.

Our school organizations are overwhelmed with problems that could never have been imagined by those who pushed to design systems of public education 150 years ago. As a public school- and university teacher of nearly two decades, I have seen the pendulum swing from one extreme to another many times. In addition to my work as a teacher in my various roles, I frequently lecture at local, state, and national conferences in areas relative to educational leadership. Seldom do I present a lecture where I do not bring out the point that teaching and learning, like the practice of medicine and law, are not exact sciences in which a specific process or procedure can be applied and realistically assumed that a particular result will ensue. Unlike the more exact sciences, the work of educators does not start with a uniform raw product. Therefore, it is a fallacy to assume that the work of educators can always be approached totally objectively, worked out systematically, and the result have no loose ends or unexplained phenomenon. This is not a popular mindset to those where political actions must be brought about and policy decisions made.

I find it alarming that our society as a whole is terribly naive and hideously gullible when confronted with matters relating to the education of the youth in this country. When I am charged with the responsibility of teaching a group of adults who will ultimately become principals and other types of educational leaders, I stress repeatedly that we must all become literate consumers of the information relative to the work we do. The ability to recognize good information from bad gives the leader the skills and tools to analyze the problems we face and take a proactive stance in these changing times.

It is my perspective that teachers and educators at all levels are the most mistreated professionals in society. Despite the myths and popular opinions concerning teachers, there is not a group of professionals in this country who work any harder and are more dedicated to their mission. It has been reported in the media for many years that by the year 2010 almost half of the nation's teaching force could be retired (Kantrowitz & Wingert, 2000). This is an alarming statistic and one would think that society would be doing everything possible to ensure teaching to be an attractive profession. But teachers still continue to persevere against insurmountable odds while continuing to be mistreated by the society they serve.

The underlying assumption to this book will be the idea that in this country educators are shabbily treated in every aspect of what they do. From the public perceptions of the work they do, the societal role they serve, what is expected of them professionally, how they are compensated, and the fact that expectations are imposed on them that would never be tolerated by comparably educated professionals in the private sector of society, the treatment of educators at all levels borders on brutal. The mistreatment continues as educators continue to be held unfairly accountable for that which is not within their power to control or influence (Fontenot, 1998).

Polite conversation perpetuating the assumption that professional education is not a "real" academic discipline when a fair, commonsense look would clarify matters is another form of mistreatment. Such myths and fallacies are not imposed on similarly educated processionals in society. Our system is not perfect and will never be so. But despite some perpetual battles in an imperfect system, and quite contrary to popular belief, the schools do successfully educate far more than they fail to educate.

This book will be divided into seven chapters. In chapter 1 I present how society at large and some educators perceive teaching, the operations of the school, and why such perceptions are so hideously misconstrued. I will argue that, historically, in this country being a teacher has never been particularly well respected (Johnson et al., 1999). Through research as well as anecdotal experience, I will counter some of the mistaken notions about the profession, what we do, and how it is supposed to be done. Far more people in society have experienced the work of far more teachers than they will have any other social service or medical professional. This seems to play out in that everyone wants the schools and their workings to be done "my way" (Hughes & Hooper, 2000).

In chapter 2 I discuss how vague, false standards and expectations are imposed on educators that would never begin to be seen in other professions. Many of the outrageous expectations imposed on educators come about from poor planning, badly executed research, and often popular opinion not supported in research and practice. There seems to persist an erroneous idea that a perfect system of education can be legislated. I will compare the professional expectations imposed on other providers of services to children and youth and society and how those expectations parallel and differ. I will likewise discuss how those of us in the profession are partly to blame for this dilemma because we do so little to stop it.

In chapter 3 I discuss how years, literally decades, of flimsy research, questionable ideas, and outrageous "research-based" practices have failed our children miserably. In our business, ideas don't simply change or evolve; they seem to run erratically—like a child chasing a rabbit. One failed reform attempt after another has led society to assume erroneously that teachers "did it all wrong" when in fact, teachers were only doing what they were told to do.

Chapter 4 will be a critical chapter in the book, for it is here that I discuss some crucial points and dispel some serious myths about our profession and the workings therein. Much of what gets presented to the public under the name of "research" is not research at all, but popular opinion that is told so often in polite conversation that it becomes complacently accepted as truth. This is much the same as people who tell stories of alligators living in the sewers of New York City, or the old story of the lady finding a nest of snakes in a bolt of fabric. This chapter will confront many of the myths that are presented in the name of "research" and will seriously address the question of "researched" versus "research-based." There are some serious misconceptions in this area that must be addressed among educational leaders. Too many leaders and policymakers are attempting to pass off a shallow, glossy rococo style of mediocrity as excellence to an ill-informed public.

In chapter 5 I discuss and argue how the past 20–30 years have plagued our system with one desperate, practically hysterical effort after another that promised to "fix" what is wrong. From the Madeline Hunter Elements of Instructional Design to Statewide Teacher Evaluation Models, through the School Restructuring Movement and now to the Standards and Accountability Movement, one effort after another has failed to produce the instant results that society seems to demand of educators. Everyone seems to want education and educational reform to be painless (Stone, 2000b).

In chapter 6 I discuss the current movement in which we are seeing an overuse and misuse of standardized tests. Most critics of the testing movement are not opposed to the idea of standardized testing but are concerned with test scores being used in ways for which they were never intended. When the use of tests reaches a point where it begins to drive instruction rather than measure it (Charlesworth, Fleege & Weitman, 1994), we find educators once again mistreated.

Finally, in chapter 7 I discuss what the working role of the educator is really like. The polite conversations that continue to throw water on men and women who are virtually drowning are grossly misinformed about the schools, the people who run them and what really goes on. In those same polite conversations, it is not hard to figure out who has been inside a school and who has not. It's just as easy to see who looks around and who listens to popular myth.

I have chosen to write this book in order to help both the academic and nonacademic portion of our public become a bit more literate consumer of the plethora of information relative to our schools but particularly what teachers and other educators do. It is often said that the "half-educated" can be far more dangerous than the uneducated. It is clearly obvious that much of what gets said in polite conversation falls into the "half-educated" category, not because anyone is inherently mean or ill intentioned, but because people simply don't know what is and is not the truth. Our American public is really quite naive about many social matters that impact the masses. Our American public is equally as naive about what constitutes excellence and what is truly in the best interest of children (Rothstein, 1993).

This book is intended to present real information about the work of the teaching profession, what teachers really do and face everyday, and demonstrate that the educators of this country are not nearly as inept or inefficient as popular belief or even polite conversation would assume.

1

✚

Perceptions of Teaching

Those who can, do. Those who can't, teach.

In my years as a teacher, I have never ceased to be amazed at the mindset of where teachers fit on the professional hierarchy. In polite conversation, when discussion centers on one's livelihood, a financial analyst might likely say "I'm a financial analyst with so-and-so firm." An attorney will likely say "I'm an attorney in private practice." A physician will likely tell you about their training, specialties, and sub-specialties. But a teacher will likely say "Well . . . I'm just a teacher." It really should come as no surprise that teaching, as a profession, is not particularly highly esteemed and never has been. In my work, I frequently make presentations for school faculties as well as local, state, and national conferences. It is interesting that I frequently see a change in people's perspectives when it is learned that I am a teacher and that I spend my workday with children. When I make presentations, it is most often assumed that I must be the principal, school psychologist, some sort of specialist, or someone far more important than a mere teacher. (After all, there is an academic title before my name.) There seems to be a mindset that a person cannot possibly work with children each day and still be an authority in any aspect of our business or a scholar or expert in any regard (Marsh, 1992). I have noticed over the years that in polite conversation, when it is told that I am a teacher, I become immediately bombarded with questions about children, the system, and how "terrible everything is." Everyone seems to have more than one good horror story about schools or teachers. Most people have some opinion as to how to fix all that is wrong. I do find a bit of joy in setting the record straight for an ill-informed public, even if it is in polite conversation, one ill-informed person at a time.

Several years ago I recall reading an article in a scholarly journal written by a Russian mathematician who had come to this country with the most sincere hope of being a university professor of mathematics. As he

1

was pursuing and nearing completion of the doctorate, he became terribly disillusioned with the perception of the teaching component of the field of research mathematics. It seemed as though among research mathematicians, it was perceived that a "good" position with a university was one that involved only research, no teaching. There seemed to be a prevailing mindset that the more scholarly and astute individuals did the research, the less able did the teaching. The man became so disillusioned over his dream that he returned to his country to teach there. In Russia, teaching is held to the same level of esteem as medicine. In fact, teachers actually earn more money than physicians do. I would suspect the man is probably doing better in his own country both in terms of salary and professional prestige! We will discuss in a later chapter that even in higher education the myth persists that the less capable do the teaching.

It should come as no surprise that such a mindset exists because such a mindset has been present since the early days of this country. During the colonial times, when the concept of the academy was taking form, there was discussion among the leaders as to the "who and how" of educating the youth population. Benjamin Franklin, even as the eminent and wise scholar of life he was, stated that the "weaker" graduates of the academies could serve as teachers for the other academy students (Johnson et al., 1999). One need only "ask around" to learn the general perception of the teaching profession.

There are myriad misperceptions about the work of teaching, the teaching profession as a whole, and what exactly goes on in schools. Likewise, there are gross misunderstandings among the population at large about what is involved in the training to become a teacher. Such misunderstandings really should come as no surprise because between teachers and other professionals who provide services to children and youth, there is a common link that is not found in other social service professions—the receivers of services are children. There does exist in our society the commonly held myth that the provision of services to children and youth is of less significance than those same services to adults or that such provision of services is considerably easier. In view of this information, it should come as no surprise that professionals in medicine, psychology, and other social sciences outside the realm of teaching feel such prejudices as well (D. Betancourt, pers. comm., May 19, 2001).

There are certain myths about teaching that are more prominent than others. What are some of the perceptions that cause the general public, in polite conversation, to dismiss the crucial role that teachers play in the ongoing society? Here I address several of them and look a bit further than polite conversation would generally allow.

RESEARCH IN THE FIELD OF TEACHER
EDUCATION IS "SOFT," NOT SCHOLARLY

Polite conversation among well-meaning individuals often discusses how formal research in the area of teacher education is "soft" and not truly of a scholarly nature (Eisner & Peshkin, 1990). When such persons refer to any research as "soft," the underlying meaning is typically that the phenomenon being studied is such that a real and accurate measure that eliminates the influence of any individual perception or bias simply is not possible. This is an inherent problem when conducting research in any of the behavioral or social sciences that the skilled researcher can allow for but never totally eliminate (Babbie, 1999). Polite conversation seems to disallow that teaching and learning are still imperfect, inexact sciences in which absolutes do not exist.

Unfortunately, it is true that there is a significant lack of formal quantitative (numerical) research in the field of education. Quantitative and qualitative (descriptive) research will be discussed more in depth in another chapter. For now, suffice it to say that the field of education has far more descriptive data than numerical, which is specifically what leads to the perception of "soft" versus scholarly research. There are reasons for this lack of a common body of information.

Formal research takes time and it is expensive. In order for the people who do research to do it well, there must an adequate amount of time allocated for what is often the most lengthy portion of a research project—to design the research. Then the researchers must select samples, cover the bases concerning ethical issues, carry out the plan of action, allow time and space for any unexpected occurrences, and write their final report (Dauwalder, 2000). Formal, quantitative research is not intended to fix or address any particular problem. It simply observes, records, and reports. When a quantitative study is complete, there is usually a new body of usable information, but the situation or phenomenon being studied usually looks exactly as it did prior to the beginning of the research. With education budgets constantly facing reductions, school systems are seldom willing to allocate money for a research project that is only going to generate information and not make anything look different, bring about any degree of change, or essentially "pay off" (Kaestle, 1993). Universities can seldom fund their own research. Grants must be written and everything must appeal to the powers that hand out the research dollars (Stone & Clements, 1998). In a subsequent chapter we will discuss the various kinds of research and how they are carried out, but it is fair to say that our profession holds a far larger body of descriptive than numerical data for the simple reason that time and money do not permit it. Lack of money dictates that any study or analyses of existing situations bring about some degree of change. Descriptive data are easy to gather in a practitioner field because everyone is working in the field anyway. The problem is that, scientifically speaking, we cannot assume that a program or project brings about a change in status or behavior without making a comparison to a group that does not receive the services of the project or program. This brings us to my next point.

Designing research on teaching and learning that falls into the category (or categories) that would not be considered "soft" by the critics requires careful work in the selection of groups. The best and strongest research projects use totally random groups, which is quite difficult in school settings because schools are generally organized in intact groups, classes, programs, and so forth, all of which are typically arranged because of similarities, not diversities. Research designs that use intact groups are more frequently done in school settings. These findings are useful, but are still considered "soft" by many critics. Additionally, completing long-term studies on children, methods programs, and so on is difficult because the typical school year includes ten months with a two-month break, causing an interruption in observations. One additional difficulty is that children can and usually do change in many ways over a period of a few months, unlike adults who have finished growing. It is erroneous to assume that completing research on children is just like doing the same for adults.

So, it should make sense that there is embarrassingly little quantitative research in the field of teacher education. The system and society that expects educators to produce scholarly findings upon which to base decisions and practices do precious little to facilitate their expectations. But the question really does go a bit deeper. Any social science research tends to focus on the practical rather than the theoretical. Society at large and polite conversation shows a significantly higher regard for the theoretical than the practical. As such, research efforts in our field are "double doomed" before they even get started.

A DEGREE IN EDUCATION IS LACKING IN CONTENT

Among scholarly people the discussion often centers on what is "training" and what is "education." In brief, we can say that training basically addresses the physical movement while education addresses the mind. As such, there are scholars of teaching and learning who insist that teacher training must become teacher education (Stout, 2000). Among scholars of teaching and learning, and among recent graduates of teacher preparation programs, I often hear that the program focused too much on the pedagogy and methods—the training—rather than on the common body of knowledge that was their area of interest (for example, history, biology, English)—the education. The amount of study in the prospective teacher's area of interest is another set of issues to be discussed later. But teacher education is not the only area in which consideration has to be given to the collection of a body of information.

In order to establish an academic discipline or area of professional specialization, those in the profession must over time gather information considered necessary to serve as a professional knowledge base in that area. Such efforts are seldom completed one time and the same body of information considered the basis of professional status forever. Never will those in a position to train in a profession agree on what is absolutely necessary for the furthering of the profession. As an example, some time ago, I was called to serve on a criminal jury involving the possible sexual abuse of a young girl. The pediatrician who was brought in to testify as an expert witness had done so many times before and was considered very much an authority in the area of child sexual abuse. When the physician took the witness stand, she was asked about her background, training, experience, and how frequently she had been certified as an expert in a court of law (which was considerable). When cross-examined by the defense attorney, she was questioned heavily about her experience in the field of child sexual abuse and if that was a "sub-specialty in the field of pediatrics." She stated it was not yet a sub-specialty because the body of information was still insufficient to create an appropriate exam that could justify additional licensure in the area. While my mind was definitely on other things as I sat in the jury box, I did come to realize that all professions have to create their own professional knowledge base. In regard to creating the professional knowledge base, it seems only educators are chastised for doing what other professions do as a matter of course (Grossman, 1989).

Every profession, including teaching, bears one major similarity—there is a common knowledge base for the profession and specializations come later. When physicians graduate from medical school, or when attorneys graduate from law school, their education to that point is pretty generic. The physician then chooses either to pursue further study in a specialty area or practice as a general practitioner. Likewise, the attorney chooses which area of legal practice to pursue. Bodies of professional information are constantly changing and the professions must change as well. Even the practice of medicine will have more widely accepted theories as well as questionable or limited practices and procedures. Likewise, there will be practitioners who will adamantly adhere to or blatantly reject such theories regardless of the existing professional knowledge (Guadagnino, 1998). For reasons that elude me, it is still assumed that a teaching degree does not entail a common language or embody a common bank of information.

THE TERMINAL DEGREE

There are certain prejudices and "folk myths" surrounding the possession of the coveted terminal degree—the doctorate. Anecdotal observation will indicate that some of these misunderstandings come about because there is an air of mysticism and awe at the holding of what so few ever pursue and even fewer attain. Some of the prejudices, however, come about from blatant arrogance. If we fairly examine the phenomenon of the doctoral degree we will find the myths and misunderstandings to be shallow and easily balanced. We will likewise find any self-perpetuating arrogance to be without merit and totally unwarranted. The purpose and scope of the terminal degree is determined by the contribution that the work makes to academia, the working world, and society at large. The terminal degree is categorized by two very different phenomena—research and practitioner.

It is generally known and accepted that the holder of the doctor of philosophy (Ph.D.) degree has demonstrated and possesses the highest skills of research and literary prowess. Generally, the Ph.D. stands alone in any academic discipline not because it is inherently superior or because the work is more difficult or meaningful, but because the coursework and writing requirements focus entirely on theory and research. Other doctoral degrees, both in and out of education, are focused on the applications of theory and practice. It is often said, not necessarily in pejorative context, that the researcher writes about the problems while the practitioner solves them. It should then stand to reason that the Ph.D. degree in education is of an entirely different scope and focus, though not necessarily inferior, to the practitioner degree, the doctor of education degree (Ed.D.). We will discuss later that other applied and social science disciplines confer a doctoral degree focused on practice rather than research. For now, our attention is focused on the Ed.D., which is so often dismissed as insignificant and inferior.

In any field or discipline the doctoral degree is conferred upon the completion of a set program of study designed to produce a person with a specific set of skills. It is often assumed that simply completing about 60 semester hours of coursework beyond the master's degree and "writing a big paper" grants the conferral of the doctorate. (To hear someone say "He practically has his doctorate" is a flawed perspective. "Practically" holding the doctorate is like being "practically pregnant"—it's an either/or situation!) The fact is that any doctoral program will have specific requirements for content and standards with checkpoints along the way to ensure that the student is progressing well through the program. The program of study will be designed to accomplish two tasks:

1. to increase the knowledge base of the student so that he/she can complete the "make-or-break" aspect of the program; and

2. the writing component called the dissertation for the Ph.D. (or any
   number of descriptive titles for the practitioner program).

This brings us to a discussion and explanation of the writing component
of any doctoral program. Polite conversation often discusses that the Ed.D.
doesn't require any "real" or "original" research and usually involves
some sort of practical project. Because the Ph.D. is entirely focused on
research, the writing component is almost always the design of some type
of quantitative (in most cases, meaning measurable) experiment intended
to investigate an appropriate research question or problem. The work for
the traditional quantitative dissertation differs significantly from the practitioner's work in that the problem is not addressed or any resolution
attempted; it simply measures and reports. To the contrary, the work for
the Ed.D. typically generates a project that identifies a problem in the real
working world (the school system, the classroom, etc.), designs a solution
to the problem, then implements the solution in the real workplace. Both
efforts are very scholarly in nature and are practically identical in scope
and magnitude. There are many other professional doctoral programs that
do not require the student to complete quantitative research. For example,
the doctor of musical arts (DMA) degree generally requires a mono-
graph—a lengthy research paper that contributes to the existing body of
knowledge but is not created via quantitative research. Instead, it is typically historical research.

There is one significant difference, however, which is usually not discussed in polite conversation. When the work of the traditional researcher
is completed, there is a contribution to "the existing body of knowledge,"
whereas when the work of the practitioner is complete, there is not only
that same level of contribution to knowledge, but documentation that a
change took place that improved a situation or solved a problem. Generating more data does not solve problems; working in the field solves
problems.

Polite conversation often leads to the conclusion that the curriculum for
the Ed.D. is inferior because it typically does not require any study of foreign language. Interestingly, this has long been an argument against the
doctorate in education, while it is generally known that most practitioner
degrees don't require the study of a foreign language as a part of the doctoral program. There are two points to be considered here. First, there are
a number of practitioner degrees such as the doctor of psychology (Psy.D.),
doctor of engineering (Eng.D.), doctor of nursing science (DNS), doctor of
public health (Dr.PH), and doctor of ministry (D.Min.) that focus on the
practice in the field, do not embody a foreign language requirement, and,
for some reason, are not perceived as inferior as the Ed.D. In fact, many traditional Ph.D. programs are moving away from the foreign language
requirement for the simple fact that it is no longer necessary. Even the doc-

tor of musical arts degree only requires the study of foreign language to the point that one can pronounce German, Italian, or French. The study of the language, literature, and customs really isn't necessary as we won't find many German, Italian, or French vocal compositions that have never been translated. One hundred or so years ago the foreign language requirement was in place because communication among the scholarly of society was very fragmented. In the global society of today, communicating via online mass communications significantly lessens the need to speak a foreign language.

Second, it has been known for years that most Ed.D. programs exchange the foreign language requirement for additional study in statistics. In most universities we find that the course work and program requirements for the Ed.D and the Ph.D. are identical except for the choice to study a foreign language or the additional coursework in statistics. Knowing a second language always puts the practitioner at an advantage, but suffice it to say that no practitioner doctoral degree program, including the doctor of medicine (MD), carries a language requirement outside that of what is absolutely necessary to the practicing of the profession. It simply is not fair to assume that because one chose to study additional statistics rather than a foreign language constitutes an inferior doctoral degree.

Where does the idea originate that real scholars do the research and the less able practice in the field? In the medical field, just like others, it is the practitioners—the physicians (MDs) who see the patients and make people well. It is generally the Ph.D.s who work in the laboratories, conduct research, write, and publish. Certainly we find physicians making the time to do these things, and those who do usually do it well. Even in the field of medicine certain false dichotomies of academia and research versus clinical practitioner exist.

In view of this information, the notion that only the Ph.D. is a "real" doctoral degree, or that the Ed.D. is a "false" doctorate (Gross, 1999) is simply absurd. But, this level of credential snobbery does continue far outside of terminal degrees in the social sciences. A friend of mine who is a veterinarian is often asked by well-meaning family, "If you spent all that time in school, why didn't you become a 'real' doctor?" These probably well-intentioned but hideously ill-informed individuals have no clue that performing a hysterectomy on a 100-pound female dog is exactly the same level of science as performing that same surgical procedure on a 100-pound female human.

I occasionally have ignorant remarks hurled my way. For example, several years ago a new vice principal approached me and asked why it is that the faculty and student body addressed me as "doctor." I informed her that I held an earned doctorate in the areas of school management and instructional leadership and that I had a number of outside interests and ongoing projects and regularly taught graduate courses in local universities. It still astounds me to think she informed me that "an Ed.D. is a second-rate Ph.D."

TEACHER EDUCATION MAJORS ARE THE "LOWEST" ACADEMICALLY

Polite conversation often discusses what is assumed to be common information—teacher education majors are the "lowest" academically. Publications and discussions abound that year after year, those choosing teaching as an academic major are less capable, less academically prepared, not as bright, score lowest on the college admissions exams, and so forth. Polite conversation generally doesn't indicate that this information is usually reported from demographic data gathered at each administration of the SAT or ACT. At the time a student registers for the exam, they are asked to declare an intended academic major. It is an interesting phenomenon that year after year the lowest segment of the distribution of scores falls to those who report their intention to major in teacher education. But somehow, polite conversation never seems to question the information much further than that. One would suspect there would be other factors that must play into this phenomenon. Although such depressing regularly reported data might make such an implication, it is doubtful that any real correlation exists between a low SAT score and the desire to become a teacher. We do find correlations between family income and SAT or ACT scores. We likewise find high positive correlations between modest socioeconomic backgrounds and the *desire* to teach. Perhaps all this points in the direction of what anecdotal observation has told us for years—that those choosing teaching as a profession tend to come from less affluent beginnings. At any rate, the commonly held belief that teacher education majors are the "lowest" is fundamentally flawed and grossly misleading for several reasons:

1. The predictive validity of SAT and ACT scores (the extent to which there is a correlational relationship between test score and subsequent academic success) is not generally discussed mostly because neither of these test scores relate particularly well to success in a teacher education program or a student's subsequent success as a teacher. These scores are presumed to be predictive of a student's success at doing college-level work (Educational Testing Service, 1998).
2. We seldom hear the percentage of students who are not admitted to teacher education programs. Contrary to popular belief, there are large numbers of students who are denied admission because they do not meet the criteria.
3. Not all students who state an intention to study teacher education

actually do. Many of the ones who state an intention to major in teacher education change their academic major to an area of the liberal arts or general studies.

4. Somehow we never hear of the low-scoring students who state an intended major of teacher education but do not last in college long enough to be admitted into the program. Most programs do not admit people until the fourth semester (Hanushek & Pace, 1994).

5. We seldom hear statistics of those who change their major to teacher education after entering college or choose to earn teacher certification later. Many students who originally chose an applied discipline, such as English, math, history, political science, pure sciences, performing arts, subsequently choose the teacher education route as a means of making themselves more marketable upon graduation (Educational Testing Service, 1998).

6. In both urban and rural areas there are growing percentages of teachers who earned certifications via alternative routes. While the data on their success rate are quite controversial, their SAT and ACT scores are not included in the gloomy data as they did not enter college as teacher education majors (Feistritzer, 1996).

7. One phenomenon further complicates this often-reported data. Nationwide, one-third to one-fourth of the persons who graduate with a degree in teacher education, regardless of test scores or how they came about to choose teacher education, will never teach (Heynes, 1988). Since most Americans do have to seek some sort of gainful employment, that translates to 33% of the "lowest academically" entering other sectors of the workforce than teaching.

But there are more current data relative to the commonly held belief that teacher education majors are the least desirable persons to be teaching children (Georgia Department of Education, 1999). A recent study by Gitomer, Latham, and Ziomek (1999) brings some refreshing news about prospective teachers and the ever-touted college admissions test. In a rather large sample of teacher education candidates who completed their university coursework and passed the state exams (in this study the exams were the Praxis series administered by ETS), their findings include:

1. Those who passed Praxis I, the test of general teaching and pedagogical knowledge, had a higher SAT or ACT score than the average graduating senior.

2. Those who passed Praxis II, the subject matter exam, had SAT or ACT scores superior to the scores of college bound seniors.

We would think the public would be pleased with such information. But the literate consumer of information must realize that either argument alone (teacher education majors as inferior as judged by test scores; those who pass exams will be truly superior teachers) is little more than a half-truth. First, the SAT or ACT is a measure of academic background, not a predictor of success as a teacher. While it is desired that the two mesh, they are still two separate phenomena. Second, saying that one has "passed" either portion of the exam is quite a relative statement. Each state sets their own cutoff scores, thereby creating inconsistencies nationwide (Latham, Gitomer, & Ziomek, 1999). Some states have set cutoff scores so low as to fall at the 23rd percentile in some areas.

Despite quality research questioning the myth of poorly trained teachers, the myth remains. Nelli (1984) completed a study to compare teacher education graduates to other university graduates. The findings of this study were similar to those of Blair (1999) and Tanner (1995). We are continuing to find prospective teachers reporting a lower than average SAT score yet outscoring other college grads in the area they intend to teach. Additionally, a study by White, Burke, and Hodges (1994) found a very strong correlation between SAT scores and the subsequent exit exam in teacher education programs. Likewise a similar correlation was found between the GPA of the first 64 undergraduate hours and subsequent passing of the exam. We would think that such findings would come as no surprise and should be welcomed by critics of teacher training programs.

Some 20–30 years ago many teacher training programs, particularly in elementary education, practically had an open-door admissions policy. When there is no screening of who enters a program, it stands to reason there will be some who make it through the program who probably should not. As society began to demand more accountability and increased standards, we began to see programs in teacher education rewritten to contain some formal and official admissions process, separate and apart from admission to the university. Universities adopted varying procedures and testing instruments that measured the professional skills and content knowledge of those seeking admission to the teacher training programs. Prior to that, practically the only way a person did not complete the teaching degree was to not pass the practice teaching component of the program. But this is not so today. Teacher education candidates are thoroughly screened each semester. We can hardly find a teacher education program without checkpoints for progress. Today, students typically must have a certain grade point average as well as often having to pass entrance exams of some sort before being admitted to a teacher education program.

In many ways the current state of teacher education in this country very much parallels the state of medical education in this country more than a century ago. In the mid-1800s medical education was so slip-shod an effort that respectable people chose other careers (Goldfien, 2000). The knowledge base was shallow at best and much of a physician's training involved little more than memorizing lists of symptoms and what the knowledge base of the time considered an appropriate treatment (Darling-Hammond, 1999). There was virtually no admission criterion to medical schools, and many who attended were barely literate. Only the privileged who could afford to travel abroad and study had any real grounding in the basic sciences. When forward-thinking individuals recognized that the knowledge base was increasing and that the system had to change to keep up, it was met with resistance by the traditional thinkers who were comfortable with the status quo. The real revelation came about when Johns Hopkins created a teaching model that included a teaching hospital. Prior to that, it had not been uncommon for a medical student to never see a patient prior to graduation (Goldfien, 2000)—similar to many teacher education programs as recent as the 1960s. It took a number of years before the medical community accepted the direction that medical education had to move—with more and more clinical training resulting in more and more specialized skills. Understandably, colleges of education are under intense pressure to meet current needs and maintain current services while continuing to upgrade standards. There is one reason it will be many years before the field of teacher education reaches this level of specialization and professionalism. Society will not support or monetarily remunerate a teaching force that has endured that amount of work, study, and commitment to the furthering of the profession.

STUDENTS EARNING TEACHER CERTIFICATION ARE LESS PREPARED IN AN ACADEMIC DISCIPLINE THAN THEIR NONEDUCATION COUNTERPARTS

Polite conversation often leads to the erroneous conclusion that university students planning to earn teacher certification are less adept in their academic discipline than their counterparts who do not choose to earn the teaching credential. In fairness to this argument, it should be stated that there is no difference in the quality or difficulty of the academic classes taken by those students who are choosing to earn teacher certification. It is and certainly should be a matter of concern that there is a difference in the number of classes in the academic area that teacher education majors are often required to take. I have spoken with a number of graduate students in my classes concerning this issue. Many who are currently teaching and in pursuit of the master's degree have shared their concern that their academic background is lacking 12–18 semester hours in their academic area than other applied graduates. One student told me that he chose to earn the B.A. degree in history and earn teacher certification later because he did not want to be part of the "less capable teacher education graduate" syndrome. Others have shared that they could not spend an additional one to two years in school. They were under pressure to graduate and get a job. This is not rocket science—it's simple economics. But when this issue is discussed in polite conversation it leads the unknowing to assume that those choosing to pursue teacher certification are basically not educated in their academic field, or that any classes they take in an academic area are "watered down" versions designed for the teacher education major (Innerst, 1999). This simply is not true. The fact that teacher education majors in some disciplines (not in music or other performance disciplines) take fewer classes—not less challenging classes—is a simple case of supply and demand. Let us examine further.

Today, a college degree in any area requires between 130–160 semester hours. Even a degree program with the bare minimum of 130 semester hours will be a challenge to complete in the traditional four years. To complete 130 semester hours of college credit in four years, eight semesters, requires the student to enroll for 16–18 semester hours each term. This is a large academic load, which requires many hours of daily study, reading, library work, lab work, writing, or practicing of a musical instrument. Taking less semester hours necessitates the student to either enroll for subsequent semesters or complete coursework in summer school. Additional periods of enrollment means additional educational expenses. A university degree in teacher education costs as much as any other. Incurring an additional one to two years of student loan debt when one expects to earn about two thirds that of the rest of society must be considered.

Typically, the teacher education major might take 12–18 semester hours less in their field than their nonteacher education counterparts. I can hardly imagine a knowledgeable person who would not agree that to require additional semester hours in the academic discipline of teacher education majors is a good idea. However, doing so will likely add an additional one to two years to the degree program that compounds another social problem—our nation is already so critically short of teachers. Having to wait one to two additional years for fresh recruits to the teaching force would further delay the nation's already hysterical efforts just to put warm bodies in classrooms.

But the question does go a bit deeper, leading one to recall the old adage "speaking out of both sides of your mouth." It is interesting to note that the very critics who, in polite conversation or academic discussion, claim that our teacher workforce is not made up of intellectual or academic people will in the next breath argue that no particular academic training should be needed to be a teacher. One is likely to hear, "If you have a college degree in math you should be allowed to walk in and teach math—period." If only it were that simple. We find repeatedly that those critics who demand an academic teaching force will likewise insist on school systems that function in such a manner that academic preparation in a subject matter is of far less importance than social management skills. There have been studies produced for years indicating that upwards of 60–70% of a teacher's workday is spent dealing with matters of social behavior as a consequence of physically and emotionally impoverished children. Obviously such phenomena will be much more evident in the schools and school systems serving student populations living below the status of "middle class." Suffice it to say, a truly academic teaching force will not likely happen until we have school systems that truly require academic preparation as a key to success.

I further find it interesting that the "both sides of the mouth" phenomenon is glaringly obvious in the work of legislators and policymakers when addressing the question of an "academic teaching force." The argument, however futile, continues that teachers are academically unprepared as a result of having spent too much time in pedagogical study rather than study in an applied discipline. Yet when legislators have an opportunity to impact this phenomenon, they perpetuate its continuance. In many states, including where I reside, there are programs in place to help teachers pursue graduate study by relinquishing some tuition costs for some classes. Many such programs, however, come with some serious strings attached. Tuition is only relinquished for courses that are "directly related to the work of the teacher," which far too often translates to courses in methods or pedagogy. Even the required courses in research are not covered under the program. In theory, advanced courses should be included, but getting them approved is so tedious that most don't bother.

Obviously, this is not a simple problem to solve, as there are many mitigating circumstances that must be considered when addressing such complexities. Twenty-four semester hours of coursework in a field is still a lot of study and academic work, but unfortunately is far from the desired standard that should exist. But it is unfair to mistreat the teaching profession by making such generic assumptions as a person having only studied 24 semester hours in an academic area, rather than the desired 36 plus semester hours, makes teachers "academically unprepared."

TEACHER EDUCATION COURSES ARE NEVER NECESSARY

It is often argued that teacher education courses that focus on historical foundations of education, current school practices, political processes of education, classroom management, and so forth are not necessary. One can scarcely imagine that physicians would not have as part of their professional education some training in the history of medicine in this country. Those who know history are less likely to repeat mistakes. Certainly a physician needs to be educated in the political and legal aspects of the practice of medicine as well as legal liability issues. Since a large portion of the medical bills of this nation are paid by Medicare, it would make sense that prospective physicians are taught about such things. A physician must be taught how to organize and set up a private practice that runs efficiently. Physicians are not just taught a body of scientific and biological information and then expected to "figure out" how to operate a clinic. One seldom sees a beginning physician in private practice right away, as most lack the resources and practically all lack the experience needed to do so.

If we compare the curriculum of graduate study (masters or doctorate) in public health and public school administration we find some striking similarities. Both curriculums will require some study in the history of the profession. Both will require the mastery of a knowledge base founded upon the existing literature. Both will focus on working in a field that is constantly evolving while they continue to provide a service to society. Both will involve training in the current body of literature relative to effective leadership practices. Finally, both will include experiences whereby the practitioner must interpret current data and make valid decisions for the betterment of those served by the profession. Polite conversation does not consider similar coursework in similar fields to be similar. Graduate coursework in education is marginalized and dismissed as inferior.

We know from anecdotal observation and formal research that those beginning teachers with little or no pedagogical training have many more management difficulties, are less prepared to face the classroom, and leave the profession far more frequently (Stone & Clements, 1998). Other professions are taught how the profession operates, yet this component of a teacher's training seems to be met with disdain. Despite how imperfect the system remains, how can it ever be reasonably assumed that teacher education courses are not necessary?

THE HIGHER THE ADMISSION STANDARDS TO THE UNIVERSITY, THE FEWER TEACHER GRADUATES

For many years there has existed a myth that the higher the academic standards of the university, the fewer teacher graduates from that university. To briefly address it here, this myth is fundamentally flawed for two reasons:

1. Any university that offers degree programs in any area, including teacher education, must graduate a certain number of students from that program in order to keep the program in existence. A university cannot pay faculty and maintain facilities without students to teach.
2. The colleges with teacher education programs that graduate relatively few teachers tend to be the private colleges that are typically considerably more expensive than state supported universities.

The correlation between admission standards and teacher education graduates really translates to the cost of the university education compared to the potential earning power of the student upon graduation. Since a degree in teacher education costs as much as any other, a huge student loan debt cannot be realistically repaid on a teacher salary. From a purely economic standpoint, a college degree is an investment, and the long-term return on that investment must always be considered. An expensive college degree does not guarantee a high paying job any more than a law degree ensures the individual will ever practice law.

There is another component to the myth of higher standards and fewer teachers. A degree from a prestigious university carries with it advantages that regional or state supported universities often do not—prestige. Teaching is not an area that carries any degree of prestige and, as is the thesis of this book, in many circles is looked upon unfavorably. It should stand to reason that a university that places such emphasis on public relations and image will be far less concerned with graduating teachers than those prepared to enter other more lucrative professions. Graduating teachers pulls down the average starting salary of the university's graduates. Teacher education does not bring nearly the prestigious research grants and funding or the public relations aspects attached to such efforts. The prestigious universities are typically private and don't want to have any ties to state department bureaucracies that would necessarily dictate programs and course requirements. The prestigious universities generally have "bigger fish to fry" than dealing with teacher education programs.

HIGHER EDUCATION

In higher education it is generally known that colleges of education are often looked upon as less scholarly entities than other divisions of universities. It is interesting that another university division that is looked upon as less scholarly is that of library science (Lorenzen, 2000). Again we see the practical that supports the theoretical being viewed as insignificant and inferior. Of further interest is that no academic discipline can exist without teachers to teach it, nor can any academic discipline further itself without the services of a library and trained staff.

In recent years forward-thinking individuals in the social sciences have made serious efforts to raise the level of awareness of those professionals who provide services intended to improve the quality of life for children and youth. In many colleges and universities we are seeing undergraduate and graduate programs focus on the training of "Child and Youth Professionals." These professional roles in society are intended to be the conception, design, implementation, and management programs that address the specific needs of the diverse child and youth population outside that of teaching. These professionals will work in schools (not necessarily as teachers), agencies, and in the ministry. But the perception does linger that working with children or educating those who do is of a lesser professional status than working with adults.

Those of us who teach in colleges of education face battles concerning academic image that professors in other university departments do not. If we compare the typical professor of education, their educational background, and work experience to professors in other areas, we find some significant differences when they enter the university realm. First of all, the typical professor of education entering the world of academia is older than beginning professors in other areas. These people have generally worked for 15–20 years teaching in the public schools or working in the teaching profession in some manner. Seldom do we find beginning professors in the colleges of education who have gone through the routine of undergraduate, master's, and doctorate and directly into the professorship. In other academic disciplines, the average age of those entering is much younger because these people typically have earned the credentials specifically to go into the field of college teaching (Ducharme & Agne, 1982).

Second, the beginning professor of education typically has a work background that is practical, not theoretical. This person's work history has been in the field in which they intend to teach. Their experience with their academic discipline has been years of working in schools, teaching children, managing instructional programs, designing and implementing programs—essentially "working in the trenches." Unlike their counterparts in other departments within the university, their working experience in their academic discipline has extended beyond years of theoretical study in a graduate department in another university.

Third, the typical professor of education has likely come from a graduate program that is practitioner focused, not focused on theory and research. Since we know that new education professors are generally older than their beginning counterparts, it would make sense they are far more likely to have home, family, and other adult responsibilities that a younger person might not. As such, they have usually had to work during the course of their graduate study and therefore completed the field based Ed.D. This fact automatically limits the person's experience in writing and publishing due to the nature of their recently completed graduate work. These people have studied and prepared to spend a career working in the field, dealing with complexities, and solving problems, not researching and writing about the field. Consequently, their perspective and outlook are unfamiliar when compared to that of those in other university departments whose graduate education has been in training to write and publish in their field rather than prepare more practitioners.

Finally, we tend to find one major difference between professors of education and their noneducation counterparts. Those who enter the field of teaching tend to come from more modest backgrounds than those who enter the more lucrative professions. Additionally, those who enter teaching do so for more intrinsic rewards than one would expect of those who choose to enter the more lucrative areas (Lebaree, 1999).

Colleges of education carry a set of expectations imposed by other departments that can only be imposed on education schools. Other university departments in the humanities, arts, and sciences depend greatly on the teaching credential offered by education schools that serve to make a degree in the humanities, arts, or sciences more marketable. As was discussed earlier in this chapter, there are many students who wish to pursue a degree in English, math, history, and so forth, but upon the realization that such a degree has no inherent market value will opt to choose to earn teacher certification as a "backup." Academic advisors in the applied disciplines often encourage students to earn teacher certification for that reason. Knowing the perception of education schools among the rest of the academic world, education schools are faced with mindset of "we don't think you do things particularly well, but keep on doing it anyway." It is almost as though other departments are saying "We need you to lend that extra credence to what we do."

The perception of education schools often causes departmental leaders and deans to succumb to pressure to implement standards and requirements above what other university departments may require. In the university where I teach, the entrance criteria, program requirements, and graduation requirements to earn a teaching degree are more rigorous than any other throughout the university. Admission into and graduation from the teacher education program requires a higher grade point average than any other program in the university. Yet, for some reason, the myth still persists that teacher education is lacking in both content and standards.

There is another factor that deserves mention here. Universities usually classify themselves as either "teaching institutions" or "research institutions." Research institutions are usually the larger universities, while the teaching institutions most often are the smaller, regional institutions that serve a particular geographic region of a state. Research institutions require the majority of professorial time to be spent doing exactly that—researching, writing, and publishing. In research institutions we more frequently find the teaching responsibilities delegated to graduate assistants who are already overworked with their own courses of study and research projects that are required for their graduate degree. In the teaching institutions we find teaching loads carried by professors with very few graduate students teaching undergraduate courses. This is an irony of sorts in that society demands that teachers be the most academically prepared. Yet the institutions that are considered the flagship of academia do exactly the opposite—assign the teaching responsibilities to less prepared graduate students while the most academically prepared are carrying heavy research and publishing workloads (Von Blum, 1986). Ravitch (1985) makes the following personal account:

> In 1972, when I had been out of college for a dozen years, I decided to get a Ph.D. in history while writing a political history of the New York City public schools. I approached a young history professor at Columbia, who told me that I was a bad bet for his department: "You have three strikes against you," he said. "First, you are a woman; second, you are more than ten years away from your B.A.: and third, you are interested in education." At Teachers College, the graduate school of education at Columbia, none of these characteristics was considered a handicap, and I pursued my studies there. This lack of interest in elementary and secondary schooling and in education as a profession and as a research field is typical of major research universities. (p. 97)

CLAIMING PROFESSIONAL STATUS

Popular ideas hang around for a long time. The "just a teacher" mindset will not likely go away soon, but it certainly will not go away until those of us in the profession redirect our own thinking on the matter. The time is long past that educators exercise the same professional autonomy as other professionals. For too many years we have complacently accepted what was considered to be the "nature of the beast." We have blindly tolerated meager to mediocre circumstances that demanded a return of excellence when other professionals would never have tolerated such. Before anyone can reasonably expect perceptions to change among the general population, perceptions must change within the profession. Educators must discard the age-old "just a teacher" mindset and demand what any other professionals would take for granted. It is time that we raise our own standards. As a profession, how do we do this?

Those of us in the profession must absolutely reject the current but longstanding warped perception of what being a teacher is all about. We must be knowledgeable of the facts that are so often selectively misquoted to minimize and discount the complexities of the work that we do. We must hold our leaders accountable for being knowledgeable of the current body of information that is so often misused to make quick but ineffective decisions. We must be prepared to look an ill-informed public in the face and say, "I'm sorry—that simply is not true. This is what really happens."

2

Professional Double Standards

In the early years of my teaching career I was often angered and frustrated by what can best be termed a "professional double standard" for educators, which is not found in other comparably educated professionals in the private sector. As a 20-year veteran of the profession, I am finding myself more and more amused than angered; recognizing the phenomenon, at worst, as a by-product of an ill-informed public or, at best, as something that exists that will not likely go away. The professional double standard to which I refer hinges on the fact that society at large, mostly out of simple misunderstanding, tends to expect a caliber of work and various practices from educators that they would never ask of other professionals. Additionally, the educator's work is usually held accountable to a degree not expected (or even allowed) of other similarly educated professionals whose work is the same inexact science as teaching and learning, beginning with the same lack of a uniform raw product (Vaughn, Klinger, & Hughes, 2000). Society at large seems to have no reservations at asking of teachers what would never be asked of a physician, accountant, attorney, or any other professional provider of services. However, I will discuss later in this chapter that those of us in the profession are partly to blame for this phenomenon.

PROFESSIONAL COMPARISONS

For purposes of clarity and to simplify comparisons, let us assume that in the school system the student is the client/ receiver of services, just as the patient is the receiver of medical services or the customer in the economic realm. The difference here is that while there are laws that require every child to attend school to a particular age, there are virtually no laws that require children to receive the services of medical professionals other than those relative to certain vaccinations or emergency matters involving the immediate health and safety of a child.

When the professional expectations imposed on, say, the family dentist are compared to those of the educator, some interesting similarities occur, but also some serious discrepancies come to the surface. Both the dentist and the educator are trained to fix something lacking in the receiver of services via standard and generally well researched and established procedures. While we must bear in mind that neither dentistry nor teaching are exact sciences, the dentist and the educator's job are similar in that the client/receiver of services comes to the dentist to receive services in order that his/her quality of life is ultimately improved. The services provided by the professional educator and the dentist are similar in that some services may initially be somewhat uncomfortable and will likely require both commitment and serious effort on the part of the client.

The work of the educator and the dentist must be completed in a workspace that is physically appropriate to the work being done. This requires certain structural standards, space requirements, equipment mandates, and furniture/equipment that allows both the provider and the client to function effectively. The client who enters the dentist's office, one that is new, well decorated, and comfortable, will likely assume the dental practice is productive and the provider of services competent. An older dentist's office, with slightly older furniture, slightly older equipment, and walls of a less fashionable color, can certainly provide the same quality of dental care, provided that professional expectations and standards are maintained. We humans, however, are naturally attracted to that which is pretty and assume that new is better. It can hardly be argued that the visual appearance of the dental workspace plays a significant role in the perception of what goes on in the workspace. Likewise, when a school is new, well decorated, and comfortable it will be assumed to be a "better" school. Old buildings, old walls, old furniture, and less fashionable paint colors do not create a less effective provision of services, only the perception thereof.

Additionally, in the dental workspace and the educational workspace, a large portion of space must be allotted for the storage and maintenance of records, information, and various data. Both the dentist and the educator must spend inordinate amounts of time recording, documenting, and justifying the decisions made and the direction of services provided. In all instances, both dental and educational, the decisions made must be defensible based upon documented data relative to standard and customary practices. The dentist and the educator face similar struggles in this regard because all data are what can be visually seen via a standard set of diagnostic tools.

The dentist and the educator will use accepted and standard diagnostic tools to determine the particular needs of the individual. Then, using his/her professional judgment each will render services using a standard set of practices and procedures, fully understanding that lacking a uniform raw product, the results of neither will be guaranteed. In most instances there will be more than one option in solving a particular dental or teaching problem. The decision as to which option to pursue will typically be an evaluative one, not a mechanical one (Gersten, Vaughn, Deshler, & Schiller, 1997).

The dentist faces many of the same obstacles as the educator when the client comes in seeking services, particularly in that the dentist has absolutely no control over what has happened prior to the client choosing to seek services. The accepted and researched practices of the dental profession cannot eliminate any inherent error factors brought about by possibly hundreds of other mitigating circumstances influencing the status of the client's current dental health, including but not limited to diet, behavior patterns, background, experiences, or social and cultural mores of the family from which the client emerges. Just like the educator, the dentist is at the mercy of the nature of the individual when assuming that standard practices will be effective.

What we have discussed so far have been external influences on the status of the client. Like the educator, the dentist can usually see with relative ease any external or environmental factors influencing the likelihood that standard practices and procedures will probably create the desired outcome. However, both professionals must contend with the possibility that there are other factors influencing the likelihood of success that are internal—factors that are particular to that client alone and are not as easily observed or easily determined by frequently used processes of measurement. Such factors could include but certainly are not limited to biological anomalies, chemical imbalances in the body, or even neurological disorders. It is fair to say that both these professionals face a myriad of questions, possibly hundreds of factors that impact the decisions to be made in rendering meaningful and beneficial services—but every one of those possibly hundreds of factors are absolutely outside the control of the provider of services.

If we were to do some formal research in the area, we would likely find additional similarities between the work and frustrations of educators and dentists. Informed people have known for many years that a high positive correlation exists between a family's income and a child's academic achievement (Bracey, 1995; Kohn, 1999). When such factors are compared in correlational studies, it supports the idea of that same high positive correlation between family income and a child's general health, including dental. When educational statistics are gathered that compare cross sections of society, we repeatedly find that areas of the country that have high poverty rates are low in academic achievement. If we accept the notion that impoverished groups of people in particular areas demonstrate similar behaviors, it would seem logical that the dentist who practices in those areas will face a client base with much higher incidences of inherent dental problems not found in more affluent parts of the population.

But here the similarities stop. When the dentist's work is complete, the client leaves. Unless the dentist has made a blatant error resulting from incompetence, injured the client, or mistreated the client, the work is done and it is considered successful to the degree possible when all external and internal factors are allowed for within the limits of standard practice. From that point forward, all responsibility becomes that of the client or the person responsible for the client. If the client chooses to leave the office, continue in the same unhealthy dental behaviors that initially caused the dental problems, or not seek follow-up services, the dentist is not held accountable. Unfortunately, this is not so with the educator (Vaughn, Klinger, & Hughes, 2000).

The professional double standard kicks in here. When the educator's client leaves the laboratory—the classroom—the educator is still accountable for the subsequent behaviors of the client, specifically, what the client does and does not know as can be determined by various measures. The professional double standard has become particularly prevalent in the era of "high-stakes testing," whereby a student's promotion or retention is being determined by one particular test score. The dental profession is not condemned because a percentage, determined by one standardized measurement, of those seeking dental services either do not uphold their responsibility or simply did not respond well to standard practices and treatments. Additionally, a dentist who practices in an area where mitigating factors increase the likelihood of a high percentage of serious dental problems in the population at large would never have his/her competence called into question because of the background and experiences of the clientele. Such dentists would not be considered "marginal," "at-risk," or any of the other currently popular vernaculars of the educational world. The dentist practicing in these areas is not likely to have teams of "experts" sent in to redefine the method of practicing dentistry under the misguided and consummately wrong notion that doing more of the same thing will correct the problems that less of the same thing did not. It is not likely that the overall work of the dental profession would be presented as "failing" when, after all the research and advances, some portion of the population receiving services will always have dental problems that standard practices and procedures simply cannot fix.

So far I have compared the work, standards, and professional expectations in dentistry and teaching. There are other comparisons illustrating a professional double standard between teaching and other comparably educated professionals in the private sector. Just as dental work closely parallels that of teaching and learning, so does the work of the physician. The physician, like the dentist and the educator, works under frameworks of accepted practices and procedures. Like the dentist and educator, the physician must make decisions based on what can and cannot be seen via standard diagnostic tools. Additionally, forces, behaviors, and personal histories that are absolutely outside the physician's control immensely impact the work of the physician. In short, the work of the physician, dentist, and educator are all very inexact, imperfect sciences that bring about no guarantees.

The professional double standard between the physician and the educator becomes obvious when we compare medical work and teaching both statistically and longitudinally. The physician's work carries no guarantees that the client will respond to standard practices and procedures. As such, it would be a very shallow assumption that any physician or team of physicians will actually cure the ills of every patient who walks through the door. It is fair, however, to assert that physicians' success rate is quite good, as they do cure far more than they fail to cure. I would suspect the mass media would become the laughing stock were they to ever present the work of the medical profession as "failing" because a percentage of humans, despite the collective efforts of the profession, simply do not respond.

The educator's odds and success rate very much parallel those of the physician in that just as it is terribly naive to assume the medical profession will cure everyone who is ill, it is equally as naive to assume that the school systems will completely and successfully educate every child. Although popular opinion might say otherwise, the fact remains that as imperfect as they are, our schools do successfully educate far more than they fail to educate.

PROFESSIONAL SUPPORT AND ASSISTANCE

It is often said that teaching is the only profession in which the practitioner is expected to do the same caliber of work on the first day as the veteran of 20 years. The science and art of teaching are like any other vocation or profession in that time and experience work to define a personal style of delivery and refine the processes so that they are most effective. Let us again compare the work of the educator and the dentist.

In all fairness I will assert that the dentist typically spends one to three additional years in school than would be required of the teacher coming out of a traditional teacher-training program and has probably amassed the commensurate student loan debt. As reforms continue to be demanded and come about, we should not be at all surprised if, within the next few years, we see teacher training and licensing programs involve as many years in school as the dentist, veterinarian, attorney, or various medical

professionals. The time spent in professional preparation is an issue but is
not the point here.

Regardless of when the dentist and the educator report for their first day
on the job, there have been some similarities leading up to that point. Both
have successfully completed their college training, earned their university
degrees, and passed their licensing exams. Both have demonstrated whatever competencies are required to demonstrate they are capable of practicing their profession. Both are ready to leave the status as student and
enter the practitioner world. Both arrive ready, and we would assume anxious, to use their newly refined skills and newly acquired credentials for
the betterment of society at large. But upon arriving, there will be some
marked differences.

The work of the dentist, except in really limited circumstances, is not
going to be supported and provided personal remuneration by public dollars. As such, the dentist will likely not be working in private practice
alone, as he/she will not be in a position to be able to operate and support
a private practice independently. Obviously, the educator does not have
the option to work in private practice as a teacher, only as a consultant or
some outside support person. This is not likely to happen with no experience in the field. The dentist will never be allowed to practice his/her profession without adequate materials, supplies, equipment, and space
because doing so puts a patient's health at risk as well as being against the
law. If the dentist does not have the requisite materials, supplies, equipment, and space to complete the dental procedures in a proper manner, the
work will shut down until such discrepancies are rectified. There can be
no rationalizing or justifying why the necessary provisions were not in
place and the license of the dentist grants the autonomy to say, "No—this
is unethical." It would be absolutely unheard of that a clinic manager
would suggest that the dentist see patients in the lobby or in a storage area.
It would be equally as absurd to suggest that the dentist see more patients
in a day than he/she can realistically serve in a professional and ethical
manner. Continuing to practice under circumstances that lessen the effectiveness of the dental work or create an inherent danger is malpractice.

But, for some reason, the same standard does not apply to those charged
with the responsibility of teaching. If practicing dentistry without the requisite materials, supplies, equipment, and space constitutes malpractice, why
are teachers subjected to such? Jonathan Kozol (1991), in his book *Savage
Inequalities,* graphically describes teaching and learning conditions that
would qualify as malpractice were such to be found in a setting providing
some type of health care. In the city schools where I teach it is not uncommon to see teachers teaching under stairwells, in closets, or even in hallways.
We see gymnasiums divided with portable partitions into as many as eight
classrooms—conditions that are hardly conducive to the desired quality of
teaching that is currently being demanded. Fortunately, there are governing

agencies that shut down dental practices that would attempt to function under these standards. Unfortunately, no such agencies exist to oversee the operation of schools. Recent political rhetoric says that failing schools will be shut down. We will discuss later why that is not likely to really happen.

SUPPLY AND DEMAND

Let us suppose that one day we looked around and our nation had less than half the dentists that we needed. We can imagine what the status of dental health in this country would look like. With only half the dentists we needed, probably 70–80% of the people in the country would have some nasty dental problems. If we were to examine carefully the entire scenario by gathering data and making some evaluative judgments, we would likely find some interesting correlations to the shortage of dentists:

1. The average salary of dentists with many years of experience and specialized education beyond the minimum required to practice dentistry would be about two thirds that of comparably educated professionals;
2. There would be an embarrassing salary differential between the novice dentist and the veteran of 20 years;
3. Approximately one third of the individuals who train as dentists would never actually practice dentistry;
4. Of those who do enter the field, one out of five will leave the profession within three years for various reasons—most of which center around salary, working conditions, and general professional prestige. Those who do leave most likely will be the best and the brightest;
5. The standard training and licensing for the dentist is suspect; polite conversation among well-intentioned individuals often focuses on the status of America's dentists and the abysmal status of the profession;
6. Dentistry as a profession is not particularly respected and never has been. The academic training for dentists is considered lacking because their study focuses on teeth and does not include a broad knowledge base. Since it's only teeth, anyone can do it;
7. The media hardly have a nice thing to say about dentists or the profession;
8. Some bizarre, totally subjective measures are recognized as determining quality in the profession, including how many of their patients subsequently never again have dental problems. Those dentists who are fortunate to have a client base with few inherent dental problems are considered "good dentists";

9. The most critical shortage of dentists is in the areas where the most specialized training is needed;
10. The workload imposed on the current dental workforce is so unrealistic as to border on inhumane and abusive;
11. The middle class and affluent of society would consistently have access to appropriate dental care;
12. There would exist an almost perfect positive correlation between a person's socioeconomic status and his/her dental health.

The shortage of dentists is so critical that policymakers have imposed some measures to alleviate the shortage in this crucial area:

1. Recruiting massively, offering attractive bonuses and "perks" to those individuals who will "join us";
2. Accept individuals who hold a college degree in any area and who have attended a three- to eight-week–long seminar to practice dentistry;
3. Collaborate with local universities and dental schools to bring the necessary coursework and training to the worksite so the dentists can earn the necessary credentials (after practicing dentistry all day).

As an additional note, since the dentist shortage has caused a situation where some less than desired individuals are practicing dentistry and there is massive political and social pressure to raise the standards, we need to make the alternative route to licensure more difficult, not necessarily in academic content, but in political and bureaucratic "mess." Also, since these alternative people did not earn their license the ordinary way, we need to further impose on the already burdened system by creating more for the existing dentists to do in terms of mentoring programs and "created" work. One final note, let's make sure if there's any policy or legislation concerning this alternative process and raising standards that we word it so ambiguously that it leaves room to "wiggle out" should our best-laid plans simply not work.

Does this sound familiar? This analogy may seem extreme, but it serves to bring home my point of a serious double standard imposed on educators and teachers that other professions and professionals would not allow or tolerate. It should go without saying that society would never tolerate dentists being literally recruited from the street. Yet, for reasons that seem to defy common logic, we have no qualms whatsoever with staffing American classrooms with whomever we can find, whomever is blindly willing to assume the challenge, and whomever will tolerate the insanity of the bureaucracy in the process. But, the aspect of this analogy that most flagrantly defies common logic is that by staffing classrooms in a manner bordering on desperation and hysteria, which would be called malpractice in other professions, some of the less informed among us will have the unmitigated gall to ask, "Why doesn't it work?"

QUALITY CONTROL

In any profession or business that provides goods and/or services, there must be some manner of determining quality control. Obviously, schools are not exempt from this need (Apple, 1999). In order to ensure that standards are maintained and that all involved are treated fairly there must be some standard method for determining if those practicing the profession are doing so in a manner that furthers the profession and provides the best service to the client. It is both interesting and sad that these processes in the teaching profession are seriously skewed in directions that would never be allowed or tolerated in other professions.

Let's again compare the dentist to the educator. It is doubtful that the American Dental Association, American Medical Association, or comparable professional organizations would even think of imposing the subjective performance evaluation processes on their members that are imposed on teachers. In a subsequent chapter we will discuss some miserably failed efforts by various states to design one universal method of determining teacher quality. At this point, suffice it to say that any effort to evaluate teacher quality is a subjective judgment based on classroom visits of less than one hour with varying frequency, sometimes as infrequent as every third year. The weaknesses, inconsistencies, and often ineffectiveness of it all are well recognized by scholars in the field. Prybylo (1998) states:

> In discussing the general nature of employee evaluation, Banks and Murphy (1985) stated that "Effective performance appraisal in organizations continues to be a compelling but unrealized goal" (p. 335). Peterson (1995) asserted that research on teacher evaluation conducted over the last seventy years provides compelling evidence that current practices in this area neither "improve teachers [nor] accurately tell what happens in classrooms" (p. 14). Further, he said that research "reveals fundamental technical and sociological flaws with present teacher evaluation" (p.15). Schmoker (1992) wrote, "Research has finally told us what many of us have suspected all along: that conventional evaluation, the kind the overwhelming majority of American teachers undergo, does not have any measurable impact on the quality of student learning." (pp. 559–560)

Wood (1992) asserts that the traditional "observe, judge, and write report" model is inherently flawed because too much of the observer's background, experiences, and personal perceptions come into play, as well as the time factor of scheduling such observations (Marshall, 1996). It is of concern that observer's unfamiliarity with the group, the teacher's methods, or the subject matter may cause the observer to misinterpret what is seen. In my own experience, several years ago a central office administrator visited my class during a middle school choral rehearsal. The administrator criticized me for allowing the students to sit every few minutes, insisting instead that they should stand for the entire rehearsal. First, choral directors of experience know that tired singers lack energy and will not produce as beautiful a sound, so sitting periodically, when standing is not necessary, is quite common. Second, it would be unreasonable to ask a group of professional singers to stand for an entire hour so how can one justify such with a group of middle school children? This administrator fit the profile described by Wood (1992). She states:

> Similarly, if a behavior or event in a teaching episode is not viewed in the context of other lessons and other teacher-student interactions that transpired on other days, the principal may misinterpret what occurred. The context is essentially unavailable to a supervisor who observes one or two 30-minute lessons and does not discuss the lesson with the teacher before and after it takes place. When the context is missing, the process is a closed one that does nothing to enhance objectivity. (pp. 55–56)

Clearly the point of teacher evaluation is the same as quality control in the noneducation business. It cannot be argued that evaluation is necessary for improvement and growth. The question is seldom "why" but most often "how" (Dunkin, 1997; Gullatt & Bullard, 1998; Mayo, 1997). In view of the inexactness of it all, many forward-thinking individuals are calling for more use of peer assessment and support, more comparable to those found in the private sector. It is thought by many that the "practitioner down the hall" has a far clearer mental picture of the inherent problems and strengths in a colleague's classroom than a central office administrator who visits the school buildings three or four times a year (Murray & Grant, 1998). Although extremely questionable, some administrators are even calling for input from students in evaluating teacher quality (Bushweller, 1998). It is clear that educators have expectations imposed on them in these areas that would never be considered in other professions.

PROFESSIONAL BOUNDARIES

The field of professional education is quite inept at setting professional boundaries. Those of us in the field are partly to blame for this phenomenon, not because we have created it, but because we do little to stop it. Unlike those in the medical, legal, and financial professions, we educators generally do a very poor job when it comes to establishing professional limits. It is a phenomenon in our business that our roles are changing as society changes and that we are having to assume more and more responsibilities we were never intended to assume. Other professionals don't say such things. Their roles have not changed in the past 100 years because their professional boundaries are quite clearly defined. Other comparably educated professionals (attorneys, accountants, physicians) apparently receive as part of their professional training some cognizance of where their professional responsibilities stop. It is not difficult to see these issues addressed in professional journals in nursing, psychology, and other medical fields. Unfortunately, these boundaries are much more nebulous for teachers. One can logically deduce that the differences stem from the fact that the receivers of services are children.

Although somewhat limited, there is a body of literature addressing professional boundaries in the social science professions that are comparable to teaching. Professions such as nursing (Mangan, 1997), counseling psychology (Lamb, 1999), social work (Zakutansky & Sirles, 1993), and the ministry (Haug, 1999) all have clearly established limits within the scope of their professional practice. These practitioners are fully aware of where their professional responsibilities stop and frequently remind themselves of such. This is not so in the business of teaching and learning. It should then come as no surprise that there is an embarrassing lack of literature addressing what teachers are expected and should be willing to do. If no one is quite sure where these boundaries lie, it should likewise come as no surprise that there is not a body of professional literature speaking to this question.

A number of years ago, I was teaching in a large suburban school system. At the time, much of the current political climate and debate focused on the homeless situation in this country. Compounding this problem was the fact that at that time, the bottom had fallen out of an oil-based economy that had been the basis of a hideously inflated housing market. As such, with people losing jobs by the hundreds, entire communities of overpriced, over-mortgaged properties were becoming vacant practically overnight. This only added to the dilemma of the perception that the homeless were a constituency that must be addressed immediately. Most people agreed that on a national scale, these were problems that needed to be addressed and be brought to the forefront of American awareness. Agency efforts and programs abounded in support of meeting the plight of those whose fate had been less than desirable. At the time, the large suburban school system had a very forward-thinking superintendent who was not at all intimidated by the problems that are inherent to a city school system. I was surprised, however, when she brought to the public an idea of creating a shelter for homeless students at one of the inner-city high schools. I was a relatively young teacher at the time and remember this being the first time I questioned the efforts of a school system's administration or perceived such efforts to be generally a bad idea. I remember discussions with colleagues and friends as to where the boundaries should stop between professionals and clients. I remember thinking at the time that physicians and psychologists may direct their services in the direction of these unfortunate individuals, but they would not extend their efforts to an area that could become questionable. While creating a shelter for homeless students was a most noble idea, creating overnight care for children is simply not the responsibility of the public schools. Out of sheer necessity, the schools have unquestionably taken on far more responsibility than they were ever intended to assume, but providing for children in this manner is such that all sorts of legal and ethical implications were imminent. Needless to say, the homeless shelter for school children idea did not last long.

Since that time, I have repeatedly asked the question as to whether other professionals, despite their empathy for the unfortunate, would allow their professional boundaries to extend beyond where it was intended to fall. I think not. In asking the question as to why, my thoughts return to the fact that the receiver of services in the field of teaching and learning are children. It would make sense that it is far easier for one's professional boundaries to become muddled when the question is the best interest of children who do not have the personal autonomy to make legal decisions for themselves and who are literally at the mercy of the system.

So how do education professionals perpetuate the professional double standard that creates such discrepancies between this profession and others? Educators at the service level (teachers, counselors, and school social workers) tend to be very complacent individuals, not personally, but professionally (Scherer, 2001). Perhaps it is an inherent flaw in the personality that chooses teaching as a profession or possibly a weak link in the professional training, but the simple fact remains that we educators do not do well when we have to say no. It is common knowledge that professional stress and burnout happen in this business far more often than others. Nebulous professional boundaries cause the educator to not only perceive, but also actually possess, less professional efficacy. Burnout in this profession or any other is not caused by too much work, too much paperwork, too much stress, unrealistic expectations, and so forth. Burnout comes about when the practitioner loses his/her perspective. When we lose the ability to back up, reassess, and see the entire picture, we need to seriously redirect our place in the situation.

Professional burnout does not happen suddenly. Burnout does not come from major trauma. Burnout comes from a "piling up" of small problems that are not addressed until the person reaches the point of the proverbial "straw that broke the camel's back." Suppose we placed a frog in a pot of water at a reasonable temperature that the frog could easily tolerate. If we begin to gently raise the temperature, the frog's cold-blooded body will adjust to the environmental temperature. As we continue to raise the temperature, the frog's body continues to adjust and he has no clue something is wrong. When the frog realizes something is wrong, it's too late. This analogy is typical of what happens to those individuals who burn out in teaching. By the nature of the work, we are asked to be flexible, a team player, and adapt easily to unexpected change. Even the most compliant of individuals has their limit. There is something about our profession in that we often realize too late that our limit has been reached.

There are the anecdotal examples of individual educators who are quite competent at establishing and maintaining boundaries as to what will and will not be tolerated. In casual observation, these individuals tend to have a much healthier outlook on the profession and the grossly unreal expectations imposed by society at large. These individuals recognize what they can and cannot control, accept these discrepancies graciously, and carry on with surprising effectiveness. However, the fact that these individuals are strong, assertive, and not pulled down by the burdens of others often leads to the perception that the person is either a "trouble maker" or "not a team player." It is unfortunate that in our business the strong individual who has the potential to do quite well and who possesses the attributes that would be greatly admired in the private sector seem to be looked upon as undesirable in our profession where they are needed so desperately. Such things have been said of me. As we shall see in subsequent chapters, there have been a number of instances over the years when I "stirred the pot" by asking questions that no one else would.

Many professional expectations in our business come about by default because the receivers of our services are children. Although it may not be a popular perspective among some policymakers and educational leaders, it can hardly be argued that effective teaching cannot come about without some of the same skills, attributes, and attitudes that are found in effective parenting. Anyone who has raised children knows that conflicts are an inevitable part of the day and as such we choose our battles very carefully.

UNREASONABLE DEMANDS

It is interesting to hear polite conversation discussing what educators are asked to do, not in the sense of the entire profession, but in the context of one client at a time. In any profession, services are provided during standard business hours because service providers are real people with a life outside their practice. Service providers, including physicians, attorneys, dentists, accountants, teachers, and ministers, usually have the same home and family responsibilities as anyone else. Polite conversation complains that seeking the services of providers causes individuals to have to rearrange schedules, take time off work, and somehow manage to see the service provider during "regular business hours." While some specialty service providers may keep slightly varied working hours due to the nature of the work, we would never think of asking our physician to work well into the evening or to see us at anytime other than regular working hours. But no one thinks twice at asking a teacher to do the same. Several years ago I had an incident with a parent who worked and was adamant that various school personnel meet with her well after school hours. She approached me, insisted that I arrange a meeting, and stated, "They'll meet me on my time or I'll go to the school board." I assured the lady that someone other than me should make such arrangements and referred her to our principal, who made it clear he could not ask teachers to stay until 5:00 in the afternoon. She did very begrudgingly acquiesce and leave her job to meet with a group of faculty. I recall a similar incident when an acquaintance of mine told in polite conversation that she went to her daughter's school after hours asking to see the teacher. The teacher was preparing to leave but reluctantly did meet the parent. In the conversation, the acquaintance stated, "She didn't care about my kid—she just wanted to get out of there." This individual is a nurse and clinic manager. I asked the question, "If someone shows up at your office right at closing time without an appointment, it's not an emergency, and your own children are waiting for you—are you particularly anxious to take your personal time to see them?" The response was, "Well—I work in a clinic. This is a school. She's a teacher and that's what she's there to do." Obviously, this individual believes in the professional double standard.

The most blatant example of demands on personal time I can give involved several other teachers and me several years ago. A vice principal issued a memo directing me and two other teachers to be at school an entire hour early on a particular morning to meet with a parent of a particularly ill-behaved child. I considered the request unreasonable and was not at all pleased to be told to be at school an entire hour early to deal with one child whose behavior was not acceptable. I handled the situation by simply informing the vice principal that being there that early was "a problem for me." Another teacher was furious and asked the vice principal, "Am I supposed to leave my own child unattended at the bus stop for an hour so I can be here to deal with someone else's child and their insolent behavior?" The vice principal was clearly outnumbered, but I'm not sure she had a clue as to what she had asked us to do. I doubt we would ask our physician, attorney, accountant, banker, or other merchant to neglect their familial responsibilities in favor of our own. We would recognize these professionals have the same responsibilities as anyone else, but for some reason, such considerations are lost when we deal with teachers.

As a teacher as well as an adult, I have never particularly objected to parents phoning me at home if there was a serious enough need to do so. But early on in my teaching career I learned to squelch unnecessary phone calls as soon as possible. On balance, I have never been tolerant of a parent call-ing me at home on my time to complain, whine, gossip about neighbors, resolve a dispute, or generally grieve over matters that can and should wait until school hours. Some years ago I was forced to deal with what had to be the most flagrant disregard of my time and privacy. There was a par-ent who apparently believed it was perfectly appropriate to call me at home two to three nights a week so she could call out the answers to her daughter's homework and I could tell her if they were correct! This obvi-ously well-intentioned parent surely wanted her child to do well but had no clue as to how she was imposing on my personal time. Each time she phoned I told her that I didn't have my teacher's edition textbooks at home and perhaps her daughter could check her work with the rest of the class. She finally got the message.

ATTENTION TO DIFFERENCES

Our schools make a most concerted and generous effort to attend to dif-ferences among individuals. The concept of individual differences, how-ever, has gone so far astray that the public seems to have no problem ask-ing teachers essentially to neglect other children for the sake of one child. Parents, administrators, and outside agency personnel often place demands on teachers that require a disproportionate amount of effort and time on the specific problems of one child to such an extent that the child-ren in the mainstream who do not exhibit such problems are essentially ignored. Often such problems are those that school personnel are neither trained nor qualified to handle. Several years ago I stirred quite a contro-versy when I said no to such an unreasonable demand. While serving on a committee that screened children who were exhibiting unusual difficul-ties, a most unusual case came forth. There was a kindergarten child, age 5, and coincidentally the worst case of childhood obesity I had ever seen. In addition to the social problems caused by the child's extreme weight, he was quite aggressive toward his classmates, but worst of all was the fact that he soiled his pants two to three times each week. It became a pattern that the child would end up sitting in the school foyer for two to three hours waiting for someone to pick him up or bring a change of clothes. The principal, generally a capable instructional leader, nearly made a regret-table error when he wrote a letter to the child's guardian stating the child could not return to school until this problem was permanently corrected. The child's grandmother then got involved and took the child to both a physician and a child psychologist. The physician determined there was nothing physically wrong that would cause the child to behave in this way, so the psychologist took over. This Ph.D.-level psychologist attended the next meeting where the child was on the agenda. She reported to us that she had designed a very elaborate plan of behavior modification whereby if the child went one hour without fighting or soiling himself, the teacher was to apply a blue sticker to the left hand. After three stickers (three hours—half the school day) the boy would get a red sticker on the right hand. After two red stickers (an entire school day) then a green sticker was placed on a chart on the wall. While the idea of this kind of structure and consistency was not inherently bad, it did create one additional thing for the poor teacher to maintain, practically to the neglect of all those children who did not fight or soil themselves. The scenario became far more interesting when she stated that she and her colleagues had been working on his "hygiene problems" and as such would insist that each time the child went to the restroom he would be accompanied by a male adult to see that he cleaned himself thoroughly! The psychologist had no idea what was being asked of us. First of all, there were three men in the building—the principal, the custodian, and me. Someone's workday would be interrupted each time the child had to go the restroom, which is frequent with small children. (Would I have to call someone to cover my class so that I could escort him?) Second, an adult in closed quarters with one child who is removing his/her clothing creates all sorts of potential ethical and legal liabilities. Third, it simply is not the responsibility of the schools, outside of some very specialized early childhood or handicap-type programs, to attend to those types of needs. I interrupted the meeting by interjecting, "I'm so sorry—I will not escort a child to the restroom to check their undergarments for bodily waste." Silence ensued as everyone in the room froze and the psychologist replied, "Well . . . perhaps we can make another arrangement." I replied, "Why don't you do that."

If I had not said no, the psychologist would have made these demands and probably expected teachers to blindly obey, regardless of the practical, ethical, and legal questions involved. In a clinical setting, it is perfectly acceptable for a physician, nurse, or nurse practitioner to examine a child's unclothed body, but that responsibility is not within the role, expectations, or qualifications of teachers. Every child in this country is entitled to a free public education, regardless of handicapping condition, in the same way that a child is guaranteed medical attention regardless of the family's ability to pay. It can hardly be imagined, however, that a team of professionals, concurring on a special case, would ask physicians to perform duties outside their scope of experience and expertise. Apparently, this psychologist thought nothing of asking that of a group of teachers.

SOMETHING FOR EVERYONE

The current push for attention to individual differences is not new. Although many writers and theorists claim otherwise, the more current vernacular of "differentiated instruction," "multiple intelligences," "individual learning styles" or "multilevel learning" all mean the same thing as what the scholars of teaching and learning in the 1960s called simply "individualized instruction." (It is interesting that some proponents of curriculum differentiation claim that the practice is not the same as the ideas that abounded in the 1970s.) The idea is very progressive in nature in that we see a focus on the efficacy of the individual rather than a common contribution to society at large. The crux of the idea is that if every student who walks into the classroom could be presented the material in the exact manner that capitalizes on their strengths and bypasses their weaknesses, then every student will succeed every single time. In theory, the idea makes sense. After all, who would not want to provide every single child with every single opportunity to succeed? But the idea is flawed for several reasons:

1. True individualized instruction, its design, and implementation are myths perpetuated by untested ideas and theories that are popular, but not substantiated by any formal investigation or study.
2. Creating every lesson 5, 10, or 15 different ways is unrealistic, impractical, and basically impossible. Asking teachers to design such groups of lessons is both extravagant and excessive. This creates the same burden for teachers as asking a cook to create a number of different meals at the same time to accommodate a variety of picky eaters.
3. The idea that every single child can and/or will be able to succeed every single time is flawed logic. Teaching and learning are the same inexact science as the practice of medicine. It would never be acceptable for a physician simply to give a person enough different drugs so they will, unquestionably, eventually get well.

Other professionals do not have such unrealistic expectations imposed on them for a couple of reasons. Most professionals provide services to one client at a time. Educators, by virtue of the nature of the work, provide services to multiple clients at a time. Individualizing service one client at a time makes sense. Truly individualizing services 30 at a time simply is not humanly possible.

There has been much written in recent years on the question of learning styles and teaching to individual differences. Those who advocate totally individualized instruction are idealists who do not have valid research data to support their positions. Those who have done studies in the area have found very little correlation between individualized instruction and increased achievement.

LICENSURE AND PROFESSIONAL
DEMAND

There is much disagreement among thinking individuals as to what should be required for professional licensure of teachers. The span of ideas that ranges from extreme to extreme is often heard in polite conversation. Some believe that simply having demonstrated mastery of a body of content in an academic discipline is sufficient. For example, not too many years ago holding a law degree was not necessary to sit for the bar exam. Although well up in years and certainly no longer practicing law, there are individuals alive today who became attorneys by simply studying and passing the bar exam. Still others believe that no particular requirements should be imposed at all—simply holding a college degree in any area is sufficient to grant licensure. The extreme of these notions is certainly an issue for thinking people but is not the point here. In theory, we can create all the exacting standards we want and upgrade programs to the point that even the most critical would agree. However, nothing will look different because of one fundamental flaw in the system—in the teaching business there absolutely must be a live, human adult in the front of that classroom. So the professional double standard really turns into a vicious cycle. We want every teacher to have met a certain criteria, but we must have teachers in the meantime whether they've met the criteria or not.

We do not see this phenomenon in other professions. A physician, dentist, attorney, accountant, psychologist, therapist, and even beauticians, barbers, and manicurists absolutely do not practice until their licensure is complete and in place. We do not find physicians practicing medicine while they work on their licensure—they have to wait until it is in place. A dentist does not touch a human tooth nor does a manicurist touch a fingernail until the licensure to practice is complete. As much as society would like it to be so, this simply cannot happen in teaching because the client/receiver of services are children. As such, the client (1) is not able to legally make decisions for themselves and (2) must be supervised at all times. The polite conversation that languishes the fact that such a large percentage of teachers in classrooms today, particularly in large cities, are not certified/licensed probably have no clue as to what they are asking. In theory it certainly would be possible to have absolutely no unlicensed teachers in a classroom anywhere, but the obvious result would be that not every child would be able to attend school. Unlike the other professions who can turn away clients, that would be a nasty decision for schools to make. But it does remain a professional double standard that mistreats educators.

One other point should be addressed concerning certification/licensure of professionals. A significant difference exists between a person being certified to teach and one being *qualified* to teach. Certification refers to a person having completed whatever requirements are necessary for the granting of a credential. *Qualification* means a person truly possesses the competence to complete a task. A person completing the required educational and testing requirements for certification/licensure in any field does not necessarily mean that person is particularly bright nor does it mean the person will provide that service particularly well. In my recent experience, an elementary principal made a serious error in attempting to force the certification issue when letting go of that mindset would undoubtedly have been a better administrative move. When class sizes were rearranged and it became necessary for a teacher to move, the principal insisted that one particular "certified" teacher move to another grade level that was required to take a high-stakes test. The teacher had no experience at that level, was leery of the principal's request, and insisted that someone else with experience at that level, certified or not, would be better suited. Rather than move another teacher who was willing to make the commitment to follow through with the grade-level requirements, the principal was adamant in having her way, causing the teacher to resign and go to teach in a neighboring school system. The unfortunate result of this administrative move was that the children who were expected to take the high-stakes test spent half the year with a series of substitutes. Many days the group had to be split among the other classes at the grade level because there was no substitute available for the day. In this instance, a certified teacher was far less important than a permanent teacher.

It is an unfortunate fact of life that we have professionals who simply are not particularly good at what they do. In all the professions, there are individuals who completed the education and licensure who probably should not have. There are physicians, attorneys, dentists, accountants, and, most certainly, teachers whose work is sloppy and whose skills are lacking, despite the fact that they completed the requirements for licensure at some time. But for some reason, the same polite conversation that laments the deplorable state of schools in this country seems to minimize the fact that there are professionals everywhere, other than teachers, who are quacks. According to American Medical Association data, for every one physician in this country there are three or four teachers. With all things being equal, it would then stand to reason that for every physician practicing medicine who should not be, there would likely be three or four teachers teaching who should not be. Furthermore, for every American who has received services from a physician, they have likely received services from 60–75 teachers. Again, with all things being equal, it would then stand to reason that the average American is 60–75 times more likely to encounter a quack teacher than a quack physician. The question is visibility, in that the teachers work is far more visible than the physicians (Lebaree, 1999). Rothstein (1999) states, "A pernicious mix of myth and reality underlies the campaign against teacher inadequacy. It needs to be examined" (p. 2).

It is no secret that our nation is critically short of teachers. The shortage of teachers in this country will be addressed further in another chapter. Despite the rhetoric surrounding the "how and why" of the teacher shortage, all the arguments fall short when a group of children go through an entire school year without a permanent teacher.

A PERSONAL REFLECTION

Several years ago the professional double standard between our profession and others became particularly real. I had just completed the doctorate and submitted a presentation proposal for a national medical conference, which to my surprise was accepted. I drove several hours to the city where the conference was to take place, checked into the hotel, and located the conference personnel. This conference was organized and put on by medical professionals, and I must assert that in all my years as an educator I had never been treated so professionally. The following morning when the presentations began, I felt like the beggar child must have felt in Mark Twain's *The Prince and the Pauper*. The facilities were exquisite, the audio-visual equipment was state of the art, and the personnel could not have been more helpful. I did not find the "just a teacher" mindset present, probably because I was the only public schoolteacher making a presentation to these groups of medical and behavioral science professionals who were considered the top in their field. The behavior of the presenters was entirely different from what I was accustomed to seeing at education-focused conferences. The content of the presentations was new information that professionals shared with one another as a tool for professional decision making, rather than more propagandized dogma. Discussions were academic and adult-focused. There was no silly role-playing or time spent elaborating upon the perfectly obvious. The refreshments put out at the session breaks were beautifully done and were presented on real dishes with real coffee cups and real flatware. I knew that such preparations had to be an enormous expense, but I likewise knew that this was not how teachers were accustomed to being treated. My experience and background naturally caused me to question if I deserved such treatment. After all, I'm only a teacher and these people were doctors! But then I realized there is a reason I saw such a difference in the organization and presentation at a medical conference as opposed to a teacher conference. I seriously doubt that a group of physicians would tolerate the deplorable treatment that teachers had come to expect. A typical teacher conference will not likely take place in a public setting but would take place in a school with the school cafeteria as the headquarters. There might be a coffeepot and, if they're lucky, some greasy doughnuts presented in the box. The presentation sessions will likely take place in classrooms with child-sized furniture and in an environment that is simply not conducive to the type of reflective academic discussion that produces true professional growth. Additionally, the presentations would be new fads and buzzwords, not findings based in hard science.

Fancy facilities, fancy pastries, fruit, and real dishes do not necessarily produce a better quality learning experience, but they do serve to support my position. There is a definite double standard in what is expected of and tolerated by our profession.

3

+

Doing What We're Told to Do

Where there is a fad there is money to be made, and bookstore shelves
are bursting not only with the usual adult self-help books but countless
teacher manuals. . . . Words like "positive discipline," "constructivist
teaching" and "authentic assessment."

Maureen Stout, *The Feel-Good Curriculum* (2000, p. 143)

Since the beginning of a system of public education in this country some
150 years ago, social science scholars and the public at large have dis-
agreed adamantly over what exactly it is that the schools are supposed to
do. It is no secret that Americans have always been leery of turning the
education of their children over to someone they probably did not
know—someone who may believe differently, think differently, live differently, or come from a different cultural or experiential background.
Good parenting has not changed in thousands of years. It should make
sense that responsible people would be cautious about relinquishing control over any matter that impacts the health, safety, and well-being of their
children (Webb & Norton, 1999).

Recently Diane Ravitch (2000), the eminent educational historian in
Left Back: A Century of Failed School Reforms, has written of what has not
worked particularly well in the past century and why. Ravitch eloquently walks the reader through various reform movements and various schools of thought and outlines most of the key political players of
the past 100 years. Practically all of the arguments of the past century are
still argued today. Simply put, mainstream America seems to want public education done their way, placing emphasis on what they consider
important with no regard for what is in the best interest of all concerned
(Hughes & Hooper, 2000). When it comes to educating the youth of this
nation, people will go to some pretty serious extremes to maintain a
squabble. But, despite all that has created the controversy and indeci-
siveness of the profession for the past 100–150 years, one factor has, with-

43

out fail, remained constant—teachers have only done what they were told to do.

Virtually all the educational squabbles of past 100–150 years have been characterized by two opposing schools of thought that have consistently created diametrically opposing positions. One school of thought is generally called the traditionalist while the other is called the progressivist. While this book is not intended to be a text in the history of American education or some comparison of educational philosophies, an understanding of the two schools of thought is necessary for us to understand how we have arrived where we are, the role that teachers have played, and how these phenomenon mistreat educators. Let us briefly explore and compare the two.

TRADITIONAL VERSUS PROGRESSIVE EDUCATION

The school of thought referred to as traditionalist is noted for the adherence to time-tested ideas, education as the imparting of a common body of information, and the same curriculum for all regardless of background, interest, long-term goals, or personal capabilities. The traditionalist mindset tends to focus on the education of the masses, ensuring that a common body of information exists among society so that communication is facilitated. Traditionalist education acknowledges intellectualism, or "knowledge for knowledge sake." In the pure traditionalist mode of thinking, there isn't much space for the individual who falls outside the mainstream.

On the other hand, although the progressivist ideas had been around for some time, they began to surface in this country around the middle of the 19th century. Americans were at a point where no one quite trusted "book learning" (Hirsch, 1995). Society was ready to abandon the rigid societal expectations and mores of the Victorian era. The progressivist education mindset is marked by a move away from the educational needs of the masses—away from standardization in curriculum, content, and instructional delivery. Under the progressive mindset, instructional goals and desired outcomes tend to be expressed in such a way that they are much broader, the success of which can be more universally interpreted. As such, more and more children can be served. The traditionalist ideals view the purpose of education as creating a commonality among the masses; whereas the progressive mindset views the school as the fundamental tool of social change. To the contrary, the progressive ideas blur the boundaries between the teaching of academic subject matter and the nurturing of the child's total existence—emotional, physical, and intellectual.

When we read into the history of the movement known as progressive education several names are quite prominent and two universities appear frequently—the University of Chicago and Teacher's College of Columbia University (Cremin, 1964; Kramer, 1997). John Dewey is credited, both favorably and unfavorably, with the founding of the progressive education movement in this country (Kramer, 1997). Dewey accepted a position at the University of Chicago in 1894, less than a decade before Chicago would see a huge growth in population, particularly among less-educated, working-class families with children. With that sector of the population growing exponentially, accommodating the educational needs of the children was paramount (Olson, 1999). Further compounding the problem was the fact that most of these children would likely not have attended school or had only been allowed a minimal education 10–15 years earlier. Social reformers from many directions were putting pressure on the schools to somehow meet the needs of this growing massive population. Olson (1999) states: "Proponents of virtually every progressive cause from the 1890's through World War I had their program for the school. Humanitarians of every stripe saw education at the heart of their effort toward social alleviation" (p. 6). Similarly, Ravitch (2000) stated:

> Experts asserted that reorganized schools could train wise consumers, stabilize family life, prepare future workers, reduce crime and improve society—but only if the schools diminished their concern for "mastery of knowledge" and concentrated instead on "pressing issues of present living." (p. 240)

Many of Dewey's contemporaries were very liberal social thinkers who had traveled extensively and been seriously impressed and influenced by the Romantic mindsets of European educators, particularly the French, who saw education as happening naturally and concurrently with the typical development of a child. Whereas the traditional mode of education had attempted to force the child to fit the mold of the school, the European idea was in direct contradiction—remake the school to fit the child (Olson, 1999).

It was during his tenure at the University of Chicago that Dewey founded the famous laboratory school where it is believed that many of the practices that today are called "progressive" or "child-centered" originated. According to Chall (2000), the school was quite small at the beginning, both in student body and faculty, but grew considerably in the seven years it operated. The teachers who were chosen for the school were far better trained as teachers than most at the time and much was demanded of them in terms of professional responsibilities. Interestingly, Chall notes that the records kept of the school's operation were sparse, so much of what is touted today about Dewey's laboratory school is suspect. In 1910, Dewey met some opposition with administration at the University of Chicago and left to accept a teaching position at Teacher's College of Columbia University.

The second major theorist we find in the progressive literature is William Heard Kilpatrick. Kilpatrick had been a student of Dewey's some years earlier and after earning his doctorate moved on to a 30-year tenure at Teacher's College of Columbia University. It is thought by many that he took a number of Dewey's ideas a step further than Dewey intended, as he was adamantly convinced that children did not experience any real learning unless it came about as a result of personal experience or hands-on engagement. Though it is argued even today, he is credited with many progressive ideas having been taken to extremes and consequently going afoul. For example, a doctoral student of Kilpatrick's, Ellsworth Collings, proposed what was at the time a very controversial topic for a dissertation. Collings designed and completed the study on the "project curriculum" and cited numerous findings in which the project style of teaching was superior to more traditional methods. Of particular interest is Collings's report of a handful of children who successfully fought an outbreak of typhoid fever in their community. This study, which likely influenced many educational decisions over the years, recently came under attack by Knoll (1996). Knoll asserts that much of the statistical data were seriously flawed by research standards of the time and that typhoid fever story was absolutely false.

In the early 1930s, Ralph Tyler at the University of Chicago undertook a massive eight-year study comparing groups of students educated at traditional high schools and progressive high schools. Briefly, the study found that those educated at the progressive high schools were only slighter better academically and after high school only fared slightly better than those educated in a more traditional setting. Even today this study is cited in support of many progressive educational theories and practices. Few people stop to realize that the study, though very well done at the time, is now around 70 years old. Older research is not inherently bad. "Good" research is that which can be generalized to the remainder of the population. Many would call into question a set of findings involving only a few hundred subjects many years ago.

The progressive movement caught on and grew at such a pace that by the 1930s and 1940s such practices were considered the norm. Few questioned their presence and use in the schools until America was embarrassed by the Russians beating us in the space program by launching *Sputnik* in 1957. Progressive education was blamed as putting America behind the rest of the world. The public began to demand more traditional methods of instruction, emphasizing math and science. But since that time, progressive education has resurfaced several times, each of which seemed to make a more dramatic move away from the original ideas of such thinkers as Dewey and Kilpatrick. Each time the movement surfaced we saw old ideas with new names taken to greater extremes.

The 1960s saw the advancement of "new math," "ungraded curricula"

(Dufay, 1966), and "open schools." The new math ideals challenged the age-old practice of having students memorize basic math facts so that recall was automatic and not a problem to be solved. New math of the 1960s, in the same progressive mindset of today, focused on process rather than content. However, the open schools movement is likely the one element of the 1960s resurgence of progressivism that went entirely afoul. Many new schools were built during that time that had no walls—essentially warehouses where children were grouped for instruction. Even some universities jumped on the bandwagon and built colleges of education with no walls. Four decades later trying to teach by today's standards in those buildings is a nightmare for reasons of simple physics. First, there is nothing to absorb or block sound or contain the noise that is inherently a part of children. Second, there often are no partitions to isolate children's field of vision to the task at hand. Obviously in these situations, distraction is the key word. The distraction problem is further compounded by well-intentioned but misguided educational leaders and administrators who insist on teaching methods that involve far more movement and physical engagement than solace and mental engagement.

From the late 1970s to the present, the traditional/progressive question has manifest itself by the same arguments over and over again. In order to meet individual needs and better serve more of the population educational leaders and policymakers are demanding less structure than is typically found in more traditional methods. But in the same vein that less structure is demanded, an absolute measure of outcomes with little or no room for interpretation is demanded. Obviously one cannot have both. At the other extreme we find those educational leaders and policymakers who demand the regimented teaching of a specific body of content but done so in such a manner that no student should experience the stress of meeting mandates and/or deadlines (Gill & Schlossman, 1996). It should be clear that the traditional/progressive education dichotomy creates the most brutal and unworkable situation for those educators charged with the responsibility of actually teaching children to read, write, add, subtract, or create a solution to a real life problem. Despite the horrendous nature of it all, teachers are only doing what they are told to do.

The traditional/progressive argument is often summed up as "teacher directed" (traditional) or "student centered" (progressive). While professional opinions and perspectives on the matter contrast sharply, it is generally recognized that teacher-centered instruction tends to focus on the teacher, their role as an adult, and the fact that teachers do know more than children as the force behind the learning. The teacher decides how the learning will occur, when it will occur and how much time will be involved, and exactly what learning will occur. The learning is measured by specific outcomes representing a sample of a specific body of content.

Conversely, the student-centered idea of instruction tends to focus on the interests and general nature of children as the force behind the learning. The interests and natural curiosity of children determine how and when the learning will occur, how much time is to be involved, and exactly what learning will occur. The learning is measured by the process and application more than against a sample of a specific body of content.

When we see the two theories compared in the professional literature, it can and often does resemble harsh political dogma. We seldom see a balanced perspective on the two, but instead the weaknesses of the opposite emphasized. Hirsch (1997b) states:

> Even today classroom language unfairly pits the two alternatives against one another. . . . Parents presented with such choices for their children's education would be unlikely to prefer traditional, merely verbal, premature, fragmented, boring and lockstep instruction to instruction that is modern, hands-on, developmentally appropriate, integrated, interesting and individualized. But of course this is a loaded and misleading contrast. (p. 2)

We must bear in mind, however, that traditionalism and progressivism are ideas that have a visual manifestation via particular practices or teaching behaviors. It is a common misunderstanding that the two extreme mindsets operate entirely in isolation of each other. It is unlikely, actually impossible, that one could ever enter a learning environment and only see behaviors, elements, or attributes that are strictly traditionalist or strictly progressivist. One would be far more likely to see a balance of attributes with a stronger tendency in one direction or another. The progressive mindset tends to claim that the traditionalist model focus is on very dry, uninspiring, fact-based, rote memorization types of instructional practices that one would assume would be unlikely to entice children to learning or spark their interest. On the contrary, the traditionalists claim that the progressive open-ended perspective undermines knowledge for the sake of knowledge and their direction is "anti-academic, anti-intellectual." So how do these opposing mindsets add up to the further mistreatment of American educators? The two opposing views drive practically every policy decision made today. Since these opposing views have been the basis for every educational squabble for at least the past 100 years, it would make sense that the practitioner is always in a lose/lose situation even when they most carefully do exactly what they're told to do. But the problem really goes much deeper than this very surface explanation and analysis. There are certain problems inherent to educating the youth in any democratic society that are so complex that no carefully refined curriculum, clarified teaching methods, or sophisticated policy mandate could ever hope to address. In a nutshell, the traditionalists seem to want the freedom of expression of the progressivists. The progressivists seem to want their results to be as measurable, boundary-oriented, and concise as the traditionalists.

So far we have looked at traditional versus progressive only in descriptive terms. It is safe to say that standing alone, one is not inherently superior to the other. The question of desirability comes forth when we know what kind of population we are serving. The socioeconomic level of the student is as great a factor here as is the outcome in standardized tests. When studies are done comparing traditional and progressive practices, several common factors begin to emerge. According to Chall (2000):

1. Students from lower socioeconomic backgrounds tend to achieve more when taught in a more traditional, teacher-directed manner;
2. Students from middle-class socioeconomic backgrounds tend to achieve about as well through one mode of instruction as the other. (It is interesting to note that parents at this level tend to prefer their children being taught in a student-centered manner.)
3. Students from upper-class or extremely wealthy socioeconomic backgrounds tend to achieve as well through either mode of instruction, but parents at this level tend to prefer the more traditional modes of instruction.

While the research and literature in either direction can be convincing that one philosophy is superior to another, it is clear that the manifestations (instructional practices) of one idea or another tend to be more effective for certain populations (Chall, 2000; Hirsch, 1995; Stone, 2000b). For example, when we see an example of a poor performing, inner-city school serving a very poor population that has "turned around," we almost invariably see a concurrent move to a more traditional mode of instruction in the core subjects.

It is of concern to many educational scholars today that the progressive ideals, despite the lack of formal evidence in their favor, are unquestionably dominant in our colleges of education and school systems (Stone, 2000a). One will be hard pressed to visit a college of education anywhere in this country and find teachers being trained in the modes of instruction that are traditional, teacher-directed, and intellectual (knowledge for knowledge sake). Most certainly we would see prospective teachers spending large amounts of instructional time being drilled in the ideals of creating the perfect learning environment, whereby a sufficient number of learning opportunities will create success for every child every single time. These are certainly noble ideas, but unfortunately, teacher training today does not present a balanced perspective between the two extremes. Hirsch (2001) states:

> Whenever I'm asked which education reform program is likely to be the most effective—better teacher training, more charter schools, or various governance reforms—my reply is that there's less need for change in the structure

of governance than for change in the structure of ruling ideas. It has been the dominance of progressive ideas, not the incompetence of education professors, which has induced our teacher-training institutions to de-emphasize subject matter, and thus produce teachers who know too little about the topics they should teach. (p. 3)

We know from a credible body of research that the progressive ideals are effective for middle-class and affluent students, primarily due to the backgrounds and experiences they bring to school. We know from that same body of credible research that more traditional modes of instruction are more effective for poor and disadvantaged students primarily due to the backgrounds and experiences they do not bring to school. It is an unfortunate reality in this country that the poor and disadvantaged students far outnumber the middle class and affluent.

There are educational writers who question why the educational ideas and practices that are known to be the most effective for the majority of the students who must be educated are minimized by the institutions that train teachers and the schools that must educate the children (Duff, 1999). It scarcely makes sense to assume that such exists because those in positions to make those decisions don't know better. It can logically be assumed that the answer is a cross between popularity, politics, and market forces that are caught in a vicious cycle. Stone (2000a) states:

Learner-centered instruction is a type of teaching idealized by most professors of education. A 1997 Public Agenda survey of teacher-educators found that the vast majority of teacher-educators hold a view of teaching "that differs markedly from that of most parents and taxpayers." . . . The term "learner-centered" implies teaching fitted to the learner's unique characteristics, e.g. the student's developmental stage or learning style or gender. In concept, it assumes that if teachers are able to "connect with learners, rather than simply covering the curriculum," students will learn more or less spontaneously, i.e. without the structure and teacher direction ordinarily considered necessary. (p. 4)

From the popularity standpoint, the schools demand teachers who are trained in the progressive ideals because such practices make a nice public presentation and are well received by students, parents, and the public at large. Such methods support the idea and create the illusion of quality, depth of study, and meaningfulness. The universities, in turn, adhere to the progressive ideals to provide what the schools demand. The political component hits hardest at the university level, as funding for research and publications, the lifeblood of universities, is typically determined by who can be impressed. More often than not, those in positions to grant funding are proponents of progressive ideas as it creates more illusions of trying something new, fresh, and invigorating (Stone, 2000b). Persons steeped in one mindset or another are not likely to grant funding on a research project that contradicts their ideas (Stone & Clements, 1998).

The market forces driving the dominance of progressive ideas in universities and school systems are not difficult to see. At the school level, programs and practices that are progressive in nature are more easily marketed, as the schools want those that will actively engage the student (often meaning physical involvement) and will create the most immediate visible difference. But at the university level such matters as licensing tests combined with progressive ideals drive much of the teacher-training curriculum. According to Cunningham (2001), 38 states in this country require the Praxis exam for certification. We will see in a subsequent chapter how one particular exam can drive curriculum and assessment in the schools. Without question, such does go on in the universities as well. He states:

> [W]hat this means is that ETS through this test is now able to exert considerable control over the curriculum of schools of education. Schools have no choice but to teach what ETS says is important. At least on the Elementary Education Curriculum, Instruction, and Assessment, ETS has made a clear and almost total commitment to progressive education. Reading items are devoted to whole language, language experience, reading writing workshops, etc. They promote a balanced approach to reading, which means that although they believe in whole language they are willing to concede that phonemic awareness is also important. They don't think it should be taught, mind you, just that it is important. Beginning readers will certainly learn it through osmosis or something. Math is completely NCTM based. Science is strictly inquiry-based. The distractors or wrong answers tend to refer to direct instruction practices such as requiring correct spelling, using tests, memorization, etc. (p. 2)

During the preparation of this book I interviewed a number of school administrators and educational leaders including principals, central office administrators, school superintendents, university faculty, and education school deans. When asked why the progressive ideas dominate the education business, the answers were remarkably similar. Not one person that I interviewed indicated a professional belief that the progressive methods are inherently superior to any other. Their answers very much paralleled the thesis of this chapter—doing as they are told to do. One school superintendent stated that the progressive ideas had come about in an effort to create a more equitable system for those less fortunate children of society. A well-intentioned effort at fairness was taken to extremes. A central office supervisor remarked that while everyone on the front lines of the classroom knows that one size does not fit all, when faced with state-level mandates that require a preponderance of progressivism, you do as you're told. One education school dean essentially stated that teaching the progressive ideology is a matter of survival for the department. As states are pushing the accountability question further and further into higher education, a thorough grounding in progressivism is necessary to ensure a high passing rate on the Praxis. From the administrative standpoint, this is becoming more and more critical as states are ranking university programs on percentages of passing scores.

Simply put, the traditional/progressive battle, with progressive being clearly dominant, is one in which practitioners can please no one and are unable to win either way. Stone (2000b) argues that teacher training and the operation of the public schools contradicts what the public demands. He states, "Not only are educators and policymakers using similar terms to refer to very different ideas about education, neither seems to understand the inconsistency" (p. 36). He further states:

> In a sense, the public schools are caught in the middle, and so are college presidents and policymakers. All are under pressure to improve achievement but all are dependent on a professional community that has been taught to think of high expectations for measured achievement as stressful, wrongheaded, and contrary to the best interests of students. (p. 37)

WHAT DO EDUCATORS DO?
AS ALWAYS, THEY DO EXACTLY AS
THEY'RE TOLD TO DO

Taken to Extremes

It is a phenomenon in the field of teaching and learning that educational leaders and various experts tend to take ideas to extremes, and that historically, teachers are notorious for complacently accepting the ideas of theorists (Ravitch, 2000). We see one small piece of an idea pushed far beyond what it was ever intended to support. Usually, such extremes in ideas emphasize an insignificant portion of an idea to the exclusion of larger and more critical aspects of the entire idea. There is a body of literature that asserts that quality education should seek a healthy balance between the two extremes. Oyler and Becker (1997) suggest that education move beyond the progressive/traditional squabble and focus on shared authority, not a handing over of authority. Let's look at some things that have gone on in the schools that are examples of the traditionalist/progressivist battle. These battles have not necessarily produced any desirable results in student achievement. In fact, most have been disastrous not necessarily because they were bad ideas but because they were taken to extremes that were not intended by the theorists who developed them.

Phonics versus Whole Language

At the time of this writing there is a generation of students, about middle-school or junior-high-school age who do not read particularly well. Many educational researchers, fairly or unfairly, attribute this dilemma to an idea that surfaced some years ago that was known as "whole language." It is well known that most children do not have to be systematically taught to speak. The spoken language is acquired by the child's immersion into the environment where the language is spoken (Norris, 1996). The idea of whole language, like many others, began in response to some rather long-standing poor teaching practices. It is rooted in the progressive mindset, extends further back into the history of reading instruction than most people realize, and begins with the flawed assumption that reading is a naturally acquired phenomenon, just as spoken language is acquired (Palmaffy, 1997). From the beginning advocates of whole language argued that reading had for too many years been a dull, dreary task, replete with worksheets and isolated skills that didn't seem relevant to reading. It was further asserted that if we would simply immerse the child in the rich array of literature available at their level, they would learn to read with or without formal instruction. In scholarly fairness I will assert that there will be some children, but a very small percentage, who will learn to read this way. It is a fact that some children upon learning the alphabet and sounds will somehow—without instruction or explanation—make the connection and begin to form words. But it will be less than 3%, which can hardly be considered significant or desirable. And like so many progressive ideas, whole language focuses on the "process" rather than "product" (Education Week, 2001). Superficially the idea makes sense, but we do need to look a bit further and make some comparisons.

There are hoards of music educators in this country whose work is greatly influenced by the musical ideas and philosophies of the people of Hungary. The Hungarian culture is so musically rich that a person who is not musically literate is considered to be illiterate. In much the same manner that groups of workers in this country form bowling leagues or softball teams, workers in Hungary form chamber groups and vocal ensembles to learn and perform traditional literature. From the time that children are born, their lives are saturated with the sounds of traditional classical musical literature. Only a child who is deaf would not possess a degree of musical literacy by the time they were 5 or 6 years old. Probably the most prominent humanitarian, music educator, and pedagogue from Hungary was Zoltán Kodály, who wrote extensively concerning the immersion of children into a musically literate culture and the development of the "mother tongue"—the folk musical literature of the culture that reinforces the beliefs and mores of the society. (The philosophies of Kodály very much parallel the writing of E. D. Hirsch and his theories of cultural literacy.) The ideas and philosophies of Kodály emerged on a grand scale in this country in the mid-1970s to the point that colleges of music began offering entire master of music degree programs in Kodály studies. Although universities aren't offering degree programs of this sort too often any more, certification programs in Kodály studies are still quite prominent, bearing prestige in the music education community and requiring a great deal of work and study to attain. There are still large numbers of people who adhere rigidly to the beliefs of Zoltán Kodály and continue to promote his work.

In a similar vein, we see a comparable idea emerge from the Asian music education mindset. Some years ago the Suzuki method became popular, particularly in providing musical instruction to small children. There are Suzuki methods for both beginning strings and beginning piano. Under the Suzuki ideas, the child is immersed in the musical literature by hearing recordings daily of the literature they are expected to play at their upcoming music lesson. The Suzuki philosophy heavily involves the parent, insisting that the parent attend every lesson with the child, and adheres to the idea of two short lessons weekly rather than the traditional one long lesson weekly.

In the same manner that a skilled architect designs a house to work with the geography of the land, both of these ideas fit naturally with the manner in which a child acquires a language, musical or spoken. With a long enough period of immersion in the correctly spoken language, the child learns what is correct and not correct. Likewise, with a long enough period of immersion into well-performed music, the child learns to recognize a good sound from bad. But, like the idea of whole language, there is one element missing. Before the child can read or write the language—musical or spoken—there must be some mode of direct instruction. There is a serious flaw in the idea that total immersion in the language will automatically generate the ability to read or write anything. If we inundate a child's environment with classical piano literature for long enough and lock them in a room with a piano, they may eventually figure how to imitate the sounds they've heard. But it is absurd to think they will "figure out" how to write musical notation, key signatures, time signatures, and so forth. It is not likely they will "figure out" the correct physical technique of creating a particular sound. Without knowing how to read and write music, essentially what would be called "decoding skills" in language instruction, the child will only be able to imitate what is heard and never be able to learn a piece of music they have not heard. But, for whatever reason, this is essentially what happened with the whole language movement.

For several years, there were thousands of children who essentially were not taught to read, and we are seeing those results in standardized test scores year after year. I have made this comparison to bring home a point. People knowledgeable in the field of reading instruction knew that discarding any other instruction in exchange for this warped perspective of whole language was not a good idea. Teachers knew full well that without some means of being able to independently decipher information that students would be in a constant state of gridlock. We had many educational leaders and administrators who were adamant that "no skill should be taught in isolation." But teachers only did what they were told to do.

Unfortunately, the story of the whole language fiasco goes further than polite conversation usually admits. According to the current authorities in the field of reading, the original intent of whole language was similar to what is now being called "balanced literacy" (S. Roark, pers. comm., January 18, 2001). The idea behind balanced literacy is little more than what most have considered and known to be quality teaching for years—a balance between the teaching of phonics/decoding skills and the use of appropriate literature to support and practice the decoding. Many scholars in the field of reading insist that the actual idea behind whole language was never intended to be anti-phonics. The anti-phonics movement was the flagrantly erroneous and overly simplistic interpretation of a very complex set of ideas. The argument continues that whole language was a disaster because "no one did it right." Teachers, however, only did what they were told to do.

It would be unfair to suggest that nothing good came of the failed whole language movement. Pressley and Rankin (1994) note that while whole language is dated, controversial, and not particularly well supported in the literature, it did bring about some attributes of curriculum awareness. They state:

> In evaluations of writing to date involving comparisons of whole language and other types of classrooms, however, there have not been large across-the-board differences in the writing of primary-grade students participating in whole language instruction compared to alternatives (Graham & Harris, 1995; Stahl, McKenna, & Pagnucco, 1994). However there have been demonstrations of gains in writing due to whole language practices on particular aspects of the writing process (e.g. Dahl & Freppon, 1995; Roberts, 1991; Varble, 1990). . . . Whole language students understand that writing is for meaning making, whereas students in conventional classrooms do not (e.g. Boljonis & Hinchman, 1988; Gambrell & Palmer, 1992; Graham & Harris, 1995; Rasinski & DeFord, 1985). (p. 159)

The whole language fiasco is only one example of projects, programs, and reform efforts that were forced upon teachers that clearly were not a good idea. But let's look at some other educational efforts that either have been or have the potential to be disastrous, again a case of teachers doing what they were told to do.

Relevance

In keeping with the progressivist philosophies, there is a mindset being
pushed today that all that is taught to children must be "relevant." The idea
sounds very academic, and teachers everywhere are pressured to justify
their methods and material as being "relevant to real life." The problem in
this line of thinking comes about from the fact that there seem to be different and extreme ideas of what constitutes relevant. One would assume that
if what children are taught is considered relevant, it must be information or
a skill that is eventually applicable and useful in real life. This is not an
unreasonable assertion if it were the accepted definition of relevant. Unfortunately, too many ill-informed educational leaders, administrators, and
policymakers—under intense pressure to create immediate differences—
have construed the definition of relevant to mean immediately useful,
even if immediately translates to short term. The pressure to make everything taught to children immediately applicable can backfire in that the
broad picture is slighted in exchange for small components of more complex skills that are quite fragmented—the very idea that progressivism
tries to avoid.

Anderson, Reder, and Simon (1996) bring forth the question of over-
playing the relevance to what is learned. Their arguments are fourfold.
First, they claim that actions are specific to situations, explaining why children can do mental math calculations at the counter of the candy store but
cannot perform those same calculations at school. Second, citing Singley
and Anderson (1989), they argue that "transfer between tasks is a function
of the degree to which the tasks share cognitive elements" (p. 7). Third,
they argue against the abstract teaching of theory with no application.
Fourth, they argue that instruction is most effective in "complex, social
environments" (p. 9).

The pressure to produce a visual manifestation of relevance has served to
produce some questionable modes of instruction that would perhaps have
been better left alone. Several years ago a consultant visited our school, making presentations on curriculum integration and relevance. This individual,
a very bright man, encouraged teachers to exercise caution in reducing the
idea to an extreme whereby the real meaning was lost. He joked of "Pterodactyl Math—since we studied the Pterodactyl today, let's make it relevant
to real life by counting the spots and dividing by two." Here we have relevance incorrectly oversimplified. It is naive to assume that anything that is
taught is going to be immediately and forever applicable.

Project Teaching, Hands-On Teaching

Classroom teachers today are bombarded with the mindset of the type of
teaching described in the 1927 doctoral dissertation of Ellsworth Collings

(Knoll, 1996). Today the practice goes by a number of descriptors. Rather described as "project teaching," "hands-on teaching," and the "activity movement" (Ravitch, 2000) or "discovery learning," to name a few, the idea being that a child is actively engaged (often translated—physically engaged) in creating something (a project?) related to the concept being learned. The hands-on idea rejects the idea of students learning scientific information by reading about scientific subject matter, writing about scientific processes, or being taught through direct instruction by the teacher. Hands-on teaching insists that children learn best and really only remember what is learned when the learning is a result of them having explored in the area of study. There is an old saying about teaching that says, "Tell me, I forget; Show me, I remember; Involve me, I understand." The idea makes sense and knowledgeable people would certainly never assert that involved student learning is not a good idea, but like many other good ideas, too many people in our profession have taken the idea to a level and extreme that was never intended, often to the detriment of the children.

In the chapter addressing the question of uses and misuses of educational research we will go further into the research in this area. But for now let us assert that there is no body of empirical evidence that would suggest or support that hands-on teaching, to the exclusion of all else, is inherently superior (Hirsch, 1995; Stone, 2000a). But ill-informed educational leaders, building administrators, curriculum supervisors, and various policymakers insist on seeing "hands-on" instruction, to the exclusion of all else, when there is no research to support that it alone creates a more desired outcome. So why is this a problem? How does this contribute to the mistreatment of educators?

Despite its popularity and frequent demand by administrators and educational leaders, it is questionable if the hands-on style of teaching reaps the greatest instructional reward in exchange for all that is involved in the preparation process and all the instructional time consumed by the activity (Stone & Clements, 1998). Meaningful hands-on, project-type teaching requires a great deal more preparation time for teachers than more traditional methods. To adequately prepare quality instruction in a hands-on format requires far more detailed planning both in modes of instruction and in the preparation of materials as well. A well-planned hands-on lesson means assigning of groups, preparation of preliminary materials outside of that found in a textbook or other traditional reference source, allocating adequate class time, including backup plans in case the activity simply does not work, and above all justifying the activity according to curricular components. All of this takes time that is so precious in a teacher's workday. Many teachers are truly doubtful that the preparation time to prepare hands-on instruction is worth the outcome, particularly in view of the fact that hands-on teaching, contrary to popular belief, often does not allow a student to delve as deeply into an area as would normally occur in a more traditional setting. An additional time question concerning hands-on instruction is the extraordinary amount of class time that is consumed in completing such projects—time that might be better spent in a more traditional mode of instruction.

Educational politics creates a much bigger question to be addressed in the push for more "project," "hands-on" styles of teaching. Teachers are so pressured to have children physically and actively "engaged" at all times that a valid connection to a specific area of content gets lost in the time-consuming projects (Sewall, 2000). I have seen such project-type activities in classrooms, such as creating models of rainforests, which, on the surface, might sound like a creative idea. There was a great deal of time involved (several instructional days) of cutting, pasting, displaying, writing short descriptions, and so forth. These projects were beautifully displayed in the halls of the school, and children and adults alike bragged about the effort and the beauty of the work. I seriously doubt if these projects produced a greater understanding of all that needs to be studied in order to comprehend thoroughly the current issues and concerns over the rainforests and their preservation. In one school where I taught, several classes created a holiday village made entirely of graham crackers, candy, and canned cake frosting. The projects were cute, the faculty and administration made a big deal over their presentation, and the local newspaper even came and took pictures. While it may be questionable that such an activity had any particularly strong relation to any area of the curriculum, it surely kept children very busy during the last four to five days of school before the winter holidays when children are typically tired, excited, and generally difficult to manage.

The question of efficient use of time in hands-on instruction can easily be related to what many parents face in raising children. Most anyone who has raised children has known the experience of "allowing the child to help" as a mode of teaching them how to cook, repair something broken, and so forth. Allowing the child to "explore" the best way to roll fish nuggets in cornmeal or place cookie dough on a baking sheet is a wonderful idea. However, reaching the objective (producing something to eat) is probably going to come about with considerable wasted time and a bigger mess than if accomplished by an adult showing the child what to do. Creating a fun experience for children that simultaneously teaches them a needed skill is certainly desirable, but not at the expense of time needed for other tasks—cleaning up the dishes, feeding the rest of the family, and so forth. When the ultimate goal is to prepare something to eat, the effort is probably better served when the child is taught directly and allowed the exploration when they have first mastered the basic concept.

Just as textbook companies claim to cover many curriculum bases by briefly mentioning, randomly commenting on, or vaguely connecting related topics, so it is with integrated projects. Under intense pressure to make everything taught relevant and connected, projects often make claims to integrate skills when in actuality they only "skim the surface" of other skills. The fact that the pictures that may be cut and pasted are in squares and rectangles can hardly be considered "integrating geometric concepts." Locating one downloadable picture from the Internet is a weak version of "integrating research and technology skills." Writing a two- or three-sentence blurb to be pasted onto the project is seriously misleading when the project claims to "integrate writing skills." In short, integrated projects often oversimplify ideas and take some serious liberties.

So how does the push for hands-on translate into the further mistreatment of educators? Quite simply, while projects are not truly known to be a better mode of instruction, they are quite visible and make a nice presentation. It is easy to show a critical public that children are working and creating "things" in school. This can be quite misleading because of the flawed assumption that "hands-on" automatically means that children are learning at higher levels. The question of quality never gets addressed until it's time to compare achievement. Consequently, we have one more situation in which methods do not really produce a viable outcome, but teachers have only done what they were told to do.

Child-Centered Instruction

Another questionable idea that educational leaders and administrators impose on teachers is that of being "child centered." This idea comes from the progressive mindset, whereby every aspect of the child's existence is nurtured, not just the academic/intellectual. Child-centered teaching is focused on the natural curiosity of children and assumes that only learning that is initiated by childish curiosity is "real learning." Some critics claim that the idea of child centeredness emphasizes the social adjustment aspect of working with children while minimizing the academic components. The idea of child centeredness seems to have been confused with "child-led." So, like many other ideas that are surely based in good intentions, this one has been misused and misconstrued to extremes never intended. In the effort to develop and nurture the social and adjustment aspects of the child, teachers everywhere are under pressure from educational leaders and administrators to design instruction in which attributes of child centeredness are visible. The problem here is that no one is quite sure what exactly is meant by the term.

Many traditionalist educators have seriously criticized the child-centered mindset for many years. The child-centered mindset is often described as the teacher as a facilitator rather than director, and any instructional efforts that are pushed by the teacher are considered outside the philosophy. In a child-centered classroom, children are encouraged to learn through discovery, that lacking adult direction is essentially play. Addi-

tionally, child-centered teaching, in theory, does not teach any concept
or skill in isolation. Concepts and skills are grouped (integrated) and
taught through projects and group activities. Finally, the child-centered
mindset adamantly opposes the use of standardized tests for any form of
evaluation.

Grossen (1998a) has written extensively criticizing the misapplication of
child-centered practices. She states:

> A problematic assumption of child-directed practices is that a child cannot
> learn from instruction that is initiated and directed by a teacher. Instead, these
> practices assume that children's learning needs are best fulfilled by allowing
> each child to pursue his or her unique interests through play. What the child
> wants is what the child needs. The reasoning for this is as follows: Each child's
> learning needs are unique and these unique learning needs are revealed
> through the child's interests, which in turn direct each child's selection of play
> activities. Therefore, no child should be inhibited from pursuing his or her
> interests, that is, from playing. "Much of young children's learning takes
> place when they direct their own play activities. . . . Such learning should not
> be inhibited by adult-established concepts of completion, achievement, and
> failure" (p. 3, NAEYC, 1987). (p. 1)

The idea of child-centeredness doesn't really stop here. When we hear
scholarly discussion around the topic, invariably another concept comes
forth—the idea of "constructivist learning." According to Hirsch (1997b),
the ideals of constructivism are not part of "mainstream psychology, and
is almost certainly incorrect" (p. 2). This is another idea that is seriously
misunderstood by many educational leaders and policymakers who in
turn, impose misguided and incorrect directives on teachers that are surely
destined to produce failure before they even begin. The idea of constructivism begins with the collection of knowledge, experiences, and facts
stored in a person's memory. All that is stored in a person's memory is not
at the front of their thought processes at all times. Facts, events, and so
forth that are stored in a person's memory come forth when they are called
upon by a current event and the memory from the past is essentially recon-
structed. It would make sense that learning cannot happen without something from the past coming forth to lend support and put the new event,
or newly learned experience, into some perspective. This is where the idea
comes about that knowledge is constructed—pieced together—with both
current experience and recalled data from the memory. The idea of constructivism refers to all that exists in the person's collective memory, not
the simple acquisition and correlation of new factual data. The idea does
go a bit further to say that if there is not sufficient data stored in the person's memory, it is unlikely that new learning will occur because there will
be no basis on which the new knowledge can be constructed. A very simplified example of this idea is the age-old scenario of needing to know how

to spell a word before you can look it up to see how it is spelled. Actually, one really only needs a degree of phonemic awareness to know approximately how to spell a word. It is well known that students who arrive at school already having mastered a rich vocabulary are more likely to do well in school. A rich vocabulary—the knowledge and understanding of lots of words—creates the basis upon which to construct the further learning of more words (Hirsch, 1995).

The idea of children's interest obviously would come to play in these ideas as people do tend to better remember what is of interest to them. When scholarly discussion centers around either child centeredness or constructivism, the idea of what is of interest to children is heavily stressed. The child-centered ideas are heavily focused on creating children that are happy and willing to learn on their own, so it would make sense that capitalizing on children's interest is not inherently a bad idea. But of course, a lack of conceptual understanding of theories tends to create procedures and practices that are not at all in keeping with the idea or intent of the theory.

But somehow, both the ideas of child centeredness and constructivism seem to lose their real meaning in an attempt by educational leaders and administrators to make very complicated ideas very simple so that we will see a quick difference in classrooms. While the idea of child centeredness puts the child and his/her interests at the center of his/her education, it is not realistic or practical to assume that an eight-year-old child can or should assume responsibility for life decisions that hundreds of thousands of educated adults have struggled with for hundreds of years, and sometimes have not done particularly well. Some time ago our school had a team of visiting experts coming through, observing the school operations, and giving feedback. One person, a local university professor who directs a master's program, told us that we should see more "child-centered activities" going on. When pressed for examples, the professor was vague in response, but I deduced that "child-centered" must mean more activities that capitalize on the individual or collective interests of the children. At a further extreme, a vice principal in my experience stood before the faculty and stated that constructivism means "children sort of construct their own knowledge so you need to sort of teach them what's interesting to them."

Raebeck (1994) makes an interesting challenge to the child-centered mindset:

> Another simplistic, either/or mindset is the one that places the student at the center of the school, as in the statement, "This is a student-centered school." Have you ever been in a school in which the students' needs were being routinely met, but the teachers' needs were being ignored? I worked in such a place for five years. This is not the model we should seek to emulate. It is just

as bad as the reverse. Instead, I ask for "person-centered" schools, in which the needs of everyone, including custodians, cafeteria workers and secretaries, are being met. Happy productive staff members cannot but benefit students—and vice versa. (p. 764)

All this translates into further mistreatment of educators because we have complex ideas, which many thinking individuals consider questionable, reduced to something nowhere near the real meaning. The non-meanings are then twisted into directives for teachers that have no basis, cannot be observed or measured, basically have no meaning, and aren't even real unless someone important decides it's not there.

Higher-Level Thinking versus Mere Facts

One of the most grossly misinterpreted, misunderstood, misapplied ideas floating among schools today is an idea that exists around a false dichotomy. In what is probably a response to pressure from the business community to produce persons who are capable of approaching problems and designing solutions, educational leaders and administrators are pushing for the teaching of "higher-level thinking." The rhetoric abounds in school district and building mission statements that we want to produce students who are "capable of learning on their own," or students who are "committed lifelong learners." Other school goals will state that "Virtually all students can and will learn at higher levels," while a clear definition of those higher levels has not yet come about. Most people would agree that the idea of "higher level" parallels what would be considered the top end of Bloom's Taxonomy—the synthesis, analysis, and evaluation level as opposed to the simple factual recall. This idea has been misinterpreted by many educational leaders and policymakers to assume that any teaching that involves the memorization of a body of information or segments of information is inherently bad (Hirsch, 2000). The companies that publish textbooks have responded by creating text materials that bypass the learning of foundational information and jump directly into what would be analytical and evaluative use of foundational information (Toch, 1991). This notion is critically flawed for various reasons.

In the mid-1980s the country went crazy over a game fad—"Trivial Pursuit." Trivia is information that may be interesting to some people, but is of little use in isolation or outside of personal interest. But, math facts, basic science information, phonics, and vocabulary relative to an academic discipline are not trivia. The idea that children can be taught a collection of skills where they will be able to learn forever whatever they choose to learn without first having mastered a basic body of knowledge is a myth. To assume that children can be taught to question, compare, criticize, or analyze without a common knowledge base to support such thought patterns is ludicrous. I find it amazing that the same educational leaders and school administrators who demand constructivist teaching methods (knowledge building upon previous knowledge) will quarrel with teachers for insisting that a body of factual information must first be in place (Sternberg, Grigorenko, & Jarvin, 2001). It is not unreasonable or undesirable to want to produce students who are thinkers. It is likewise both reasonable and desirable to produce students who have the background and experiences to learn on their own. But it is unrealistic and illogical to assume that such thinkers and problem solvers can be produced without a solid foundation in the "lower level thinking" (Wu, 1999). It is disturbing to see, for example, math textbooks being published and adopted that emphasize relatively complex problem solving while basically neglecting a thorough foundation in basic math facts. The idea that memorizing facts is wrong simply does not make sense. As an example of real life applications of math concepts, it is not probable that students will be able to find the square footage of drywall needed to build a wall without having to use an electronic calculator to do simple multiplication. But for some reason, educational leaders continue to insist that teachers adamantly avoid the rote memorization of basic factual information in exchange for "higher-order thinking," when the fact will forever remain that the former must always be in place before the latter can come about. American educators are mistreated when forced by leaders and administrators to bypass the teaching of basic factual information in exchange for the mythical "higher thinking" when such has not and never will happen.

Unfairly Accountable

For years being held unfairly accountable for poor decisions and policies made by legislators has mistreated America's educators. This scenario is quite similar to the plight of our country's physicians over the HMO problem. Much of the professional autonomy of the physicians has been undermined by cost factors and not what is in the best interest of the patient. There is a plethora of published horror stories over the shabby medical treatment brought about by HMOs putting cost before need. Likewise, the shift from traditional insurance to HMO has caused physicians to carry patient loads far greater than that for which they can adequately provide medical service. Just like educators, none of this was the fault of the physicians—they were only doing what they were told to do. The major difference here is that there is not an overriding public perception of physicians having done things "wrong." Yet educators continue to be held in contempt for having only done what was expected of them.

4

Driven by Research

Widespread belief in some things that are untrue seems to be part of the human condition.

Berliner & Biddle (1995, p. 9)

In any of the professions, most of what is chosen as professional direction is based upon what earlier professionals have studied and investigated. We are then able to make informed decisions as to what is good and not so good. One of the most frequently used, and seemingly strongest arguments when making decisions and implementing policy is "But the research says . . ." (Walker, 1996). Unfortunately, the field of professional education is one in which most practices and procedures are claimed to be driven by research but with no recognition that research in any discipline varies greatly in both style and quality. Due to the inexactness of teaching and learning, the field of educational research seems to stay in a constant state of disarray (Kaestle, 1993; Ravitch, 1998). There is often little or no consensus relative to quality or effective practices (Grossen, 1996). In other professions, reform and practice decisions are made based on scientific findings; whereas in our profession reforms come about based on ideology, not science (Slavin, 2001).

I have taught graduate courses in research methods at the university level for several years as well as listened to many lectures and presentations by administrators and educational leaders whose intentions were sincere and whose best interests was the welfare of the children we serve. I have seen some hideous discrepancies in what research findings actually present and how those finding are implemented. It is alarming how many people in positions of leadership have a very shallow, novice perspective of the phenomenon of research (Stone & Clements, 1998). Many intelligent people are both intrigued and intimidated by research, apparently from a lack of conceptual understanding of what research is about, what research does, but most important, what research does not do. This chapter will present some fundamental concepts of research so that we are all informed about good and bad decisions. It is necessary to have a general conceptual understanding of research processes in order to understand how often these processes are misused, abused, or not used at all in the design of programs and policies. The wrong use and dismissal of quality educational research (Hirsch, 1995; Savage, 1989) translates into the mistreatment of educators.

BASICS OF RESEARCH

There are some basic tenets of research that are recognized in other professions but seem to be all but lost when using educational research (Slavin, 2001). For example, we find many in the field of education who often assume that when a research procedure has produced a particular finding, or set of findings, that these findings are of absolute truth, to be accepted without question. This is a very naive and dangerous misunderstanding in any area of research. Any form of research that is completed in any academic discipline is always open to question and will contain inherent errors that can be statistically allowed for, but never removed entirely. A research study of any sort in the social sciences is an experiment conducted on a basically intangible phenomenon. In my work as a teacher, professor, and lecturer, I state quite often that teaching and learning, like the practice of medicine and law, are "imperfect, inexact sciences which do not begin with a uniform raw product."

There are two very frequently misunderstood tenets of research in any academic, social science, or scientific discipline. First, research findings represent the aggregate, not the anecdote. As such, a researcher or group of researchers can conduct an experiment 1,000 times and each time reap similar findings. If, for example, the 1,001st such experiment yields a different set of findings, they are not wrong, only different. Likewise, the first 1,000 sets of findings cannot be considered "wrong" because other findings surfaced. As an example, several years ago in a graduate course in research, the discussion focused around studies that have repeatedly found a correlational link between family income and student achievement. An enthusiastic student interjected, "That's not true. I taught a child last year who was very poor but made good grades." I had to explain that tens of thousands of correlational studies are not wrong because we knew a child who did not fit that profile. Competent researchers and educational leaders know that an aggregate of 1,000 sets of findings certainly offers a stronger conclusion than one anecdotal set of findings. Unfortunately, in the business of teaching and learning many policy decisions are based on the anecdote rather than the aggregate. It should likewise be noted that research findings in any discipline, whether we are discussing aggregates or anecdotes, indicate tendencies and not absolutes.

Second, research findings are for the purpose of informing the scholarly population, not for directing field practice (Davis, 2001). It is a common concern among educational leaders that too many decisions are made based on scant evidence that may appeal to the sensibilities of compassionate and well-meaning people but is insufficient to support or justify massive reforms.

QUALITATIVE VERSUS QUANTITATIVE FINDINGS

Depending on the question to be investigated or the problem to be studied, there are many styles and types of research and numerous ways in which an experiment can be designed. Research that is conducted in educational circles generally falls into two very broad categories—quantitative and qualitative. Briefly, quantitative research methods investigate questions and problems through very standard, numerical, and statistical processes and typically seek to determine if differences occurred by chance. On balance, qualitative research methods, which may and usually do involve quantitative/numerical measures, are more descriptive in nature, only presenting what the researchers have been able to see, not necessarily what the researchers think. Both categories of research design can create useful findings and certainly allow a basis for making professional decisions, but there are inherent differences that do not allow one style of research design to fit all questions or problems to be investigated. The quantitative/qualitative question is one that is wrought with sharp opinions and controversy. For many years there has been an argument among professional researchers as to whether quantitative or qualitative designs are the most useful, or even if qualitative designs should be allowed or considered "real research." It is argued that since qualitative designs are descriptive in nature and, unlike quantitative designs, not backed by "hard data" that their findings can be too broadly interpreted and don't scientifically support one position or another. Since qualitative findings are more useful in making evaluative decisions than supporting a hypothesis, it is often argued that such findings are "soft." Regardless of one's conviction concerning research design, uses, and applicability of findings, it is fair to say that no one research design can answer all the complex questions that come about in the running of the schools. Grossen (1998b) admonishes educators for practices that are quite common—information going from an idea to widespread use with nothing in between. Most educational leaders assert that an idea must first be supported by data, then carefully tested on a small scale, and finally tried on a larger scale. If the

idea is successful at this point it becomes part of the professional knowledge base. Grossen (1998b) states:

> The education profession in America differs from other highly successful pro-
> fessions in one significant way. Most other professions ensure to some extent
> that the procedures shared across the profession actually work to increase the
> success of all members of the profession. To ensure that they work, proce-
> dures are first tested in some way. These shared procedures form the profes-
> sional knowledge base of the profession. New procedures come into the pro-
> fessional knowledge base only if they have been shown to yield better results
> than the old procedures they replace. . . . Education is an unfortunate excep-
> tion to this pattern of professional behavior. (pp. 23–24)

This brings us to another area in which the general public and many educational leaders are grossly unfamiliar—evaluation. Often the terms
research and evaluation are used interchangeably when they have entirely
different meanings, are entirely different processes, and are used by policymakers for different reasons (Worthen, Sanders, & Fitzpatrick, 1997).
Although research processes differ, research can be defined as "the systematic inquiry into a question or problem." Evaluation, on the other hand,
involves the gathering of data to make informed decisions, and unlike
research, always involves a judgment call. Both research and evaluation are
necessary for the design, implementation, maintenance, and improvement
of programs, but the two are very different entities and serve very different
purposes. Research looks for truth (just the facts), while evaluation works
to make decisions (did we use these facts well?). The findings of good
research are generalizable to the remainder of the population and can be
replicated (Walker, 1996), while the findings of an evaluation tend to be
specific to one situation. In the business of teaching and learning, leaders
and policymakers often make serious decisions based on evaluative data
(specific to one situation and quite subjective) rather than on research findings (generalizable to other populations and based on scientific comparison). We will see later how dangerous this lack of information can be to our
schools.

RESEARCH VERSUS RESEARCH BASED

It is not difficult to figure out that the problems/issues that arise when
addressing the question of "what the research is telling us" in the education field come about because those who create policy don't do things quite
the same way as other pure science or social science fields. In the past 15–20
years, the professional direction of the education field has become dominated by a less sophisticated research genre that most refer to as "research
based." This terminology sounds impressive in both written and spoken

professional communication, but the term is grossly misleading for two reasons. First, it implies a false degree of credibility to a piece of verbiage, a practice, procedure, process method, or policy. Second, getting new ideas to stay in place while the school continues to function is always a problem (Klinger, Vaughn, Hughes, & Arguelles, 1999; Stone & Clements, 1998). Programs abound that claim to be "research based" and are presented in the same professional light as those that are truly researched (rigorous testing and controlled comparisons). Since the American public is basically intimidated by the word "research," most people naively assume that "research based" means quality. This causes concern among educational leaders as many funding proposal requests often state that proposals must be "research based" rather than "researched." According to Slavin (pers. comm., February, 1999), states are "funding just about anything." A more realistic idea of what research based actually means is an effort to apply theory to practice (Gernsten and Brengleman, 1996). Since well-placed ideas do not mistreat educators, let's look at the wrong side of research based.

According to Slavin (pers. comm., February, 1999) research based can mean "anything you want it to mean—you can use someone else's work to support what you would do anyway." Research based does not mean that any idea, process, procedure, or program has been tested in any way, or that there is any credible data that would support the effectiveness of an idea. Research based essentially means that someone else's writing, research, or opinion is cited to support what sounds like a good idea (Grossen, 1996; Hirsch, 1997a). In view of what is being presented here, it should not be assumed that "research based" is bad and "researched" is good. When a research-based program is put into place, implemented properly, and carried out according to plan, they are usually effective. If a research-based program is carried out correctly and children do get a second chance, do learn to read, and succeed rather than fall through the bureaucratic cracks of the system, it really doesn't matter if the program is researched or research based. My concern is that there are so many people in positions of leadership who are grossly misinformed and therefore are making decisions every day that may be based on flawed or fallacious information. There is an old saying that the half-educated can be far more dangerous than the uneducated. Needless to say, an ill-informed leadership is dangerous. Hirsch (1997a) states:

> The enormous problems faced in basing policy on research is that it is almost impossible to make educational policy that is not based on research. Almost every educational practice that has ever been pursued has been supported with data by somebody. I don't know of a single failed policy, ranging from the naturalistic teaching of reading, to the open classroom, to the teaching of abstract set-theory in third-grade math that hasn't been research-based. Experts have advocated almost every conceivable practice short of inflicting

physical bodily harm. . . . So we need to discriminate between reliable and unreliable research. . . . When lawmakers say that education policy should be based on research, the spirit of the law implies reliable, consensus research. Any other interpretation would mean, and has meant, carrying out unwarranted human experimentation on our own children. (pp. 1–2)

How does the terminology of "research based" lend a false credibility to practices and procedures that are happening in classrooms? Simply put, the ill-informed educational leader likely assumes that research based means that an idea has been tested and shown to support that a process, procedure, or method (referred to as the "treatment" in experimental research) is what causes a change to come about. This is quite misleading for the following reasons:

1. The data that are cited to support the idea, process, program, or method may not necessarily be the result of some systematic inquiry or methodical investigation (Grossen, 1996). Many citations from the literature that are used to support an idea are descriptive in nature or even citations of writers expressing their own opinions about an idea, process, program, or method. Opinions of experts are useful, but do not support that one phenomenon or another brings about desired changes. According to Grossen (1996), citations of opinion look just like citations of experimental comparison.
2. In order to support that an idea, process, program, or method is the true reason for change to come about and to negate the idea that other factors could have impacted the change there must be more than simply citations of researcher's observations or opinions. There must have been some sort of comparison made between two statistically identical groups where one group gets the "treatment" and the other does not. Only when groups are compared in this way can it truly be said that "the research supports this idea or that."

While I would never assert that all research-based practices are inherently bad, there are some common misunderstandings and problems that tend to recur when such programs are put into place. First, research-based programs are typically not a collection of activities, skills, or curricular components. Such programs are an idea or a philosophical base evidenced by supporting activities. Second, the surface application of the activities, which are a manifestation of the program or idea, is not program implementation (S. Brumfield, pers. comm., 1994). Third, previous programs are frequently discarded under the assumption that the new program will fix the problems. Finally, many programs and the changes to instructional processes and practices do not stay in place long enough to see any significant difference in outcomes (Gersten, Chard, & Baker, 2000).

There are some common weak links in the training and implementation of many research-based programs. First, training in such programs is both time consuming and costly. Time and money are equally precious in the school system. Second, there is often little data to support long-term use of research-based programs. Third, full implementation of a program often takes two to three years. The political pressure on schools is for quick results. Next, educational leaders often focus on one or two components of a program that will cause the situation to quickly look different with no provision for long-term implementation or follow-up. Finally, program maintenance is (generally) almost as expensive as the initial implementation.

Research-based programs are finding their way into prominence in large and small school systems. Educational leaders across the country are finding ways to justify spending hoards of tax money putting programs in place that have not been tested in the long term or on a broad enough basis to assert that the procedure in question truly does what it is intended to do. We will see later in this chapter that many research-based programs have their own methods of gathering data to support their effectiveness. Often the data-gathering process contradicts standard data-gathering processes in conventional or mainstream research (Grossen, Coulter, & Ruggles, 1998). Hirsch (1997b) argues that an insistence on one ideal or direction with no regard for other possibilities can create bad science. Yet, despite a lack of data to support such administrative decisions, we continue to see school systems spend money and effort trying to put these efforts in place.

The sparse body of literature addressing research-based practices discusses the problem of such practices not staying in place for long, but is somewhat limited in that the focus is mostly in special education. In any of the professions portions of the body of research will be recognized by some and dismissed by others (Gersten, Vaughn, Deshler, & Schiller, 1997). In the pure/applied sciences or the social sciences, practitioners recognize and apply the body of literature when it can realistically be seen as applicable to real work, real practice, and real problems. It is generally known that if theory to practice efforts are shallow or superficial, the desired change is less likely to remain in place beyond a minimum. Gersten and Brengleman (1996) (citing McLaughlin, 1991) state the three components that contribute to ineffective research-based practices are lack of concreteness, lack of specificity, and lack of intensity. But the primary factor found in the research is the quality of follow-up efforts (Klinger et al., 1999). Practitioners tend to retain research-based practices when there is adequate long-term support in their use. The phenomenon in educational professional staff development known as the "one-shot–workshop" is well known to be the least effective (Goldenberg & Gillimore, 1991).

What are some of the current research-based programs we are seeing reach the peak of popularity? I spent several years teaching in a relatively affluent suburban school system that was notorious for its "progressive mindset" and its use of "research-based practices," some of which were not "practices" at all, but rather an erroneous attempt at creating a process from nothing. Let us tour about five years of teachers' staff development directives and how effective these efforts were in bringing about desired changes in outcomes in individual classrooms and the school district as a whole. We will see how the misuse of such programs translates into the mistreatment of teachers.

MULTIPLE INTELLIGENCES

If I start at the time of this writing and go back five years, I was a middle school teacher in a particular "progressive" suburban school system. The first really big efforts on the part of the system in "training in research-based practices" (to which I was exposed) came about when Howard Gardner's theories of multiple intelligences were at the height of popularity. Gardner, a brilliant psychologist at Harvard, developed the theories of multiple intelligences in an effort to redirect the concept of intelligence and the measure thereof. It has long been argued that intelligence is not a phenomenon that can truly be measured, and it has long been accepted among the scholarly community that attempting to test for intelligence is really nothing more than an elaborate measure of the person's academic background to date (Yekovitch, 1994). However, as long as the testing process called intelligence testing has been around, it has always been done via a single language/linguistic and logical/mathematical perspective (McGrath, 2001). Gardner's idea was that people were intelligent in other ways, and that everyone possessed certain strengths that were not necessarily visible through a measurement from a linguistic or mathematical perspective (Brualdi, 1996). It should be remembered that Gardner is not an educator and really never intended for his work to become the basis of an entire school curriculum. His work is less about curriculum and instruction and more about determining intellectual strengths and educational assessment (Gardner & Hatch, 1990). In interviews, he has stated that much of what he wrote about has gone directions he did not intend (Grossen, 1996). But some writers assert that school systems have jumped on his work under the misguided notion that since we're all good at different things, if teachers will simply present material in such a manner as to reach each child through his/her "strength," then every child will be able to succeed at everything. This logic and directive is hideously flawed in that it assumes that everyone can be good at the same thing and that approaching the same topic from a different direction will ensure that no one is perceived to be deficient. This interpretation contradicts the real meaning of "multiple intelligences," as Gardner's position was about diversity, not uniformity. It would seem logical that the use of the theory to make everyone good at everything would be outside the scope of the theory. So, how does this fit into the picture of research-based practices?

When this progressive, suburban school system jumped on the bandwagon of multiple intelligences, it was done so with the same misguided idea—that approaching every topic from seven different directions—would ensure that all children would be totally successful at absolutely everything. Over the course of almost two school years, several professional workshop days and untold amounts of staff development funds were spent with consultants and in-house turn-around trainers teaching the teachers what everyone assumed was a groundbreaking body of information that was going to revolutionize our daily work. Every classroom in the school had some sort of display presenting the multiple intelligences. One classroom had a huge ice cream cone on the wall with seven scoops—each one representing a different intelligence. After a few months, the teachers were being told to teach the theories of multiple intelligences to the children supposedly so that they would be aware of their own strengths and would seek out their learning by way of their strength. Even at the time, I privately questioned that if the theories of multiple intelligences are complex enough that semester-length graduate courses could be taught on the topic, what was to be gained by pushing this vague, theoretical construct at sixth graders? Nevertheless, we did as we were told and taught multiple intelligences to middle school children. It didn't last long after that.

Following the massive effort to immerse the entire middle school level of the district in multiple intelligences came the other portion of what we tend to do ad nauseam in the field of professional education—document your efforts. New lesson plan forms were developed that required every teacher to correlate every instructional objective and every method of attaining the objective to one of the multiple intelligences. Teachers spent untold hours cross correlating everything they did to the multiple intelligences. The educational world went equally as crazy in the early 1960s when the theories of Bloom's Taxonomy were prevalent and used to support the notion that behavioral objectives were the answer to increased student achievement. There were other taxonomical theories around at the time, but none were quite as popular as Bloom's. Hundreds of thousands of hours were spent cross-correlating every instructional objective to various levels of the taxonomy when the simple fact of the matter was that there was absolutely no instructional value to be obtained by doing so. For some reason, no one in a position to make a difference ever asked, "Why are we doing this?" (Popham, 1993). To this day I am unclear as to how this approach to the theories of multiple intelligences was supposed to improve instruction.

The question should come forth: "Are the multiple intelligences researched or research based?" The answer is neither. The theories of multiple intelligences is exactly what it states—a theory. In the science and research fields, a theory is the lowest level of cognition. A theory comes about because someone is curious or has observed phenomena that should be investigated. It is only after a theory is tested repeatedly and similar findings resulted that it can be called a hypothesis. When further testing of the hypothesis results in repeated similar findings, it then becomes part of an accepted professional knowledge base. Gardner's theories of multiple intelligences has not reached the second or third level because it is only a theory. As such, school systems everywhere (not just the school system where I taught) are doing with Gardner's work what Gardner never intended. Such is considered "bad science"—allowing a theory to go from conceptual idea to where it is presumed to be the accepted professional knowledge base with nothing in between. Is it any wonder why such efforts do not reap any particular benefit? The theories of multiple intelligences have not progressed past the point of theory. There is no real body of evidence to support that any use or program of instruction designed around multiple intelligences creates any difference or brings about any desired changes in academic behavior (Grossen, 1996).

THE RESPONSIVE CLASSROOM

The next effort was the "responsive classroom," a research-based program set up and operated by the Northeast Foundation for Children (NEFC). The program is successfully in use in schools around the country. The teaching models advocated by the program are certainly desirable by the teaching standards of today. The reader should not deduce from this section that something is inherently wrong with the program. The problems in my experience came about from a poor conception and implementation of the program by persons who did not understand research in the traditional sense.

The responsive classroom is based on a set of seven tenets:

1. The social curriculum is as important as the academic curriculum.
2. How children learn is as important as what they learn.
3. The greatest cognitive growth occurs through social interaction.
4. There is a set of social skills that children need to learn and practice in order to be successful. They form the acronym CARES—Cooperation, Assertion, Responsibility, Empathy, and Self-Control.

5. Educators must know children individually, culturally, and developmentally.
6. All parents want what's best for their children and educators must work with parents as partners.
7. The principals of *The Responsive Classroom* must be practiced by educators in their interactions with each other, with the children and with the parents. (NEFC, 2000)

The thesis behind the tenets of the responsive classroom certainly makes sense. It is no secret to anyone who has been a teacher at any level, including the university and graduate levels, that the greatest deterrent to instruction comes about from a lack of social skills, or at least a lack of the awareness of such. It would seem logical to anyone who has taught middle school that if children of this age were to develop the social skills desired in more mature students, there would be far less instructional time lost to dealing with such social discrepancies and that same energy would be spent productively. Obviously, who would not want to teach students who were cooperative, assertive, responsible, empathetic, and self-controlled? Teachers were told at the time that the responsive classroom had typically been used at the upper elementary level, not so much at the junior high or middle school level. The progressive school system announced their intention to implement the tenets of responsive classroom at the middle school level.

The middle school teachers of the district, just like in previous staff development programs, spent at least an entire school year being trained in what was presented as "The Responsive Classroom," when in actuality only tiny pieces of the bigger idea were presented. For example, we spent untold hours learning the correct way to create a chart of greetings, questions, and general information that would catch the students' attention at the door of the classroom each morning. In at least one of the middle schools, there were faculty appointed to monitor and see that every teacher was correctly creating the charts. They jokingly, yet caustically, referred to themselves as the "chart police." Additionally, we spent untold hours being shown the correct way to seat the children in a circle, the correct way to demonstrate to children how to ask questions and respond in a share session, and ridiculous amounts of time demonstrating and redemonstrating activities to groups of 40–60 adults.

It was during this time that I came to realize that the majority of our professional days were being spent engaged in a very surface application of the activities that are a manifestation of the philosophy behind the responsive classroom with practically no grounding in the ideas behind the philosophy. It concerned me greatly at the time that we were being expected to make a difference in the behaviors of children by being shown a few movement or musically oriented social activities and writing a morning chart with absolutely no study in the philosophy guiding these activities. As I was doing the research for this book I came to realize that much of what teachers experienced during those years under the misguided notion of theory to practice fell very much within the scope of poor practice as described by Gersten and Brengleman (1996). They state:

> In other words, to be useful, research must be able to be translated into manageable and comprehensible teaching strategies and procedures. Further, these strategies must reflect and fit within the details of day-to-day classroom instruction. (p. 68)

Clearly, what we were being asked to do never came close to strategies and procedures that would bring about change for the better. While I certainly questioned the idea of this program being "researched," I was more concerned with things that were being said not by the consultants, but by the local turn-around trainers. For example, we kept hearing that "The Responsive Classroom is a social curriculum." This does not mean the same thing as tenet number 1 of the responsive classroom philosophy. Such statements are a gross oversimplification of a much bigger picture. The responsive classroom is an idea just as in the study of geometry, a point, line, or plane is an idea. As such, the activities are only an example of the idea, just as the sharpened end of a pencil is an example of a point, the crack between floor tiles is an example of a line, and the entire floor in the room is an example of a plane. Geometric examples are not in and of themselves the whole of the study of geometry nor are charts and group circles the entirety of the responsive classroom. I have come to realize that the responsive classroom is the epitome of the progressivist/traditionalist question, in that the entire emphasis is on the social, empathetic, and emotional rather than a specific body of content. This is not inherently bad. The question to be considered is what we expect to accomplish.

I became disillusioned with many of the people who made the presentations. Many of those who were chosen to serve as local "turn-around" trainers seemed to have lost their place in the big picture of the responsive classroom. Their perspective seemed to be that we can take a very complicated idea like the responsive classroom, reduce it to a few very visible and overdone components, and still expect it to work. Much of what came back to the schools was a half-baked perspective of a very complex set of ideas. For example, in order for the responsive classroom to be successfully implemented, a faculty must accept a buy-in assumption that "children basically want to be good." One turn-around trainer returned to school only to inform a large group of professional educators that, "You have to remember—every single child wants to be good." I would never presume to argue the point as to whether every single child wanted to be good, but there is a significant difference between what this person said and the original presentation of the program, that "children basically want to be good." What is frightening is that we had someone teaching teachers who did not seem to understand the difference.

As an interesting side note, at about this same time the district implemented a district-wide in-school suspension plan for the students who simply could not function in a socially appropriate manner. We were told that since research supported that statistically 5% of the population was incorrigible, and our current suspension rate was at about 14%, this program was intended to catch and help the 9% who might not respond to traditional methods. Two years after the massive effort to train and implement the responsive classroom, not much had changed in terms of discipline problems, discipline referrals, and students assigned to the alternative program. One middle school trainer stood in a faculty meeting at the beginning of the following year and announced that "Since we are still referring as many children as ever, we obviously need to do more responsive classroom."

Following the effort to implement the responsive classroom, the district embarked on a similar research-based program for upper elementary, which was the work of Jane Nelsen. Consultants came to the local elementary schools to train the faculty in the components of positive discipline. Positive discipline and responsive classroom were similar in their progressive mindset of nurturing the social as well as the cognitive aspects of the child. During these training sessions, it was interesting to note that there were several teachers whose assignments were itinerant between both elementary and middle school levels, and these teachers had already been exposed to the responsive classroom and recognized the similarities. When one teacher brought this to the attention of the consultant and questioned the difference between the two programs and two philosophies, the consultant rather coldly replied, "I don't know anything about responsive classroom." Perhaps it was a turf question, but at any rate, positive discipline didn't last long because the following year the district spent nearly $100,000 to train all upper elementary teachers in the components of the responsive classroom. Unfortunately, such efforts often do not bring about the desired result because those in charge take a tiny piece of the bigger picture and overdo it to the point of being silly. It is sad that we see these things go on every day in schools across the country, most claiming, "the research says. . . ."

Early on in this five-year period, about the time that the school system was hitting the multiple intelligences so hard, the state's annual school report cards came forth. The state annually publishes these documents that compare a number of components of each school to other schools in the district and the state. One of the components compared is the number of teachers who hold an advanced degree. In most states, there is some additional stipend paid for having pursued and attained an advanced degree.

The local news media reported that this progressive school system, which, at the time, was the highest paying district in the state, had a noticeably low percentage of teachers who had gone on to earn a graduate degree (Ramos, 1996). When the media contacted the school system for a comment, members of the central office staff stated that they really weren't concerned about advanced degrees since they provided most of their staff development through district seminars. One principal stated that an advanced degree was probably less valuable than the in-district seminars because the advanced degree was "all theory." I had recently completed the doctorate and considered both that perspective and response to be arrogant at the very least. I was incensed that the school system would value these shallow, ill-prepared, narrowly focused workshops, most of which are based on a tiny, fragmented segment of usually questionable research, to be of the same academic caliber as graduate study in a university (Ramos, 1996). It was also interesting that about this time, something bizarre began to happen all over the district. Charts appeared on the walls of teachers' lounges that indicated the "research based practices" in which each teacher had received training. There were blocks for Frameworks, Writing Across the Curriculum, Cooperative Learning, and probably a half dozen others. Their wall life in some schools was short lived, as most teachers were absolutely livid. I privately chuckled that teachers would be recognized in a rather tacky fashion for spending personal time in these shallow, questionable activities, while minimizing graduate study in a university.

RESEARCH AND POPULAR OPINION

Those practitioners who are what can be termed "research literate" are always amazed at the information that is touted, flaunted, and passed around in our profession that is called "research" that has absolutely no clinical, comparative, or numerical basis (Walker, 1996). Every day in schools across the country directives are given, curriculums designed, and lessons planned around tenets and ideas that are presumed to be based in research. It is amazing that an idea that is spoken of frequently enough eventually reaches the point that it is accepted as truth. As an example, Tanner (1998) refers to the media hype often reporting the illiteracy of our adult population. According to Tanner, the reported sale of books in this country is hardly indicative of an illiterate population. We should examine some of these popular opinions that are talked of so freely that it is assumed they are either the result of research or based in some sort of credible research. Some current writers have asked if this is "truth-making or truth-finding" (Stout, 2000).

In the previous chapter, the progressive education mindset was discussed along with many practices that are advocated by those whose ideology leans in that direction. I will assert again that there really is no such thing as a bad theory. The problem comes about when a theory goes from being an idea to an accepted knowledge base with no experimentation or comparison to support it (Grossen, 1996; Slavin, 1987a; Stone & Clements, 1998). As such it becomes "bad science." Many educational leaders who claim to be working in the progressive mindset tend to focus on many ideas that have never been researched in the comparison manner. As such, many of these ideas keep hanging around with the assumption of an unerring truth attached (Hirsch, 1997a; Tanner, 1998). For example, there is a huge movement in our schools centering around the idea of self-esteem. This movement is so strong that many instructional decisions are made with self-esteem as the basis, and not real academic achievement. Our business seems to be driven by this misguided notion that if we, the teachers, will create an environment for everyone where no conflicts can occur and everyone is happy all the time, to the exclusion of all else, children will achieve more. Parenting experience, teaching experience, and simple common sense dictates that not only is such an effort futile but is also devoid of logic in the assumption that positive self-esteem causes higher academic achievement. Logic should assert that genuine achievement brings about positive self-esteem. But teachers continue to be told to design instruction and classroom activities so that children will feel good about themselves, as though feeling good is the desired outcome, not functional literacy (Stone & Clements, 1998).

Much has been written recently concerning the overpowering self-esteem movement in our schools. In her book *The Feel-Good Curriculum*, Maureen Stout (2000) criticizes the school systems and universities for placing extreme emphasis on a student's self-concept rather than the mastery of a knowledge base necessary to function in real life. I never cease to be amazed at the professional meetings where a new idea is shared and teachers are told:

1. If you teach this way students will be successful;
2. Their self esteem will increase;
3. With increased self-esteem will come increased academic achievement.

This idea is passed off quite often as unerring information in the professional knowledge base of teachers and is usually not questioned. For some reason, seldom does anyone ever ask, "Is there any research to back up that idea, or is it merely popular opinion?" The fact is, there is not a body of research that would support the idea that self-esteem increases achievement (Stone & Clements, 1998). This is so for a couple of reasons. First, self-esteem is a difficult, practically impossible thing to measure. It is not really something you can observe and identify via some sort of observational checklist. About as close as you will ever get to measuring self-esteem will be some sort of "self-reporting" by those being studied. If we are able to design some sort of standardized self-reporting instrument, we are a step ahead provided that we can measure the same thing on every child. Second, self-reporting does not actually measure the construct, it merely quantifies the person's perception of the construct—specifically their perception of their own self-esteem. Of course, this causes the findings of a "self-esteem study" to immediately fall into the "questionable" category because we have not actually measured the self-esteem, only the person's reporting of their perception of their own self-esteem.

Despite this inherent, inalienable flaw, decent research has been done attempting to demonstrate a relationship between self-esteem and academic achievement. When such studies have been completed, it is interesting that the findings invariably are that those students who report a high level of self-esteem do not do as well academically as those who report a modest or low self-esteem. Understandably, any research in the area of self-esteem will immediately be suspect by virtue of the fact that we are essentially trying to measure the unmeasurable. But what has been found in research indicates the exact opposite of what is passed off as part of the professional knowledge base in the teaching profession (Scheirer & Kraut, 1979).

Another unfounded myth that is assumed to be supported by research is that of "hands-on instruction." While this was discussed at some length in a previous chapter, suffice it to say that teachers are bombarded every day with the erroneous idea that hands-on, project-type teaching, to the exclusion of other types of instruction, is inherently superior. Many of those in charge of supervising instruction adamantly insist on seeing teachers design their instruction so that children are moving, touching, and always creating something. Again, this is not necessarily in and of itself a bad idea, but when the idea is pushed to extremes the desired outcome gets lost. Most teachers use hands-on, project-type activities to reinforce what has already been taught because the fundamental concepts are already in place. There is no research anywhere to support the idea that the exclusive use of hands-on instruction is superior to more traditional teacher-directed methods when first presenting the material (Stone & Clements, 1998). Let us examine this a bit further.

This is a question that would easily be examined using a quasi-experimental design, whereby two statistically alike groups were taught the same material—one using hands-on instruction exclusively and the other using more traditional teacher-directed methods. Such studies have been done numerous times and have repeatedly shown the traditional methods of instruction to be superior when first presenting new material. Some time ago at the first faculty meeting of the school year, the person charged with presiding over the meeting encouraged teachers to use the "hands-on" type of teaching. The person stated, "The research has proven over and over again that children learn more when you teach this way." This meeting was certainly not my place to question what was being said, but two things went entirely against my sense of logic. First, as I discussed earlier, research does not prove—it supports or suggests. Second, there is no body of research supporting what this person had just stated. This poor, uninformed person was wrong on both points.

Another mistaken notion driving our profession is the idea of cooperative learning. Unlike some other ideas, there is a body of research supporting the use of cooperative, group-type teaching methods, but not to the extent that it is being pushed today (Grossen, 1996). My first exposure to the tenets of cooperative learning happened about 10 years ago at the first faculty meeting of the school year. The principal, generally a capable leader in most respects, stated that as central office personnel would be visiting the schools periodically to observe instruction, it had been indicated they preferred to see "less whole class instruction and more cooperative grouping." When questioned as to the meaning of cooperative grouping the principal informed us that it was a new idea they were trying in California. The man stated that basically, the children are organized in groups and allowed to work by themselves while the teacher walks around the room monitoring and supervising as needed. This was the extent of the. training in cooperative learning that central office personnel were expecting to observe. Needless to say, central office personnel didn't see much cooperative grouping going on during that school year!

It is generally accepted that the push for the cooperative group type of teaching appears to come from the mindset that businesses are putting pressure on the schools to produce people who can "solve problems, design solutions, work as members of a team, and so forth." This is a reasonable assumption since it's not difficult to see that most businesses are not organized in "top-down" style that was considered the norm 30–50 years ago. And while there is a body of information and research supporting that cooperative learning strategies do produce what they claim to produce when used as they are intended to be used, it is a very naive assumption that cooperative learning is totally good to the total exclusion of all else. The push for cooperative learning is flawed in that a person cannot cooperatively perform a task or solve a problem without first having the ability, background, or experience to do so singly. In order for any group to communicate and function cooperatively, the group must first collectively possess a common body of information relative to the task at hand. By its very nature, cooperative learning emphasizes the socialization with the academic content in the background—not the academics with the socialization in the background.

Although not a popular topic in polite conversation, the education business is driven by the same economic factors as any other. Tax dollars are a finite entity and as such, educational leaders and policymakers must necessarily design programs of instruction that serve the largest number of students possible using as few personnel as possible and costing as little as possible—essentially creating the "biggest bang for the buck." Nowhere does this phenomenon manifest itself any more clearly than in the question of class size. School systems are quick to report their data concerning "average teacher/pupil ratio" and present their organizational structure as exemplary of meeting all the diverse individualized needs of the masses. Polite conversation seldom addresses that teacher/student ratio data can be compiled in a number of ways, and that the report that an "average teacher/pupil ratio of 18" does not necessarily mean that a visitor walking through the school system will never see more than 18 children in a class. Likewise, the class size question is highly politicized by flawed data and faulty assumptions. Let us examine further how such erroneously reported data are often misleading, placing unrealistic demands on teachers.

The student/teacher ratio question is often misleading because there are so many ways in which the data can be gathered. It is assumed that the data are gathered by dividing the total number of students by the number of teachers. Most of the time, the number reported as "teachers" actually refers to "certificated personnel," which serves to skew the numbers considerably. In any school system there are many people who are certified teachers who do not actually teach children, such as superintendents, principals and other building level administrators, central office administrators, program directors, and school counselors. Additionally, there are other teaching personnel who teach more specialized areas and either serve an entire school or a very small portion of the entire school such as reading specialists, various specialists for programs serving the physically handicapped, physical education, home-based instruction, vocal or instrumental music, or foreign language. Further skewing such data is the role of those certified personnel in special education who often have serious class size mandates imposed on their teaching load, sometimes limiting class sizes from four to eight students (Boze, 1999).

We can easily see how the simple reporting of a single ratio is misleading, but the problem can become even more complex, which further mistreats some teachers. Regardless of the reported student/teacher ratio, individual schools are assigned an allotment of teachers based on the number of students enrolled. Most school principals have the autonomy to organize their school and assign teachers in any manner they so choose. I recently witnessed a novice middle school principal take this autonomy to a serious extreme that brought about some serious repercussions, not only in faculty morale but some management and instructional problems as well. Because the 8th-grade students are required to take the state mandated, "high-stakes" test, the principal made the decision to place more teachers in eight grade than in sixth or seventh. This allowed the classes in eighth grade, where the exam was to be given, to be about half the size of the 6th- and 7th-grade classes. One 7th-grade teacher reported, "I have 32 students in a pre-algebra class." This was a serious error on the part of the novice principal because about 30% of the faculty left that year. In addition to the problems created when 30% of a faculty is new to the school, the 8th-grade test scores did not improve significantly, which made circumstances even more difficult the following year. The effort to reduce class size in order to impact test scores brings us to the second set of questions.

The question of class size is probably discussed in more political rhetoric than mere polite conversation. Seldom does a politician run for office that we don't hear, "We're going to reduce class sizes to improve achievement and give teachers more individual time with children." This logic is critically flawed for two reasons, the first of which is the myth of "individual time." For simplicity, let us suppose that we have a class of 30 children and exactly one hour (not including time to check roll, and so forth) to teach them. If it were possible to divide those 60 minutes so that every child had an equal number of minutes of a teacher's undivided, individual time, each child would have exactly 2 minutes with the teacher. If we reduce the class size to 25 and divide that hour equally among every child, then we have every child receiving 2.4 minutes, which translates to 2 minutes, 24 seconds. While this does in fact provide each child with more theoretical "individual time" with the teacher, common sense would dictate that 24 seconds isn't good for much. If we could be so fortunate as to reduce the class size by half to 15, that would give each child 4 theoretical individual minutes, which would be better than 2, but the "individual attention" idea is still a myth. It is a fallacy to assume that a teacher can ever realistically give every child in a class their undivided attention for any amount of time. Even at the optimum in this example, 4 minutes of individual time can't do any child a great deal of good. Additionally, that would mean 14 other children would go 56 minutes with no teacher direction or supervision at all. Yet for some reason, this myth persists.

The second reason the smaller class size idea is flawed is that there really is not a body of information that would support the idea that simply reducing class size will improve instruction or achievement. In order to use research to assert such a claim, studies would have to be done that compare a class that has been reduced in size to another that has not. This would be a difficult question to investigate because so many other variables would come into play that probably could not be allowed for, and as such, any findings would be so open to question. While the research on reduced class sizes is unclear on many things, it is clear on two points. First, class size reduction alone does little to improve achievement (Boze, 1999). Second, there are mitigating factors outside the control of the teacher or the school that produce a much stronger correlation on achievement than reducing the number of students in the class (Hall, 1998). Does this mean that reducing class size is not a good idea? Absolutely not. There are many things to be gained and a number of benefits to be found with smaller classes, but there is not a body of research that would support that improved instruction or student achievement are among them.

These unsubstantiated myths are perpetuated for one reason. It is erroneously assumed that quality classroom management is an automatic recipe for academic achievement. Each of these myths is a question of management, not achievement, because when each of these theoretical ideas is present in a classroom, a group of children are inherently easier to control. It is no secret that a group of children who are happy, content, and emotionally nurtured will be easier to manage than a group who is forced to face social maturity before they would ordinarily make that decision themselves. Likewise, if we are constantly doing cooperative learning or project-type activities, children are free to waste inordinate amounts of time and it's far more difficult to hold them accountable, as what is produced is likely to be more individualistic than criterion oriented.

NO EXCUSES

There is absolutely no excuse for those who are leaders in the teaching profession to not be literate of the field of research, research processes, and the most current body of information that we have available for our use. Likewise, the practitioners in the field cannot assume that someone else will be responsible for making them literate about research in general or research in our field. It is the responsibility of the practitioner to know the body of literature and to recognize researched ideas as opposed to questionable popular opinion. Most important of all, practitioners must insist that educational leaders and administrators know the body of literature as well (Ravitch, 1998). We must hold leaders and administrators accountable for knowing the literature and for making decisions that are based on good research, not flawed or inconsistent findings. As a profession we can bypass some of the mistreatment of educators via bad information and policy decisions by simply asking, "Why?" or better yet, "On which base of empirical research has this decision been made?" Educational leadership roles, by their very nature, are quite political. A wise educational leader will not likely push a decision when the subordinate majority clearly know the decision is weak and not particularly defensible. Slavin (2001) states:

> Evidence-based reform, backed by informed leaders, could finally bring education to the point where evidence is the lifeblood of progress. . . . It is ironic

that the field of education, with its value on knowledge, has so embraced ideology rather than knowledge in its own reform process. Evidence-based reform honors the best traditions of our profession and promises to transform schooling for all children. (p. 29)

In a field where formal study of a question tends to intimidate people, knowledge of the process translates to power. It is a basic tenet of sociology that the educated will always have superiority over the uneducated. Being knowledgeable of the research in our field puts the practitioner in the position to say no. Practitioners who are educated cannot be controlled and/or mistreated.

5

Quick Fixes

While few lawmakers would presume to tell physicians when to recommend dialysis, many think nothing of dictating a particular method of teaching children to read.

Alfie Kohn, *The Schools Our Children Deserve* (1999, p. 94)

There is a mindset driving much of what goes on in our schools that is as much a by-product of a fast paced society as a series of errors in policy development. In society at large, no one is willing to wait a reasonable amount of time for results. We want complicated questions answered quickly, correctly the first time, and with no room for interpretation or analysis. We all want answers that don't impose the inconvenience of "gray areas." Gray areas force us to think, slow us down, and necessitate that decisions be justified by available data. Nice, succinct answers to complicated questions, even if they don't consider the entire question, might appear to solve problems when they actually create a false sense of direction.

Nowhere in society does the quick fix mindset create more problems than in our schools. The schools are a small cross section of society, so every element that exists in society, including the problems, will exist in the schools. As the makeup of society becomes more complex, so do the problems, and likewise the problems that must be addressed by the schools. Other professions are directed to build upon previous experience, hold on to good ideas, and discard the rest. Unfortunately, those who are supposed to guide and make decisions in the teaching profession tend to "chase rabbits." Anyone who has ever tried to chase a rabbit knows the correlation to educational reform. They move quickly and don't move in a single direction very long.

EDUCATIONAL PANIC

The "quick-fix" mindset is relatively easy to trace. One event in the late 1950s triggered the massive changes that we have witnessed in our schools. One element has been present in every reform or improvement effort since—the element of panic. When the Russians launched *Sputnik* in 1957, America was terribly embarrassed that another nation beat them in the race to outer space. Prior to that time, the schools had functioned in the same way for the previous 60–80 years—a relaxed manner that generally didn't attempt to educate every single child regardless of handicapping condition or regardless of those factors that the schools cannot directly impact (Popham, 1993). When I was a relatively new teacher, I recall asking one of my elderly aunts (who has since passed away) about her days in elementary school and if students were ever socially promoted. A woman of this age had no concept of students being promoted simply because they were too old to be in a particular grade. When I asked what happened to the children who, for example, in second grade had not learned to read, she replied, "Well, hell—they just stayed back till they got it." Based on the practicality that society depended on at the time, I would suspect that we did not really find 14-year-old children in second grade. They likely dropped out to work and go on to make some sort of productive lives.

In one of the graduate courses I teach, which is the "foundations" course for those students seeking alternative teacher certification, I often have the students interview the oldest person they know and report back to the group how schools operated 40, 50, or 60 years ago. I have noticed that each semester I tend to hear the same things from those individuals who attended school in the 1930s and 1940s. Public education was viewed as a privilege, not an obligation, and only those who were fortunate to be able to attend school and could meet the requirements and expectations did so. People of that age tend to report a very basic, standard curriculum with some study in the social studies and current events. Very few services were provided for students such as food service or transportation. Many of those people talk of walking home for lunch or bringing their lunch because they lived too far away from school. They likewise tend to report very few discipline problems because the children who, for whatever reason, could not behave appropriately simply did not attend school. By the 1950s, the schools had moved in a direction that allowed for more job-type training in the mechanical sciences and business skills, but was still quite basic. But all that changed when the Russians beat America into outer space. In what would become a typical reaction to school matters (panic), our federal government began handing out major dollars for education like it had never been done before. But we know the federal government does not hand out money for anything without strings attached. So it was directed that any program or project financed with federal dollars be "evaluated." At the time, the field of educational or program evaluation was practically nonexistent, as anyone who would have had anywhere near the background to systematically gather data for any reason was typically trained in the traditional quantitative style of data gathering and interpretation (Worthen et al., 1997).

Unlike the field of scholarly research, the field of educational evaluation is far more particularistic. Research findings draw conclusions while evaluative findings support making decisions. Evaluative findings tend to be more relative to one time and one place. This phenomenon perpetuates the "quick-fix" mindset because evaluation, unlike research, is a far more subjective process that goes further than simply measuring and reporting. Evaluation work is done for the purpose of finding what one is setting out to look for. Since evaluation is inherently the basis for issuing a value judgment, those who are charged with the responsibility of making policy are in a far easier position to make quick decisions with far less numerical or comparative data than would ordinarily be considered necessary. As such, jumping from one extreme to another is much easier to justify (Worthen et al., 1997).

UNHEALTHY BEHAVIORS

Anyone who has been in an unhealthy relationship of any sort, whether it be marriage, work, social organization, or whatever, will quickly learn to recognize patterns of behavior that are considered unhealthy, destructive, or to coin a rather dated term, dysfunctional. Our schools have for years engaged in cycles of destructive behaviors that very much resemble bad or troubled relationships. Such troubled relationships are essentially a set of behaviors that work together like a beautifully engineered set of gears. It takes both sides of an unhealthy relationship to make it work well, and the behaviors continue as each side better refines keeping the balance of power in such a manner as to see that no one ever wins. Such destructive/unhealthy behavioral patterns are easy to recognize, analyze, and address by behavioral science professionals via several common factors:

1. Every confrontation comes about in response to the same question or difference;
2. The same actions trigger the same confrontational behaviors;
3. Every argument is the same argument;
4. In every argument, the same words are spoken.

To fix an unhealthy relationship requires a great deal of work. When behavioral science professionals are called upon for assistance, the person essentially isolates the unhealthy behaviors and helps the individual break the cycle by not responding in the usual way. Unfortunately, in our schools the unhealthy balance has continued for more than 150 years. We have repeatedly seen an unhealthy pattern of "problem/quick-fix . . . problem/quick-fix." To the detriment of the system and the teaching profession, much of what is touted as "innovation" is really a shallow effort to undo years of damage. I am of the opinion that the time is long past that the rest of the world should notice the same patterns of destructive behaviors.

RECOGNIZING A MOVEMENT

The trends in which our business seems to run are often called "movements." There are certain easily recognizable professional behaviors that can identify a movement in the making:

1. A new idea surfaces that is basically good, holds a fresh perspective to an old problem, and is based in reality. While the idea may be a generally good one, it is neither conclusive nor comprehensive. But while the idea is based in reality, it will not have enough information backing it to be considered part of the professional knowledge base.
2. Educational leaders and policymakers will vigorously jump on the idea with little planning or forethought. Educational leaders and policymakers will begin designing and implementing programs based around the idea, although there is not enough information to make informed decisions about the program or idea.
3. Across the nation educational leaders and policymakers skew the idea to meet particularistic needs in specific areas. This is usually a futile attempt to make one idea conclusive and comprehensive. It is likewise an attempt to create an element of universal applicability.
4. The lack of cohesive planning, the wide-scale misuse and fragmentation of implementation efforts causes the movement to result in a lot of effort that brings about no appreciable change.

In the past 25 years, a number of ideas have come and gone that have all promised to "fix" what is wrong with our schools, our teachers, our system of education, and all that goes into the science of teaching and learning. Some of these ideas have been challenges to intrinsically held philosophical ideals, while others have focused on content, expectations, instructional management, and teacher behaviors. I have outlined four major "reform" movements from the past 25 years that have mistreated teachers and created a lot of turmoil but not significantly impacted our schools or the work they do. One should be amazed that what did not work in one place is repeatedly tried in another with the same dismal results. The four major "reform" efforts of the past 25 years that we will address are:

1. The Madeline Hunter Elements of Instructional Design;
2. Statewide systems for evaluating instruction;
3. The School Restructuring Movement.
4. Minimum Standards, Essential Elements, Standards and Benchmarks, the "Standards Movement"; Accountability.

MADELINE HUNTER ELEMENTS OF INSTRUCTIONAL DESIGN

Probably the most overblown "quick-fix" effort of the past 25 years surfaced around 1977 as the instructional model designed by Madeline Hunter. The late Dr. Madeline Hunter was a professor of education at UCLA for many years and also the principal of the UCLA Lab School. She created a model of instructional design that became extremely popular for many reasons, some of them not particularly good reasons. While this is not a book on curriculum and instruction, an overview of the instructional model might be appropriate.

The original model contained several elements, the most popular and frequently cited of which was the anticipatory set. (The origin of this phrase is questioned—most think that it is not a term created by Hunter. Many educational leaders think this term caused the model to catch on so quickly because people liked the way it sounded!) This concise, quite measurable idea caught on quickly and dominated much of the curricular/instructional thinking of this age. While considered by some to be a stroke of genius and the definitive answer to all instructional questions, others questioned its validity beyond that of any other theory. The stiffly formal, precise elements that can coherently create a beautifully executed instructional lesson became popular among those in charge of evaluating instruction to the point that many school districts and some states devised district-wide and statewide plans for the evaluation of instruction built around the Madeline Hunter Elements of Instructional Design. Although the use of the model was refuted by many, there were many educational authorities who were convinced that if every teacher would design every lesson around this model that children's learning would be greatly enhanced. Many teachers became over-dependent on the model partly because of the surface simplicity and partly due to the lack of understanding of the model (Gibbony, 1987).

The Hunter model was not in and of itself a bad thing. What many in our system did with the model, however, went far beyond that, bordering on heinous (Coulombe, 1994). Hunter was an adamant believer in the "teacher as decision maker," and her idea was to create a model that would allow teachers a framework for making decisions (Magestro, 1994). She refuted numerous times that the model was intended to be used to design every lesson in every classroom across the country. Hunter (1985) stated:

> To begin, the Hunter model isn't a program or recipe. It's a decision-making tool. That is, no one can tell a teacher what will be appropriate or applicable to all situations. But we can tell, based on research, what he or she needs to know and think about before deciding what to do. (p. 58)

As is typical in our business, massive reform efforts often happen before there is enough information to know if we're making the right decisions. At the time, it was argued repeatedly that there was not enough data to support such wide use of the Hunter model. To make so many decisions on one theory with no supporting comparative data was shortsighted and dangerous. Slavin (1987a) said:

> One of the most important reasons for the continuing existence of the educational pendulum is that educators rarely wait for or demand hard evidence before adopting practices on a wide scale. Of course, every innovator claims research support for his or her new methods; at a minimum, there is usually a "gee whiz" story or two about a school or district that was "turned around" by the innovation. Alternatively, a developer may claim that, while a program itself has not been formally evaluated, the principles on which it is based are supported by research. . . . The Hunter Model is appealing, practical, and well grounded in education and psychological theory. But does it work? Fortunately, there is no ambiguity about Hunter's objective, which is stated in the title of one of her books, *Teach More—Faster!* Asking rather Hunter's model works clearly means asking, "Do students taught by the ITIP-trained teachers learn more (and learn faster) than students taught by other teachers?" (p. 754)

Gibbony (1987), another prominent educational researcher, questioned the widespread use of the Hunter model:

> The lack of any pattern of research to support her claim for improved learning also confounds Hunter's starting point. . . . Hunter's model starts with learning theory, moves to prescriptions for teaching, and, finally to claims for increased student achievement. Ignoring the fact that her learning theory is based in part on research with lower animals that lack both the capacity for higher cognitive functions and culture, her view is inconsistent with at least one major theorist who embraced a generalized method of science. . . . Without a solid pattern of evidence to support the claim for improved learning, there is no scientific basis for the Hunter model. (p. 48)

With its surface simplicity many school administrators and policymakers found the model to be an easy way to measure what they are supposed to be supervising with little or no regard to the appropriateness or applicability of the model. Berg and Clough (1991) stated:

> Administrators, swayed by public and professional pressure, prefer codified teaching modules because of the accountability they seem to provide. Moreover, because administrators seldom have time to remain abreast of current research in each discipline's content and specialized pedagogical research, some are drawn to claims of "universal applicability." Unfortunately, generic models may conform to many traditional beliefs governing teaching and learning. Finally, busy administrators seldom have enough time to thoroughly investigate the claims made by the creators of these systems or keep abreast of literature critiquing specific lesson design models. (p. 27)

Hunter and many others were quite insistent that her model was based on research. In retrospect, it would appear that much of the research cited to validate the model was more evaluation of the model than research principles upon which the model was based. I am of the firm opinion that effective educational leaders must take the initiative to become literate consumers of the information relative to program development and implementation. I am also of the firm opinion that it didn't happen here.

How then, was the overuse/misuse of the Hunter model a mistreatment of America's educators? As a classroom teacher, I was always leery of those individuals who insisted that every lesson in every classroom had to be a carbon copy of the Hunter model. The adamant adherence to the model made the naive assumption that students were expected to know nothing at the beginning of a lesson and demonstrate mastery at the end. This is a gross oversimplification of a complex process and is in direct contradiction to what we know about higher-level learning. There were a number of arguments that were prominent during the era of the Hunter model popularity. But, suffice it to say, the model, in its proper context, very much served as a framework for an effective lesson. Eliminating the research argument, common sense would dictate that the teacher behaviors advocated in the model enhance the quality of instructional delivery when used in the context for which they were intended. When used as intended the teacher served as the professional decision maker in choosing which elements to use, modify, or correlate, or not to use the model at all.

The argument that the Hunter model emphasized technique over content was valid but not necessarily negative. The model was quite generic and not really intended to meet the need of any one instructional area. It only made sense that technique is the emphasis when the elements of the model were teacher behaviors. The argument that the model stripped all creativity from the act of instruction was valid if the user allowed the model to do so. The culprit was not the model itself, but the interpretation of how the model was used. As such, it would be unfair to make a general statement of the effect that the elements of the model were never appropriate for use in teaching higher-level thinking skills.

The entire Hunter controversy was a direct result of the model being used in a manner inconsistent with its purpose, especially in the area of instructional supervision. The horror stories abound of school buildings, school districts, and even states having become so dependent on the Hunter model that any other instructional model or ideas were totally disregarded. The overuse of the model clearly indicated the desire then, just as today, for a generic, standardized base for the facilitation and assessment of instruction. But in addressing the need for streamlining and standardizing what happens in classrooms anyway, it is critical not to lose sight of the ultimate purpose. Years of effort and untold tax dollars were spent trying to create one way to teach that would "fix" all that was wrong. Too many misinformed leaders assumed that the universal applicability of the Hunter model was the answer. It was simply too easy to take the complex ideas of a brilliant researcher and reduce them to a checklist. This misuse of the Hunter model led to another era of teacher mistreatment—the statewide programs of teacher evaluation.

STATEWIDE TEACHER EVALUATION
MODELS

As a result of much of the country having jumped on the Madeline Hunter bandwagon another effort to improve instruction began to surface as a model for teacher evaluation that would be used statewide. This movement was based on the assumption that although there was no way in which any educational leader could be knowledgeable in every subject area, there were "instructional behaviors" that were known to be effective and as such a measurement instrument could be designed that would be applicable in determining the quality of teaching in any class. It was argued that these evaluation models would not be based on any particular theory but would be based on a compilation of ideas, theories, methods, and practices that had been shown to be effective.

Teachers were assured that these evaluation models allowed for individual differences in teaching styles and would not result in carbon copy classrooms across the state. More often than not, however, those "desired teacher behaviors" translated to a paraphrase of the Hunter model, often with the same verbiage such as "set," "modeling," and "closure." Several Southern states, particularly Georgia, Texas, and eventually Louisiana, embarked on such efforts over a period of several years and all had similar experiences that caused the programs to be very short lived. Minnesota made an attempt at such a program but shut it down in 1989 (Block, 1992).

Of course, persons who are knowledgeable in the field of educational measurement knew that such efforts are immediately suspect for three reasons: (1) the question of the validity of the measurement; (2) the question of consistency in the training and implementation of the program; and (3) the question of provisions for modifications.

The issue of validity in any measurement instrument has traditionally posed the question as to whether or not the instrument truly measures what it claims to measure. More recent textbooks in testing, measurement, and evaluation have extended the definition to include that validity refers to the "inferences" that can be made from the findings of the instrument (Popham, 1993). From the beginning, it was argued that because the evaluation of instruction involves the subjective assigning of a judgment of value, it was not possible to design one instrument that would be a valid measure of instructional quality in every possible instructional situation anywhere in the state. At the time it was also argued that the current body of literature did not support any set of instructional practices as highly related to instructional effectiveness (Block, 1992). Also at the time there was concern that such models would not allow for more open-ended teaching practices as typically found in honors and gifted classes (Searfoss & Eng, 1996). Educational leaders were cautioned that reducing instruction to what amounted to a very lengthy checklist not only limited instructional opportunities but was a deprofessionalization of the act of instruction. Assuming that complex problems can be reduced to an observation-type checklist is both naive and dangerous. We assume that the intent of a program of teacher evaluation is to see that teachers are delivering quality instruction, and we likewise assume that a given instrument is truly a valid measure to this end. Logic would then dictate that the instrument was intended to generate a holistic picture of the teacher's performance. It was told that this program was intended to see what the teacher is capable of doing, not necessarily what the teacher might routinely do. Such statements serve to assert that the intent of the program was probably not a comprehensive evaluation of a teacher's effectiveness, but instead a view of one performance at one time, which would then be generalized into an evaluation of questionable quality. To this day, I find that perspective flawed, as the instrument obviously was not intended to present anything other than a short-term, one-shot picture of what goes on in classrooms.

The convenience of universal applicability brings with it the burden of consistency. This question proved to be one of the greatest challenges to such programs. For one thing, decisions concerning curriculum and delivery of programs are intended to be local decisions with evaluations to be determined by local needs. Training personnel to implement a statewide program that is so specific can be a nightmare because two school districts 10 miles apart may very well interpret directives in an entirely different manner. One school system may hire individuals who do nothing but complete teacher evaluations, while the other may use classroom teachers who are released periodically to complete teacher evaluations. Immediately there will be inconsistencies because of the perspective(s) of the person who teaches every day and will themselves have to be evaluated as opposed to the person whose responsibility is strictly scheduling classroom observations and writing reports. One school system may choose to schedule every classroom observation, while others may not have chosen to do so. As I spoke with a friend of mine who was involved with the model at the state level, I learned that some school systems allowed the evaluators to take notes during the observation, while others only allowed the evaluator to observe and complete the report from what they could remember. I likewise learned from my friend that the training for evaluators was quite intense, involving many days of lectures, discussions, and videotape reviewing of model lessons for training purposes. As the inconsistency issues began to surface, the trainers of the evaluators had to resort to reading parts of the training verbatim in order to ensure that everyone received exactly the same training.

Whether one is building a house, planning a wedding, or designing a statewide program of teacher evaluation, even the most skilled and experienced planner will not be able to think of everything that may go wrong. Provisions must always be in place for modifications in the event that the most carefully laid plans simply don't work. When these programs were put into place, there was an embarrassing lack of preparation and as such, massive revisions had to be made very early on, some of which made a mockery of the system. One would assume that such a blatant lack of planning would be a source of embarrassment for the state.

My own experience with such programs was a disaster. When this effort was at its height, I was teaching in a very progressive suburban school district in one of the early states to take on this process. I was a relatively young teacher at the time and had completed the master's degree less than a year earlier. The school system did very little to prepare staff for the onset of the program, as training for the program consisted of a brief discussion at the first faculty meeting, a short very propagandized video, and a copy of the handbook that did little more than present an overview. The district chose to bring the process about by hiring several people whose sole responsibility was scheduling classroom observations and writing reports. This person visited the school and talked informally with teachers in the teacher's lounge, but the anxiety level was high as people were unsure of this new thing and what was to be expected. Teachers knew this process was coming but were virtually ignorant as to what they were expected to present during a classroom observation or what teaching behaviors needed to be presented for the sake of the observation. As would be written into any traditional plan for personnel evaluation, there were some vague notions about a teacher receiving a poor evaluation and subsequent plans for remediation. But generally the perception of this new program was one of anxiety, apprehension, and uncertainty. When I met the person who was to serve as our "evaluator," I attempted to ask some specific questions to alleviate some discomfort, but the answers I received were the kind of vague, elusive remarks of a person who is generally unclear on what they are to be doing. I quickly concluded this person was not someone to be trusted with your professional standing. My concerns seemed to be confirmed rather quickly as the classroom observations began. Teachers' responses to the observations and feedback ranged from concern to anger to outright hysteria. Many teachers who had for years earned most positive evaluations were suddenly being evaluated as "marginal" or "marginally acceptable" for very subjective and highly questionable reasons.

It was interesting that no one saw the actual instrument until the observations began. The instrument contained 71 "indicators" (desired teaching behaviors very similar to the Hunter model) that were divided into 5 "domains" (planning, management, professional behaviors, instructional delivery, and so forth). Each of the 71 indicators was rated as "Not Observed," "Observed," or "Exceptional Quality." It was clear that the scoring criteria for this new instrument was such that only if the evaluator saw all 71 items would the evaluation be considered "acceptable." Any rating to be earned on any indicator above the level of merely "acceptable" had to come about as a result of what was explained as "a preponderance of the evidence" and would be noted as "EQ" (meaning exceptional quality) next to the appropriate of the 71 indicators. It was most discouraging and demoralizing to hear teacher conversation asking "How many EQs did you get?" as though the EQ were the determining factor as to the quality of your teaching. As the classroom observations continued, so did the horror stories. Teachers reported being denied credit for various indicators on the basis of papers being passed out after the lesson began (rather than at an appropriate point during the lesson) or not having clearly articulated the objective to the lesson (according to the evaluator). Other teachers reported a loss of points over such matters as having worded an explanation in a manner that did not please the evaluator or the classroom seating not having pleased the evaluator, and so forth. When it was told that "It was marked against me for not making the objective clear," teachers began writing the objective on the board and having the children read it aloud so there could be no question that it was brought forth. When another teacher was told she did not include "closure" (a clear indication that the lesson was concluded), teachers began to use the word "closure" or to bring closure to the lesson two or three times "too make sure I got it in." It certainly makes sense that all this only served to feed the hysteria that we were all doomed, no matter how well you prepared or delivered instruction. One can understand that I, and everyone else who had yet to be observed and evaluated, was on the verge of panic. So, when my scheduled time for the dreaded classroom visit came about (about the fourth week of school), I did the only thing I knew to do. I prepared the lesson as meticulously as I knew how, set up the classroom with a particular place for the evaluator to sit, and when she entered the room I turned on a small audiotape recorder. I had no idea that word of such a small gesture would make its way across the entire school system in only a few hours! My intention was not to further stir the hysteria, but instead to be able to defend myself if needed.

That afternoon, the vice principal cornered me in the hall asking if I had taped the lesson. This vice principal was quite competent at what she did but was in an awkward situation because in taping the lesson, I had not broken any rules—I had simply made the evaluator furious. She advised me that it might be a "nice gesture" if I made a copy of the tape and gave it to the evaluator. I replied that I had no objection to making a copy of the tape, but I knew full well that I was under no legal obligation whatsoever to do so (I had long since checked with a teacher union attorney on that matter). The following day when the evaluator confronted me in the hall-way, the conversation was not nearly so polite. She asked for a copy of the tape and I told her, too, that I was glad to do so but knew full well that I was under no legal obligation to do so. She was furious and said, "I didn't appreciate you doing that. I'm only human, I can only see and observe so much. I can't compete with an audiotape that hears everything. This process is still new and everyone is still learning." While I understood her concern, I was adamant in my position. If I was expected to teach "correctly," from the beginning, according to this new instrument, she should be held accountable to the same standard and likewise be expected to evaluate "correctly," from the beginning according to the instrument. She didn't see my point of view and seemed to expect teachers to be patient while she learned the system but was not willing to do the same for them. But, the problems with the entire process, both locally and statewide, were only beginning to surface. The problems this poor lady was preparing to face were likewise only beginning as well. This was the first of several strained and nasty conversations she and I would have. As I look back at all that I have learned, there is a part of me that wonders if perhaps I should be ashamed at the amount of grief I dealt this individual. But on the other hand, common adult sense tells you that even the most gentle of animals, when cornered and frightened, will likely bare their fangs and claws. By frightening the predator, they protect themselves. Likewise, when teachers, generally mild-mannered and complacent people, are cornered and frightened for their professional lives, they will likely come out swinging. This individual was probably doing what she believed she was there to do, but so was everyone else. It was never my intention to be mean to the lady. I was only doing what I believed I had to do in order to survive the situation.

As the classroom visits and observations continued, so did the horror stories, but the horror stories did not seem so extreme in other parts of the school district. In our building, teachers' responses were of such concern that many had follow-up conferences with the principal, vice principal, or other central office/supervisory personnel. One teacher bypassed the building administration and took her concerns all the way to the associate superintendent. Some teachers left the post-observation conference in tears, others in varying states of hysteria, but the general feeling was that they had been slapped in the face. If there was a single teacher who did believe they had been observed and evaluated fairly, it was not told in general conversation. Unfortunately, the school principal(s) was not really in a position to intervene in these matters. Regardless of the trouble created among the faculty as a result of the obviously inappropriately completed observations and evaluations, all they were able to do was to assure teachers to hold their head up and keep on trying. Understandably, they could not agree or disagree with either side of this battle, and they did their best to "keep the peace." The principal(s) likewise had to complete two such observations on each teacher, but the teachers did not respond so vehemently to these observations and evaluations because they were perceived as fair and constructive, not caustic and destructive.

So it should be easy to see that before too many weeks word came down that some changes would be made for the observations that would occur in the spring semester of the year. Teachers received written propaganda indicating that "changes will be made for the spring semester," although the only concrete example of what to expect was that if the evaluator did not observe a particular indicator, "the zero next to the indicator would no longer be circled." This information came from a beautifully prepared letter from the teacher of the year who, coincidentally, had come from the school system and was now working in a position in the state Department of Education. Being given such nebulous information that didn't mean a great deal did little to subside teachers' concerns. In response, I wrote a letter to this individual expressing my anger at the entire system and my disgust at such propaganda that insults the intelligence of adults. I described what had happened in our school and asked the question, "Do we really think that simply no longer circling the zeros makes everything okay?" I never got a response from the teacher of the year. About that time, additional word came down concerning the fact that since some school districts had scheduled observations and some had not, that the issue had come before the state board, an elected body. The literature told which board members had voted in favor of totally unannounced visits and which ones had not. Again, I took the time to write to each of the 15 board members, thanking those who had voted against further brutalizing the process and told each of those who had voted in favor of the measure that "I hope your constituents will vote you out of office." One board member who had voted in favor of the measure did respond, thanking me for my "concerns and concrete examples of inconsistencies," assuring me that she had the best interest of all concerned at heart, and "truly wanted to see the system work in a fair and equitable manner."

By this time the poor evaluator understandably kept as low a profile as possible, but her problems did not. In the spring semester another teacher who was most unhappy with the previous classroom observation did exactly as I had done and made an audiotape of the lesson. The evaluator asked for a copy of the tape and he said no. The following afternoon he came into my classroom to show me a letter prepared by the vice principal (who probably had far more important things to do than get involved in another squabble). The letter essentially stated, "you were observed at this time and date; you made an audiotape of the lesson; you were asked to submit a copy of the tape and have refused; this letter is being placed in your file." The man went home that afternoon and called a teacher union attorney who immediately phoned the associate superintendent and made it clear that what the man was being asked to do was blatantly against the law. The following afternoon the man came back to my classroom, chuckling, with another letter from the same vice principal that essentially stated, "please disregard the previous letter; it has been removed from your file."

Since teachers were being asked to be patient with the new system as the problems were addressed, I took what I considered a good idea to the principal. The evaluator had been insistent that everyone was learning, as this was a new process so it stood to reason that perhaps she may be seeing things a bit more clearly by the end of the first term. If this was true, it may be likely that the people she observed at the end of the first term were observed differently from those observed at the beginning of the term (as I had been). As such, it may serve to equalize matters if she would visit teachers in the reverse order of what she had done in the fall semester. The principal did not object to the idea and said she would make the suggestion. In a couple of days the evaluator appeared at my classroom door and I presented my position to her. She was not particularly receptive to the idea that she may need to improve her skills in the use of the instrument, but agreed to reverse the order of the classroom observations to the extent that she was able. Near the end of the term when my second observation came about, I knew the procedure well. I meticulously planned the lesson trying to be prepared for any and every horror story that had been experienced during the school year as well as prepared the tape recorder. This was my fourth and final classroom visit for the year so I took the evaluation results from the previous three and created a bar graph for comparison purposes. As I prepared my graphs, I left space so that the results of this final observation could quickly be penciled in at the post-observation conference. Two of the three had been the observation work of my principal, and the scores in all areas were significantly higher than the one visit from her early in the school year. At the post-observation conference she was furious that I would present such data to her. In fairness, I will say that there were tiny matters she called to my attention that were constructive. But the scores again were noticeably lower than the other two observations from my principal. I concluded the conference by stating, "I will never believe you have done this fairly." Within a couple of days I composed a letter to the supervisor of the evaluators clearly outlining my concerns with the evaluator and the blatant inconsistencies in her methods. I never received a response.

The following school year so many changes had come about to the instrument that it was hardly recognizable as the mode of trauma that so many had endured the year before. This many years later, that state now provides school systems a choice of the state instrument (in its current form) or one created locally. Teachers' collective anger over the entire fiasco can be traced to several things:

1. Several other states had already attempted such programs and had failed at bringing about any serious changes that resulted in better schools, better performance, better anything;
2. It did not take a team of psychometricians to figure out that one instrument to be used on such a large scale is questionable at best; those individuals who pushed the idea had to know it was a bad idea;
3. It was very early in the process that the fundamental flaws in the system (which were considerable) became evident and the attempts to remedy them were little more than propagandized window-dressing;
4. Teachers were not told the truth about the failure of the system; likewise, teachers' integrity and professionalism was patronized;
5. The school where I served was unfortunate to have had an evaluator who did it very poorly;
6. Teachers were subjected to this brutal, demoralizing process for nothing. Nothing changed, nothing worked better, teachers did not teach more effectively, children did not learn more. All that happened in this two-year process is that a lot of needless hysteria was generated that contributed to the further mistreatment of teachers.

THE SCHOOL RESTRUCTURING
MOVEMENT

In the late 1980s and early 1990s schools were undergoing the fashionable quick-fix that became known as "school restructuring." This movement came about as a reaction to the criticisms of the business community. It has long been discussed that the organization and management of our schools resembles the early factory models that came about during the beginning of the Industrial Revolution in this country. Critics argue both sides of this issue claiming that schools cannot be run like a business, while others argue that the schools will only improve if the same practices used in private business are applied to public education. Whether this idea is feasible or ethical is another discussion for another time. Suffice it to say, however, that the school restructuring movement came about in an effort to make the management of our schools look more like the current practices in business management.

I was a first-year doctoral student when I heard my first lecture on the school restructuring movement, but I did not attend the lecture in my role as a doctoral student. My first exposure to the school restructuring movement was part of new employee orientation in a very progressive school system. I was intrigued at the time, but in retrospect I can see that their efforts in presenting the school restructuring movement were very much in line with their efforts to present information in other areas. Those in charge of staff development in the school system were notorious for presenting a small piece of a very large picture. The small piece was typically twisted and squeezed to the point that the practitioners only knew enough about the idea to recognize it as familiar and perhaps drop a few "buzzwords." Outside of that, not enough critical information was presented to discuss it intelligently among truly scholarly people. For example, we were told that the school restructuring movement was an effort to "make the schools work better—not differently." This perspective struck me as odd for a couple of reasons. First, this perspective implied the need to "fine tune the status quo" as opposed to the demands for massive reforms that had been the basis for typical political squabbles for many years. It did not seem logical that after all the years of being told how terrible everything was and some pretty embarrassing failed reforms, that suddenly all was okay and the schools only needed to reorganize a bit to be considered acceptable. Second, any effort that genuinely brings about improvement must be *different* from what went on before. It makes sense that we can have change without improvement, but improvement without change simply is not possible. The concept of change is quite threatening to the human condition. As such, the years of the school restructuring movement, like most other movements, kept a lot of people very busy, created a lot of highly paid, bureaucratic positions, and generated a lot of very impressive but generally nebulous verbiage. In the end, however, school restructuring created a lot of work for educators without any consistency and with no real idea of how to determine success or failure.

We all know the visible signs that a "movement" is taking off in the teaching profession. The restructuring movement fell right into the profile of "good idea, slightly different perspective, everyone jumps on it, everyone doing it differently." But the one idea that did seem to be consistent across the country was the need to realign the power and decision-making hierarchy in the schools. The big talk among proponents of the restructuring movement was the need to shift decision-making power from a central location (generally meaning the administration building of the school system) to the individual school site. Most agreed this was a wonderful idea since it had long been argued that the traditional "factory model" of organizational structure, with decisions made at the top and "trickling down," was no longer appropriate for schools. People were excited at the idea of reshaping district hierarchy and redefining some traditional roles. With the powers and authorities distributed differently, educators would have greater professional autonomy where little or none had existed before. It was assumed that reorganized hierarchies would allow educators at the building levels to make decisions concerning budgets, staffing, instruction, program implementation, and general management, which would be most appropriate for the individual population being served. Making decisions at the building level pushes efforts forward in a far more timely and efficient manner than having to go to the top of the organization and back again.

What could possibly have gone wrong with such a wonderful idea? Quite simply, the school restructuring movement fell victim to the same destructive cycles as previous movements. First, when an organization makes changes and redistributes responsibilities, every individual cannot keep all previous responsibilities and take on others. Common sense would dictate that if a concern for teachers everywhere is the time to prepare and teach what needs to be taught, more responsibility outside of instruction is probably not a good idea. Many "restructured" schools found teachers with full teaching loads but spending inordinate amounts of after school and personal time involved with matters that further complicated the school day. Second, within school systems there are decisions that must be uniformly applied. During the school restructuring movement everyone heard glowing reports of a school faculty somewhere that had been able to decide to hire para-educators in place of an additional teacher in order to use personnel funds more efficiently. But such stories were clearly the exception to the rule. In short, the school restructuring movement created a lot for teachers to do, often resulting in fragmented programs that did not stay in place very long.

THE STANDARDS AND ACCOUNTABILITY MOVEMENT

The mid- to late 1990s saw efforts surface within our schools that can be called the "standards and accountability movement." For years, legislators and educational policymakers have increasingly been under pressure to improve schools with one failed reform after another standing as a tribute to the best-laid plans. We have clearly seen how we spent nearly 20 years trying to get everyone to do things the same way. Since that didn't work, the most recent mindset seems to be "Let's set a standard and allow everyone to get there by whatever means they so desire, and hold them accountable if they don't." This mindset supposedly bypasses the heated and politically charged question of a common curriculum. Such reform efforts have been called various things in various places: essential elements, minimum standards, standards and benchmarks, and so forth. The standards movement has been marked by such practices as "high stakes testing," whereby one standardized test score is the determining factor in whether a student is promoted or retained. At the time of this writing, 49 of the 50 states have adopted some form of academic standards. Iowa requires each district to create individual standards (Jones, 2000). "Accountability," the other buzzword of the standards movement, generally means that schools that do not perform according to plan face the possibility of corrective action, or at worst, being shut down and reopened as an entirely different organization. For the very same reasons that other hard-hitting quick fixes have faltered, the standards and accountability movement is experiencing difficulties such as: poor planning, political pressure, and inconsistency.

It is not difficult to see that the standards and accountability movement thus far has resulted in many rules that are inconsistent on a large scale and basically cannot be enforced. Like many others, this movement is quite politically charged and got off to a furious start but fumbled quickly. Like others, little wide-scope or long-term planning took place before educational leaders and policymakers tried to "slap a bandage on a big, nasty sore spot."

At this point the standards and accountability movement has some serious "holes" in it because the definition and scope are so varied. States everywhere have written standards that address the content—the "what" we are to teach children. Very few, however, have addressed the performance standard—the "how well" students are supposed to do the "what." It is not difficult to see the weak link here. National standards have been written by various professional organizations representing the various disciplines such as National Council for Teachers of Mathematics (NCTM), English, Social Studies, and so forth. Many of these standards are so vague and ethereal, so devoid of direction that they can mean just about anything, sometimes with no regard for the complexities of teaching (Nelson, 1997). For example, Tanner (1998) refers to a science standard whereby it is expected that 4th-grade students will "express themselves eloquently in spoken and written form." Obviously the perception of eloquent makes this a difficult standard to quantify. It's hard to place a measurement standard against something that doesn't have particularly clear boundaries.

With so many standards being written that can be interpreted so many different ways and not particularly measurable at the same time, it should stand to reason there will be inconsistencies between two classrooms next door to each other (Donlevy, 2000; Thomas B. Fordham Foundation, 1995–1996). Is there any wonder that there is so much inconsistency between school systems and states?

Finn, Petrelli, and Vanourek (1998) make some arguments as to why so many standards-based reform movements are failing. First, too many currently adopted standards are so vague as to basically allow anyone to do things any way they choose. Second, the question of "skills versus real knowledge" is seldom addressed to the satisfaction of most. Third is the relevance question. Too many standards focus on the immediate so that the long-term picture is lost in the verbiage. Finally, these writers argue, along with many others, that standards are often worded in such a way as to become standards of teaching rather than standards of learning.

It is interesting that the standards movement so directly contradicts the use of "behavioral objectives" that was so heavily advocated in the 1970s. Teaching to an objective has never been a bad idea, but around the early 1970s educational thinkers decided that objectives needed to be specific and stated in terms of learner behaviors that could be visibly observed. No longer did one assume that the learner would appreciate, understand, or experience. Instead, instructional objectives had to state that the learner would "say," "add," "list," "arrange," "identify," and so forth—actions that could be visibly observed by the teacher. Usually attached to this was some sort of criterion whereby the teacher would be able to assert that the objective had been met. For example, "The student will correctly choose the noun in the sentence 4 of 5 times." If the student only chose the noun three times, the objective was not met. Such thinking led to very fragmented modes of instruction that focused on smaller and smaller bits of information that were only part of "the big picture." This thinking is in direct contradiction to the thinking of today that seems to be "Comprehend the big picture without mastering the small pieces leading up to it." I recall as an undergraduate student being drilled ad nauseam on the correct way to write a behavioral objective. Although I know that we have learned a great deal since then and that ideas have certainly changed, that early teacher training that focused on the specificity of ideas is firmly entrenched in my memory. It is still difficult for me to state that children will "understand" because that's not something that can be "observed." Hadderman (2000) argues that too many standards seem to violate what standards are about—an exact measure at the end. She states:

> Some parents, students, educators and other stakeholders are alarmed by unintended consequences of imperfectly designed and implemented standards-based reforms. Some states "are using tests in ways that directly contradict the

recommendations of the National Academy of Sciences, the Department of Education's Office of Civil Rights, and other experts," and advise that "one shot assessments" should never determine major decisions about a student's academic future. (p. 3)

The question of "school accountability" has loomed over educators' heads for some time. Political rhetoric speaks of holding schools accountable in such a manner as cutting off funding, bringing in external support, or even shutting down schools that do not meet the expectations, which translates into schools that present poor test scores. To make a very long story short, in our state the idea was that schools that did not perform well would first be subjected to corrective action—bringing in teams of experts to rework programs so that children did succeed. Failing corrective action would/could mean further corrective action—more experts, very serious monitoring, and so forth. Failing further corrective action could mean the school being shut down—the doors temporarily closed, administration, and teachers reassigned or dismissed, and reopened as a different school with a different population. When I heard this for the first time, I had to chuckle for two reasons—the money to make it happen and the political pressure to keep it from happening. Political pressure is not hard to come by—money is!

At this point in the accountability movement I have seen many schools coupled with teams of experts to lend support. I have not seen a single school shut down. I seriously doubt we will ever see such a thing actually happen for several reasons:

1. It is not terribly difficult to justify reassigning a principal or even a few teachers. It is difficult to justify dismissing a principal or teachers because of students test scores. There are so many factors that impact how well students perform on standardized tests that are not related to instruction or programs, and such factors are known to far more significantly impact test performance than anything related to instruction. Dismissing school personnel based upon student test scores has never been done because of the legal nightmare it would create. (School systems that choose to dismiss personnel typically do so by creating such a miserable situation that the person voluntarily leaves.)

2. The schools that tend to perform poorly on standardized tests are typically inner-city schools with populations of extreme poverty. Closing the doors of the school will mean significant burdens on the families and the school system, as well as requiring the school system to provide some alternative (the instructional program and transportation to it)—which means money.

3. Moving children from the disadvantaged and poorer performing

schools will mean displacing children in the more desired schools where test scores are higher. What is the likelihood of the middle class parents tolerating these poor performing students coming into the school and bringing down the school average? What is the likelihood that the middle class parents are going to tolerate their child being displaced and moved to one of the "former poor performing schools," which typically are in the less desirable areas?

Common sense dictates that closing the doors to a school is not likely to happen—hence the accountability movement has made another rule that it cannot enforce. But the other component of the accountability movement that has not held up is that of the "high stakes testing." High stakes testing will be further discussed in the next chapter, but for now recognize that the states that have attempted a mode of school accountability via high stakes testing have generally failed or at least it has not stayed in place for long. There are simply too many factors to be considered that one test score alone cannot account for. Although legislators, policymakers, and educational leaders are not saying so, our experience has been similar (Robelen, 2000). Our state dictated that a student who did not pass the state mandated standardized test at the 4th- and 8th-grade levels would not be promoted. Although far more students did present better scores than was originally predicted, there were no provisions made for or funding allocated to enforce the nonpromotion aspect of the program. Out of a lack of anything else to do, the state then lessened their criteria and placed the student who did not pass the first administration of the test (or a subsequent administration following summer school) into a class labeled as 4.5—a transitional grade. A new curriculum was created, whereby, in theory, those students would be "taught 5th-grade material but remediated on 4th-grade material" with the expectation that they would retake the test at the end of the transitional year. One member of the state board of education stated in the media that there was no provision to retain the child after the third test administration. The law allows the child to go on (after the transitional year) but still "complete" summer school. It does not take high level logic to figure out that if they do pass the test after the transitional year and are then promoted to sixth grade, they have essentially been in fifth grade for the year. To further muddy the waters, the state legislature announced early in the fall semester of the transitional year that a "loophole" had been created that would allow students to be promoted anyway, but "the 8th-grade students will still be held accountable for passing the Graduate Exit Exam." So much for accountability.

But in the accountability argument a phrase keeps coming forth that questions the entire process—the question of true accountability. It would make sense that what we are seeing—rules created that cannot be enforced and therefore become more and more "watered down" as time goes on—

epitomizes the question of true accountability. Many critics have argued that the system will never have true accountability until everyone whose work and decisions impacts the working of the schools and the achievement of students is held accountable. Recently the following letter appeared (in part) in a local newspaper:

> Accountability should begin at the top of the educational ladder. Legislators and other elected officials who make political decisions at the expense of sound education should be accountable. Governors who allow themselves to be influenced by well-paid "experts" with the one, true answer to education's problems should be accountable. Educational leaders who spend our tax dollars to recklessly follow unproven trends, discard these trends and search for new ones as they bend to the desires of book companies and consultants should be accountable. Citizens who don't vote or don't require excellence from candidates should be accountable. Society, which places more value on entertainment, roads and prisons than it does on children and their school buildings, should be accountable. Parents who don't value their children's educational needs, who don't ensure daily attendance and who don't demand maximum effort and acceptable behavior from their children should be accountable. Apathetic and disruptive students who deny education to others should be accountable. (Fontenot, 1998)

That would mean that the student who does not pass the high stakes test is unquestionably not allowed to promote to the next grade. It would likewise mean that the teacher who cannot produce documentation that the requisite material was taught and mastery demonstrated is held to answer for discrepancies. Additionally, it would mean that school administrators who created school climates, teaching environments, and working situations that were not absolutely conducive to the teaching and mastery of the curriculum would be held to answer for their decisions. In the same context, the central office administrator who disallows budgets to hire additional staff to adequately prepare the student body for the high stakes exam will be held to answer for their decisions. Hoover, Farber, & Armaline (2000) asserts that we will see true accountability when states are held to answer for failing to provide funding and resources to implement mandated programs and reforms. This is not a problem that is peculiar to education—business and industry find themselves asking for governmental help quite often to implement mandates. Likewise, we will see true accountability when the funds and resources are made available to enforce the rules made by the legislators.

Much of the thinking behind the accountability movement is a well-meaning effort to put information before the public that the public has a right to know. Unfortunately, some information is not particularly useful to the public and might lead to some erroneous conclusions when not presented in its full context. We are seeing one such example in the push for institutional accountability in higher education. States are preparing to publish data concerning the percentage of teacher graduates from individual institutions who pass whatever licensing exam on the first administration. Likewise, states are preparing data to present to the public concerning such matters as the percentage of teacher education graduates from individual institutions who do enter teaching, who are still teaching three years later, and even which ones stay in the state. Such information is certainly of use to those working in the areas of institutional development and university recruiting, but presenting such data to the public under the false notion that one institution is superior to another is simply not fair.

But one point is missed in all the rhetoric surrounding standards, accountability, and raising expectations. They all must be both reasonable and realistic. We can create all the standards, rules, expectations, and difficult tests we want but not much will change until we correct the problem at the bottom of it all—the lack of resources that make for such discrepancies. We often hear it said that simply raising expectations will correct what is wrong in schools. No one can argue that raising expectations is not a good idea, but the idea alone stops short. We can raise the expectations of the bathtub to include cooking rice. We can put rice and water in the tub but until some resources are in place—namely a controlled source of heat and a lid to contain the heat—the rice will never cook. Raising expectations without the supporting resources will never bring about the desired changes.

As we can see, the question of true accountability is a complicated one that is hardly treated fairly in polite conversation. But for some reason, the failings of the system don't seem to point fingers at those who have created unworkable situations and unenforceable rules. The only fingers pointed seem to be at the teachers, which translates to one more way in which American teachers are mistreated by the society they serve.

MORE OF THE SAME

We can see clearly how there exists in our schools an unhealthy cycle of behaviors that are reactive to the pressures placed upon the schools. This unhealthy cycle mistreats teachers by continuing to create more things to do, more unreasonable and unrealistic responsibilities, often without basis, that do not produce any benefit or increase in student achievement. More recently, an idea has surfaced that has caused leaders, policymakers, and critics alike to pay attention and question if this is another "quick fix." One of the current buzzwords we are hearing around schools is that of brain research. All over, educational leaders and administrators are quoting selected pieces of supposedly high level "brain research" that support their ideas and positions. We are hearing everything from "brain research indicates that children learn better and retain more information longer when their bodies are hydrated, so it's a good idea to allow them to keep a bottle of water near their desk during standardized tests." Another brain research idea that has circulated is that peppermint stimulates the brain, so allowing student to eat mints during a test might help their performance. The terminology of "brain research" sounds quite scholarly and is a bit intimidating to the average individual. After all, we have already learned that the average person in the general public assumes that when the word "research" is attached to an idea, it must be valid, worthy, and truly intellectual. But more than just the "R" word, it is affiliated with the brain, which of course makes it far more convincing than any old common research on something like observable behaviors. It is not my intention to discount or minimize the work of neurological researchers but instead to put their work in the appropriate perspective. Stone and Clements (1998) state:

> Any educational proposition gains an aura of credibility if it can be tied to research in the hard sciences, and that is indeed the way in which brain-based learning makes use of neuroscience. The neuroscience on which brain-based learning is based is the product of legitimate research in the medical and biological sciences. Brain-based learning principles, however, are dubious interpretations of neuroscience, and the educational application is wholly untested (Bruer, 1997). (p. 11)

In searching through the literature on brain research we see several different levels of writings on the question of implicating brain research into teaching. On one level we see writers such as Languis (1998) and Kovalik and Olsen (1998) enthusiastically reporting some broad generalities in what neuroresearchers have found, or perhaps have known for some time, about the functions of the brains. Educators at all levels certainly need to be aware of this emerging knowledge base and the inevitability of its influence on the work we do. Then there are writers such as Bruer (1997), Abbott (1998), and Abbott and Ryan (1999) who advise practitioners to be aware that our traditional systems are about to undergo some serious rethinking, and that practitioners must be ready. Abbott (1998) states:

> For such models to emerge, the whole system must be changed significantly, and such change is not likely to happen of its own volition. If change were as simple as applying what we know, the researchers, educators and policy analysts would have arrived at large dissemination plans long ago. Radical new ways of education entail very long and hard pathways for change to be widespread. (p. 21)

Cohen (1995) cites some rather extreme perspectives that include throwing out practically everything that is currently in use and starting over.

Such radical thinking leads us to the positions of such writers such as Sousa (1998b), Davis (2000–2001), Stone and Clements (1998), and Sylwester (1998), who seriously caution educational leaders and policymakers not to use this new knowledge base as many others have been. The brain research findings that are currently discussed as having educational implications are still quite preliminary, far from conclusive, and open to broad interpretation. The profession of teaching and learning must not allow this new information to go from theory to bandwagon to "bad science." Wheeler (1998) writes that although imaging technologies are creating remarkable findings, they are rudimentary and only marginally support earlier brain research. In short, educators must not be too quick to create programs based on such findings. Sylwester (1998) states:

> It's a good time, not a bad time. We're in this for the long haul. We shouldn't rush to claims that brain research supports something if we can't cite the research that proves it. It's not necessary to add the totem of brain research to every successful educational practice. . . . Let's rather take the time and expend the energy to do it right. (p. 10)

If the profession truly expects to use neurological research findings to reshape how schools function, then the research must be used in a scholarly and scientific manner (Sousa, 1998a). It goes without saying that a one- or two-day workshop on brain research will not truly equip teachers to bring about desired changes. Educational leaders must be realistic in determining time frames for instructional reform. Sousa (1998a) states:

> Before we can decide how to use the research productively, we have to learn much more about these scientific endeavors. We should read the appropriate research and engage in conversations among ourselves and with the scientific community. Only when we understand the science involved can we then devise strategies and techniques that translate the research into effective classroom practice. (p. 25)

We are seeing reform initiatives based on brain research emerging. Schools Attuned is a program intended to train teachers in learning style differences though the collection of neurological research of Dr. Mel Levine. Dr. Levine is a most distinguished pediatrician at the University of North Carolina who has for many years expressed and shared an interest in how children learn. It is his honorable intention to get information about how children learn to the ranks of those who can best use the information—educators. The reports vary from 15–25 years of research while the type and style of research are not mentioned—simply "years of research." Levine's program sounds as though it carries a great deal of scientific credibility. We don't need to look too deeply, however, to realize that the focus of the program is learning style differences (O'Sullivan

& Page, 2000). The design of the program doesn't differ a great deal from others except that the research used as a basis comes from the medical aspect rather than the social sciences. Those of us who are a bit skeptical anyway would be inclined to ask if this information, even coming from a medical perspective, will really tell us a great deal more than we already know from the research that has been done for years in the social sciences. People who are knowledgeable about learning styles and educational leadership will likely be leery of Levine's work not because it would be considered questionable but because it fits so nicely into the pattern of the "quick-fix." Typically, the "quick-fix" pattern falls this way:

1. Years of clinical data, gathered by unknown means, supporting a person's idea, and claiming to either "fix" what is wrong or serve as a "tool to fix what is wrong" are compressed into a weeklong seminar with teachers as the focus audience.
2. A large teacher audience feels enthralled, enlightened, and empowered at a new perspective to an old problem.
3. Since training in the program is quite expensive, school systems send a few people to the training. Groups of people who have trained in the program return to their school system to train others. What had previously been many years of work and research compressed into a week is now further compressed into two or three days.
4. These people return to their individual schools to present in three to four hours what had previously been a week of intense work, based on possibly years of research and study.
5. Teachers, through no fault of their own, are then so poorly prepared that the program fails miserably. Interestingly, someone will ask "why?" In all likelihood, teachers will be blamed for "not having done it correctly."

My position here is certainly not to question if Levine's program is reputable. I'm sure it is. I applaud the man for bringing some staff development effort to teachers that contains some real academic content as opposed to what is typically handed to teachers as "professional development" (Norris, 2001). My "devil's advocate" position here is to make the practitioner aware by challenging thinkers to ask the questions that need to be asked. Schools Attuned is a program, like so many others, that is research-based. At this time there is no quantitative or comparison data to support that using Levine's strategies will improve student achievement. Schools Attuned doesn't offer any intervention to accommodate individual differences that we haven't already seen. The selling point of the program is that the techniques for recognizing learning style differences have particularly scientific names attached to them, although they really don't mean anything more than the names given to individual strengths by Howard Gardner when he wrote on the theories of multiple intelligences.

CONCLUDING THOUGHTS

Amid reports of an aging teaching force, of which a large percentage is dangerously close to retirement, it would seem logical that a large portion are veterans. It should then be understandable how the majority of the teaching force is angry and frustrated at years of slip-shod practices that have been a reaction to hysteria rather than a response to changing needs. A colleague of mine, a 20-year veteran of teaching, recently stated, "When I first started teaching, I would go into rages about the absurd things that go on. Today, I just don't have the energy to get angry." Unfortunately, we often see this perspective from those who have worked in the business for enough years to see the patterns of behavior.

The same polite conversation that laments the deplorable status of schools forgets to mention the years of brutal treatment against teachers and students as one oversimplified fix after another has been slapped in place while the business of schools still had to go on and educators still had to survive. It should embarrass the thinking sector of society to know that the majority of reform efforts in the schools have amounted to little more than repairing a broken water main with bubble gum. It is doubtful that the polite conversationalists recognize how often educators, particularly the classroom teacher, is given a tiny piece of information and expected to bring about real and permanent change. This pattern of behavior in a clinical psychology setting would bring forth a different set of answers. While the issues are quite complex, one fact does remain stable—the quick fix pattern mistreats educators because the American population is not yet tired enough of it.

6

✠

Tested Beyond Reason

Virtually anything can be produced with less quality and sold at a cheaper cost. Those who consider price alone are this man's lawful prey.

Unknown

Many years ago when I was a small child I saw the epigraph to this chapter on a sign at the cash register of an auto parts store. I asked my father to explain what it meant, which essentially is the old saying "you get what you pay for." One may pay a lesser price today, but the poorer quality product will not work as well, provide as useful a service, and in all likelihood will have to be replaced in a relatively short time. The extra time and money spent now will likely mean less to be spent in the future. When I understood, the lesson learned has stayed with me for these years. This is a lesson that many educational leaders and policymakers should heed.

There is a phenomenon that is both particular and peculiar to the teaching profession, causing professional grief unlike any experienced by other professions—standardized testing. The current overdependence on standardized test scores creates exactly that to which the statement refers—a product of lesser quality that is sold at seemingly less cost.

The perspectives of critics and experts in the field of educational testing are as varied as the types and kinds of tests available. There are critics who adamantly oppose any form of standardized testing (Kohn, 1999). There are others who refute the majority of the literature, insisting that the public demands more standardized testing (Phelps, 1998) and that U.S. students are not tested to an extent beyond that of other nations (Phelps, 1997). It is a safe assertion, however, that most who are critical of testing are not opposed to the idea of testing as a necessary though less desirable part of the total educational experience. Instead, they are opposed to the manner in which test scores have begun to be used (Kohn, 2000) or in some cases not being used. The testing mania in this country did not come about just recently (Madaus, 1985). It has gradually crept into the American edu-

115

cational culture over so many years that few people now even question how or why it is done. The amount of would-be instructional time that is spent in acquiescence to testing is staggering. Some reports suggest that as many 200 million instructional days per school year are spent in preparation and administration of tests. Even more staggering is the amount of money spent to support the practice of testing. Reports of testing costs in the entire country range from $500 million (Charlesworth et al., 1994) to in excess of $900 million annually (Berliner & Biddle, 1995).

Recently, Nicholas Leman (1999), in his book *The Big Test: The Secret History of the American Meritocracy,* has written an exhaustive explanation as to the origin of the SAT and its use. The SAT was originally intended to be a totally objective, scientific method of identifying the best and the brightest young minds. As such, what was perceived to be a truly scientific measure would give deserving students from modest backgrounds the same advantages as those from affluent backgrounds. Unfortunately, a "good score" on the SAT has become seemingly one of the primary goals of secondary education. Those early thinkers who advocated for a scientific method of choosing the best and brightest had no idea that test scores would one day influence real estate values. It is safe to say that 60–70 years ago, no one could have imagined that the science of mental testing would become the out of control phenomenon that it has (Lemann, 1999). My argument in this chapter has less to do with college admissions and more with the types of standardized tests that are administered to millions of children each year under the guise of educational measurement, instructional management, or quality control. It is easy to see from Lemann's expose how well-intentioned ideas have grown far beyond what they were ever intended. The overdependence on standardized tests is possibly the most heinous mistreatment of American educators partly because of what it does to the art and science of teaching and partly because of what it forces educators to do to children (Gordon & Reese, 1997). Although not a popular topic for testing proponents, in this chapter we will see how the current use of tests moves from an effort to "formulate correct questions to ask about curriculum mastery" (Taylor & Baker, 2001) to the force that drives instruction (Charlesworth et al., 1994). We will see that driving instruction via testing does not improve quality, but instead pushes for a poorer quality of teaching for the sake of testing (Sacks, 1999). As the adage stated, those who consider price alone will surely be disappointed. Likewise, those who consider test scores alone will surely be disappointed.

WHY TEST?

In any organization that provides services or sells a product there must be some method of determining if the organization's efforts have been successful as well as to make decisions on areas in which improvement is needed. It can hardly be argued that some measure of quality control must be present in any organization. This is no different in a school setting. Of course this is far more easily accomplished in a business or hard science setting than in any organization whose focus is in the social sciences. When surveys are done we find few people who are opposed to any type of testing as a means of quality control or design of improvement. What we find is widespread concern over the use of educational tests in ways for which they were never intended to be used. The problems arise when: we try to impose exact measures on what is not exactly measurable and we make important decisions based on a seemingly scientific measure that is markedly deceptive (Popham, 1993).

Quality control is an important expense in running a service organization. It is not unreasonable for educational leaders and legislators to want a simple, relatively inexpensive and universally applicable manner in which to determine if our schools are doing the job they were designed to do (Linn, 1993). To a point, the current market of standardized tests does exactly that, and when used correctly and in the manner intended, can do it well. However, like any well-intentioned idea, the purpose and effect becomes skewed and finally vanishes when the idea is taken to a dangerous extreme. As a result, no one is quite sure why the testing mania has taken off or if it is doing what we want. Bracey (2000) states:

> Looking at the frenzy about testing, two questions immediately come to the fore: The first: Why? The second: Are the testing programs having their desired impact? The short answer to the first question is, "A loss of trust in teachers and administrators." The answer to the second is, "No." (p. 3)

Let us examine further by viewing a clever analogy made by Linda Darling-Hammond (1985):

> Once upon a time in Wonderland, a prestigious national commission declared that the state of health care in that country was abominable. There were so many unhealthy people walking around that the commission declared the nation at risk and called for sweeping reforms. In response, a major hospital decided to institute performance measures of patient outcomes and to tie decisions on patient dismissals as well as doctor's salaries to those measurers. The most widely used instrument for assessing health in Wonderland was a simple tool that produced a single score with proved reliability. That instrument, called a thermometer, had the added advantage of being easy to administer and record. No one had to spend a great deal of time trying to decipher doctors' illegible handwriting or solicit their subjective opinions about patient health. When the doctors discovered that their competence would be judged by how many of their patients had temperatures as measured by the thermometer as normal or below, some complained that it was not a comprehensive

measure of health. Their complaints were dismissed as defensive and self-serving. The administrators, to insure that their efforts would not be subverted by recalcitrant doctors, then specified that subjective assessments of patient well-being would not be used in making decisions. Furthermore, any medicines or treatment tools not known to directly influence thermometer scores would no longer be purchased.

After a year of working under this new system, more patients were dismissed from the hospital with temperatures at or below normal. Prescriptions of aspirin had skyrocketed, and the uses of other treatments had substantially declined. Many doctors had also left the hospital. Heart disease and cancer specialists left in the greatest numbers, arguing obtusely that their obligation to patients required them to pay more attention to other things than to scores on the thermometer. Since thermometer scores were the only measure that could be used to ascertain patient health, there was no way to argue whether they were right or wrong.

Some years later, during the centennial Wonderland census, the census takers discovered that the population had declined dramatically and that mortality rates had increased. As people in Wonderland were wont to do, they shook their heads and sighed, "Curiouser and curiouser." And they appointed another commission. (pp. 247–248)

While some may consider this analogy trite and overly simplified, it cleverly demonstrates the social and political issues faced by educators in the current race to determine educational quality by test scores alone. Let us consider some other aspects of the testing race that are detrimental to the educational process as well as a mistreatment of educators.

BASICS OF TESTING

The testing mania is deeply entrenched in the American educational culture, yet the American public is terribly ill informed concerning the science of standardized testing, test scores, how they are contrived, what they mean, and how they should be interpreted. While this is not intended to be a textbook on educational testing and measurement, it would do well to establish some baseline data about educational testing in general as it relates to public schoolchildren. While there are variations of testing types in many areas, in the realm of educational testing we find two general categories—those considered norm-referenced and those considered criterion-referenced.

The norm-referenced test measures a sample of what a child is supposed to know and reports those findings in relation to what other students who took the test at the same time are reported to know. The norm-referenced score is a comparison of the individual in relation to every other individual and is usually reported in "percentiles," which of course sounds very scientific but can be seriously misleading. For example, to say that a student scored at the 80th percentile sounds like the student did well. This score does not indicate that the student demonstrated mastery of 80% of the sample of content but instead that the student scored better than 80 out of a theoretical group of 100 students. If the students tested were particularly ill prepared and 80 of them only demonstrated mastery of 35–40% of the sample of content, the score of 80th percentile is quite misleading. Likewise, in the reverse setting, let us assume the group of students tested were particularly bright and demonstrated mastery of 85–90% of the sample of content. If this student only demonstrated mastery of 80%, the percentile score may very well fall into the range of the 60th percentile—not nearly as desirable a score. Norm-referenced test scores are useful in making some decisions about groups, but it should be of serious concern to parents and educators when high stakes decisions regarding promotion and retention are made based on one particular set of numbers.

The criterion-referenced measure is often more useful when making decisions about the individual. A criterion-referenced measure compares a student's individual performance against a set of standards, a body of academic content, or a group of performance competencies.

So if either realm of educational testing can yield useful results, where does the problem lie? Quite simply, that answer comes back to the premise of this chapter—the misuse of the tests. When the focus of schooling becomes a pseudo-measurement via testing rather than true learning, what is likely to occur? When the factor determining good or bad is that collection of test scores, what is likely to happen to the modes of instruction we see in classrooms every day? Obviously, instruction will become focused in such a manner as to be subservient to the test rather than the test simply measuring what has been taught.

It has been argued for years that when the pressure is on to raise test scores, teachers will "teach to the test." There is really no question that such does occur every day. In many school systems such practices are blindly allowed under the misguided notion that the end (raising test scores) justifies the means (Bushweller, 1997; Kaufhold, 1998). It certainly stands to reason that any prudent adult who is being held accountable to one set of numbers is going to do whatever is necessary to make those numbers "look good." Berliner and Biddle (1995) describe this practice:

> Teachers who work in schools subjected to such programs report that their worries about the school's status and the shallowness of accountability evaluations consume their time and energy. Over time, these programs tend to generate the three A's, Anxiety, Anger, and Alienation. Teachers feel anxious when their schools face accountability systems—particularly systems that are imposed by higher authorities, and that are used to make important decisions about their lives. They feel anger when they discover that those accountabil-

ity systems are used unfairly—when they provide rewards or impose pun-
ishments on undeserving schools. And when teachers learn they have little
ability to change unfair accountability systems, they become alienated—
passive-aggressive members of a community, acting as obstructionists for
other new ideas that come along. To say the least, this does not sound like a
good recipe for improving American education. (p. 196)

An interesting twist to this argument is the question of how frequently
test coaching, teaching to the test, or whatever actually influences score
outcomes. In response to the pressure for increased test scores, everyone
would like to believe that such coaching and test-prep efforts produce a
"good return" on the investment of time, resources, and money. While
there are data from such organizations as Kaplan and Sylvan Learning
Centers indicating score increases after completing their test prep courses,
there is relatively little in the professional literature addressing such.
Apparently such studies that do exist tend to focus on college admissions
exams and less on standardized tests in general (Allalouf & Ben-Shakhar,
1998). However, a study completed by Herman, Abedi, and Golan (1994)
investigated the effects of "teaching to the test." Their findings state:

Regarding the meaning of test scores, the study found little to suggest that test
scores are a function of teaching to the test—either in terms of school attention, teachers' concentration on test objectives in instructional planning and
delivery, or in time devoted to test preparation. More interesting were the
strong effects associated with SES. Classes in which disadvantaged students
are a majority are more affected by mandated testing than those serving their
more advantaged peers. In the former classrooms, students are exposed to a
more meager curriculum—with less attention to science, art, thinking skills,
and skills and content not specifically included in the standardized tests.
According to study results, teachers serving disadvantaged students are
under greater pressure to improve test scores and are more driven to focus on
test content and to emphasize test preparation in their instructional programs.
(p. 481)

Shepard (1990) offers a less negative perspective on the phenomenon of
teaching to the test:

The phrase, *teaching to the test,* is evocative but, in fact, has too many meanings to be directly useful. Although it has a negative connotation to most
members of the public, many educators take it to mean teaching to the domain
of knowledge represented by the test. In framing our interview questions
with state testing directors or their representatives, we avoided this pejorative
phrase with its multiple interpretations. Instead, we asked about a wide range
of policies and practices, beginning with the uses of the test data, the process
of test selection, time spent on teaching the test objectives, and test preparation efforts. (p. 17)

In the education business we are masters at losing the point in our verbiage, creating buzzwords that are not particularly clear in meaning or purpose. One of the current buzzwords in the testing dilemma is "curriculum alignment"—theoretically meaning that if the test and the curriculum are "aligned," the test will be a true measure of instruction (Bushweller, 1997). This idea sounds plausible and is readily accepted by many but is flawed for one reason. No test is ever a comprehensive measure of what a student is expected to learn. A test is only a sample of the content a student is expected to master. The part of the content of which mastery is expected and is included on any particular test is determined by the whim of the test makers. Consequently, "aligning" the curriculum to the test often means deleting some content from the total curriculum—obviously that which will not be tested (Toch, 1991). It is an unfortunate fact in this business that many reasonable ideas get lost when taken to extremes and viewed as a quick fix. Curriculum alignment is no exception but it should not be assumed that such practice is inherently a bad thing. Wraga (1999) cautions against the wrong uses of curriculum alignment by first creating the test and then creating the curriculum to support that test. Drawing heavily from the writing of Fenwick English, Wraga states:

> English identifies two methods for establishing a fit between the curriculum and the test: "frontloading" and "backloading." Frontloading "means that the educator writes his or her curriculum first and then searches for an appropriate test to measure or assess whether or not students have learned what the curriculum includes." Backloading "refers to the practice of establishing the match [between the curriculum and the test] by working from the test 'back to' the curriculum. It means the test becomes the curriculum." Backloading the curriculum—that is, aligning the local curriculum to the content of standardized tests—is the modus operandi of curriculum alignment. In short, for English, curriculum alignment is "a process to improve the match between the formal instruction that occurs in the school and the classroom and that which any test will measure." (p. 6)

As an example I recently attended an afternoon workshop titled "Using Data to Plan for Instruction." It did not take long to realize this was an attempt at the wrong kind of "curriculum alignment" for the upcoming state-mandated standardized test. Teachers were presented with a detailed layout of the specific skills to be tested as well as how many questions on the test actually addressed that particular skill. (Apparently that information was readily available for the asking.) Teachers were told to "emphasize" the math and language arts skills that would be tested several times (10–20 test items) and "not waste instructional time" on those skills that may only be tested three or four times. I was appalled and asked if this was not essentially "teaching to the test." I was told, "No . . . we're giving teachers this information so that instruction can be designed to most improve test scores." I'm still not sure I see the difference. I do know, however, that in this case we had the test content driving instruction rather than measuring it.

Most reasonable ideas are certainly intended to further the quality of instruction, but when squeezed in directions they were not intended, this does not happen. When educators, particularly classroom teachers, are essentially forced by ill-informed leaders to incorrectly implement what should be a good and reasonable idea, the results are usually disastrous. Glatthorn (1999) discusses the good and bad of curriculum alignment:

> One step toward the reconciliation of advocacy and dissent about curriculum alignment is the realization that the process is only a tool, one that can be used foolishly or wisely. Used foolishly, curriculum alignment diminishes the art of teaching, sterilizes the curriculum, and makes the classroom a boring place. Used wisely, it offers teachers a practical method by which they may ensure that their students are well prepared for the mandated test. This wise and practical use of alignment was advocated by several experienced teachers. In writing personal essays on how they respond to standards, accountability, and high-stakes tests, most replied, "We cope creatively." (p. 27)

There is another way in which the wrong kind of curriculum alignment not only annihilates good teaching but can likely backfire when dire efforts are made to inflate test scores. This will be discussed in further detail later in this chapter, but for now suffice it to say that by the very nature of standardized tests, they will always contain questions that are not calculated into the student's score. As such, having focused instruction heavily in a skill area that is to be addressed more frequently on the test may actually be of little benefit because no one has any way of knowing which test items are being field tested and which are calculated into the score. Emphasis in that area may actually hurt the final score as other "pertinent" information has been ignored.

Unfortunately, too many testing experts seem to miss this point. Phelps (1999) argues that with instructional time limited, choices must be made as to how time is spent. One view of "curriculum narrowing" as it is sometimes called is that the more humanitarian subjects, such as the expressive arts and foreign language, are minimized or omitted entirely in exchange for more instructional time in the "basics." As a teacher in the arts, I take issue with Phelps when he further argues that "the public wants students to master the 'basics' before they go on to explore the rest of the possible curriculum" (p. 76). We have known for years that exposure in the arts and humanities complements, supports, and most often increases student achievement. What is happening goes much further than simply omitting classes in music, art, foreign language, and the like. As we can see from my own experience, teachers are being pressured to narrow the focus of even the "basics" to that which is addressed on standardized tests.

A school administrator in my experience showed how easily leaders bow to the pressure of testing. When an elective class teacher left an elementary school to accept another position, the administrator unilaterally made the decision to replace the elective class with what would be termed an "academic" subject. (How is it that the study of a foreign language, music, or art could not be considered "academic"?) Obviously, this erroneous idea of an "academic subject" often translates to "that which will be tested" (Skinner, 1968). A new math class was created for the sole and express purpose of "practice and reinforcement of tested math skills." The logic here is seriously flawed by virtue of the fact that if what teachers are currently doing is not working (translated—artificially raising test scores), doing more of the same will not make it work better. A comparable incident was cited by Taylor and Baker (2001), both of which resulted in what is known in statistical terms as the "regression to the mean." In this phenomenon, the top scores do not remain stable while the lower scores improve. Instead, the bottom scores improve slightly and the top scores regress more than slightly toward the mean score.

Another practice we are seeing frequently in teacher workshops and even in university courses is that of "curriculum mapping." The basic idea makes sense in that teachers across all subject matters can plan the school year so that certain aspects of certain subjects are being taught at about the same time. As such, instructional content between reading, math, science, and social studies will be less fragmented. However, when the idea is reduced to an oversimplified format, it contradicts itself in that there are many components of reading and math instruction that must be taught sequentially to ensure smooth progression and ultimately mastery. Hopping around from one segment to another to keep "every subject together" often creates more fragmented instruction than had matters simply been left alone. The ultimate beauty of curriculum mapping done well is that professionals can easily know what others are doing (Jacobs, 1997). Just like curriculum alignment, when curriculum mapping is done badly, it actually plays a part in the testing mania. Recently when I took part in a two-day workshop on curriculum mapping, a central office administrator visited the school to view our efforts. In casual conversation the administrator stated that efforts of this sort allowed teachers to pace instruction so that tested skills were taught prior to test administration and would also allow teachers to "leave out what would not be tested."

What we have discussed so far are questionable practices that have essentially been legitimized through educational verbiage. There are practices seen at test administrations that are equally as unethical, done as often, but hidden in the same manner as the Southern colloquialism of "hiding the crazy relatives." Such practices involve the unethical removal of students from the testing situation who will likely negatively impact the school's average scores. In my own experience I have seen testing administrators go to some serious extremes to be able to isolate students in such a manner as to test them, but not have their scores "included." Just as many well-meaning parents have gone to extremes to find some physical or psychological niche to allow their high school student extended time on the SAT, any possible "catch" that will disallow questionable scores to be included in the aggregate is pursued. Recently I was standing in the office of a school on testing day when a parent attempted to enroll a child who, coincidentally, was of the age that the state-mandated high stakes test would have been required. The principal gently encouraged the parent to wait until later in the week to register the child "when testing would be complete." When the parent and child had gone, the principal remarked that since we had no clue as to the child's background or ability, he/she may "pull down the school average." But more serious breeches of ethics do occur for the sake of salvaging test scores, even temporarily. McGill-Franzen and Allington (1993) report school systems testing children with a district created "pre-test" at the end of the year prior to the year in which a high stakes test will be given. Serious efforts are made to retain those children who demonstrate any likelihood of not doing well the following year. Such efforts at "school-extending" do little to help those individual children who are not going to do well anyway, but create a false sense of accomplishment for the school as well as seriously pollute test data.

Other such questionable practices include the overclassification of students to special education. Serious efforts to place children in special education who would ordinarily "hurt" the school and school district score aggregates is not only unethical but can have serious backlashes. A suburban school system in my experience that was predominantly white and middle class was very proud of their high test scores and for many years wore the test score numbers as a badge of honor. To their dismay, the Office of Civil Rights took note and when the school system records were audited they were found to have an "overrepresentation of minorities in special education." It is doubtful that the school system deliberately made such placement decisions, but two very unfortunate facts remained afterward. First, the district was forced to monitor the ethnicity of the population receiving special education services—a matter that should never have to be considered. Second, their generally high test scores for a number of years would be suspect.

McGill-Franzen and Allington (1993) argue that too many school systems are allowing their testing and accountability data to be contaminated, rendering them useless for making decisions and best serving the needs of all children. They state:

> We submit that the placement practices discussed here not only pollute, but outright *contaminate* (emphasis in original) the accountability reports, rendering them useless for their intended purposes—to ensure equity and fair treat-

ment for all children, but particularly the neediest. Instead, the contamination of accountability reports with unethical placement practices contributes to lost expectations for low-achieving children, lost opportunities for children's development, and lost resources for genuine inquiry and change. At the very least, we would suggest that present policies for conducting high-stakes assessment be revised to eliminate any incentive that school districts might have to contaminate their results with unethical placement practices. (p. 22)

Obviously to those of us in the teaching profession it is of great concern how much power the test score yields on what takes place in classrooms across the country every day. Not only do we see generally good teaching strategies reduced to poor, we see well-thought-out ideas bastardized by the reduction to a quick-fix mindset. Let us examine some pretty standard practices happening in classrooms across the country that are done in the name of "test preparation" but that actually hinder instruction and learning.

TEST PREPARATION

Just as the doctors in the fictional analogy quoted above were not allowed to use any treatment that did not directly influence thermometer scores, educational leaders and policymakers continue to press for increased test scores with no regard for how those scores are raised. It is not unrealistic to think that teachers and building-level administrators are going to respond as would any prudent individual by doing whatever is necessary to increase the test scores, regardless of their personal convictions or professional knowledge or what common sense says about ethics. It should alarm the public to see things going on in classrooms under the guise of "test prep" that translate to little more than relatively poor quality teaching narrowed and focused to the sample of content on a particular test (Ravitch, 1985).

With test scores dictating so much of what is done in schools it should come as no surprise that we are seeing school administrators and leaders spending massive amounts of money on published material that allows students to "practice" taking tests. Many such materials are questionable and designed less to reinforce academic content than to acquaint children with test formats (Shea, 2000). To those knowledgeable about testing and measurement, the impact of excessive test prep on score validity is a concern (Killian, 1992). It is the nature of standardized tests that what is named as a particular skill in class each day is approached from an entirely different manner at testing time. For example, most students practice spelling new words as part of the total language arts program and are likely to have an orally dictated spelling test each week. But when standardized tests come about, spelling will be tested not in the format of writing down what is heard, but in choosing the one misspelled word out of four. While this is called "spelling," the two testing formats are looking at entirely different skills. Many of the published test prep materials consume hours of what should be instructional time simply having children become familiar with the look and layout of a test as well as how test questions will typically be worded.

In test prep efforts, the verbiage of "problem solving strategies" surfaces quite often. It is of great concern to many educators that spending time on "strategies" that give clues to the desired answer in the typical standardized test question negate the thought processes involved in solving the problem. McNeil (2000) reports schools holding testing pep rallies where students are taught such strategies as recognizing that three same answers in a row likely indicates one of the answers is incorrect. A typical test prep strategy taught to children would include a math problem asking a student to add two even numbers. By the laws of mathematics, the answer will be an even number. Rather than solving the problem the student can know by the process of elimination that any answer choices that are an odd number cannot be correct. This strategy does not necessarily mean the student demonstrated the thought processes to correctly solve the problem but instead simply "beat" the test. Other strategies that are alarming educators and parents involve the writing samples typically called for on criterion-referenced tests. We repeatedly find children being coached to take the writing prompt and essentially fill in a "template" to produce a written response. Such a strategy may allow the student to create a written sample that will meet whatever criteria is used to score the writing samples, but it can hardly be said that this is a particularly good way to teach writing. Among some educators, the writing strategy question is often referred to as "real writing versus test writing."

As testing processes and procedures become more prominent in school operations many educators are concerned that private, for-profit companies are using the testing mania as a market niche. According to Charters (1998, 1999) companies that produce test prep/practice materials are working diligently to create appropriate materials for every possible grade level that is subjected to standardized testing—from primary school to graduate and professional schools. Other educational leaders are expressing concerns that the huge focus on test prep is causing schools to become "test-prep centers," often taking one hour daily for a semester or more on test prep materials. According to Shea (2000), some school districts are spending from $20,000–100,000 annually in local funds and grants to bring SAT prep programs and materials to schools.

Under pressure to raise test scores, educators are likewise spending large amounts of money on computer software that allow students to practice test-prep strategies, but also for teachers to generate classroom tests that are in the same format as standardized tests. I recently sat in on a school meeting where the faculty, with the support of the principal, made the decision to purchase a software program that was for the sole purpose of generating classroom assessments in any one of several particular test formats. This particular piece of software cost several thousand dollars and was not for use by students at all. Teachers simply clicked which particular skills they needed a test to cover and the software would generate a multiple-choice test in the format of the state-mandated test. Interestingly, this piece of software was designed to be of use in preparation for a number of standardized tests currently on the market. Is it possible that test preparation materials, both printed and electronic, have reached a point of higher priority than chalk, copy paper, very standard teaching materials, and time with students?

FLAWS IN TESTING

It is very well known and understood that testing, as sophisticated as it has become, is still a very inexact science. The arguments against the science of testing are pretty standard. The descriptive and quantitative literature is replete with consistent criticisms that standardized tests are very limited in the skills and knowledge they measure. The truth is that any test is going to be limited in the knowledge and skills it can measure. Others claim that standardized tests cannot truly measure "higher order thinking skills," "problem solving ability," or "creativity." Test makers are working diligently to bridge this gap by creating test questions that involve several steps before an answer can be formulated. Further, critics argue that standardized tests focus on one predetermined answer with no regard to the thought processes involved in reaching the predetermined answer. Perhaps the most vocal criticism is that standardized tests penalize the student whose background is exceptionally rich in academic and cultural exposure or who thinks very critically. For example, I ran across this musical test question several years ago:

> "Emperor" refers to:
> (a) a piano concerto
> (b) a woodwind quintet
> (c) a string ensemble
> (d) an operatic aria

Most likely, the predetermined "correct" answer to this question would be "a" referring to the Emperor Piano Concerto by Beethoven. A student whose background has exposed him/her to classical music may very well know that a less well-known piece, a woodwind quintet by Haydn, is also referred to as the Emperor Quintet. Another example comes to mind that I encountered a number of years ago:

The people of Antarctica are good farmers. (True or False).

The question is intended to determine the student's knowledge of the geography of Antarctica, but the wording can be misleading for a child who thinks particularly analytically. An especially bright child may interpret the previous question differently than if it were worded to say "The climate of Antarctica allows the people to farm." The scoring machine has no way of knowing that the student has demonstrated exceptional thought in answering these questions, only that the answers are "wrong."

Gardner (1989) addresses the scenario just described. No standardized test can ever provide real or usable information as to why a student answered questions as they did. It is only in knowing why a student missed the question that the problem can be addressed. Gardner states:

It is common, especially for critics of testing, to confuse the information provided by a test score with interpretations of what caused the behavior described by the score. A test score is a numerical description of a sample of performance at a given point in time. A test score gives no information as to why the individual performed as reported. (p. 2)

The writing sample often required by criterion-referenced measures falls prey to another testing flaw by virtue of the fact that it cannot be scored by a machine that is absolutely objective. As such, untold inconsistencies will automatically exist, as literally hundreds of humans somewhere must read all the writing samples and attempt to apply some sort of consistent criteria to each. Test manufacturers go to great extremes to train readers according to a matrix of criteria to see that all are looking for and applying the same criteria. As a safeguard, numerous "spot checks" are made to see if differences in scoring are found. Regardless, this is so human a process that the possibility of total objectivity simply cannot exist. Studies have been done showing that a paper read nine times can be given nine different grades (Hirsch, 1995). It is not hard to see how teachers responsible for teaching writing for a criterion-referenced test may very well resort to the "template" style of writing.

All the arguments against testing can be reduced to a simple phenomenon very aptly pointed out by Popham (2000). No standardized test will ever be a comprehensive measure of anything, only a sampling of what someone, or a team of experts, has determined that students need to know (Popham, 2000). Taylor and Baker (2001) state:

Since each test represents a small sample of essential learning, testing to prepare for testing is ineffective. We are reminded of the adage, "You can't fatten a pig by weighing it." We can only view this activity as "taking the temperature" of learning—and tests are thermometers, not thermostats. The tiny sample of essential learning featured on any test makes suspect the practice of directly revising curriculum based on test data. Examining all student performances associated with the domains tests is a critical step to take before changing curriculum or instructional practice. (p. 3)

Popham (1987) brings an interesting twist to one argument against testing in general but particularly in high stakes tests—the idea that such measurement instruments do not and cannot consider the needs of specific populations. Some educators have attempted to bypass this problem by working to create high stakes tests locally. Popham advises against such efforts for several reasons. First, teachers and central office personnel usually do not have the skill and expertise in measurement to create such tests. Second, teachers would not necessarily be the best professionals to call on in standardized test construction as their focus is primarily in the classroom teaching children. Likewise, the focus of building level and central office administrators is solving the day-to-day problems of the school system. Third, using local personnel can easily call conflicts of interest into question.

But there is one issue surrounding the testing question that is occasionally discussed in academic circles, seldom in polite conversation, but always treated gently. As long as there have been tests there have been discrepancies between the performance of black and white students. It is well known that the two social phenomenon of nonwhite and poor influence test performance more so than any other. It is also well known that nonwhite and poor are almost always connected. The level of experience and background of the nonwhite and poor are known to correlate almost perfectly with performance discrepancies (Willie, 1985).

Educators continue to be mistreated by being held perfectly accountable for an imperfect measure that can be influenced by literally hundreds of factors over which they have no control.

FACTORS INFLUENCING TEST SCORES

As long as there have been standardized tests there have been people whose job it was to gather data about the tests and those who took them (Camilli, 1999). As long as there have been standardized tests one fact has remained. There has always been a high positive correlation between the socioeconomic status of the student and how well they scored on standardized tests. In the world of research, correlational findings are useful but are often misinterpreted to mean that a high positive correlation between two variables indicates a cause-effect relationship. While the statistical link may exist, it should never be assumed that a high socio-economic status causes students to perform better on tests nor should the reverse be assumed. But we know that students from a more affluent background bring to school and ultimately the testing situation experiences not found in the backgrounds of poor students. For example, students from more affluent homes are most likely going to have parents who are educated beyond high school. As such, a value is placed on children's education that may not be found in poorer homes. College-educated parents are more likely to read, engage in challenging conversation, but above all, will likely speak standard English and demand such of their children. Further influencing what students bring to the testing situation will be the students' previous experiences. Students from more affluent homes will likely have traveled and seen other parts of the country or even other parts of the world. Students whose parents are professionals are likely to have seen and to some degree experienced the work of their parents in their professional role and as such have a conception of what academic and professional success is about. Obviously the student who has toured Italy, France, and Germany has a far greater advantage in many areas than a student who has never ventured beyond his/her own section of the town or city where he/she lives. But the greatest factor influencing what students brings to the testing situation is their general literacy. A student who has always heard Standard English spoken and who has consistently been engaged in challenging and meaningful conversation with educated adults has the advantage of a rich vocabulary. Children do not develop an articulate and fluid speaking vocabulary by only talking with other children. This comes about by talking with adults. It is well known through literacy research that the student who possesses an advanced vocabulary will have the added advantage of being able to learn more than those of a limited vocabulary (Hirsch, 1995).

So what could account for the advantaged children consistently scoring better on standardized tests? The research is quite plentiful supporting that test performance is far more greatly influence by what comes to school than what happens at school (Chall, Jacobs, & Baldwin, 1990; Kellaghan, Sloane, Alvarez, 1993; Steinberg, Brown, & Dornbusch, 1996). Popham (2000) illustrates through testing research that as much as 40–60% of what is asked on a typical standardized test has less to do with what the student learns at school than what the student brings from home. He states:

> [Y]ou'll find far too many items that assess things learned outside of school. To be more specific, these items measure skills or knowledge flowing from the kinds of experiences that are more common to children from higher socioeconomic status than to children from lower socioeconomic status levels. (p. 55)

MISUSE OF TEST SCORES

Polite conversation often discusses student testing and even will generate seriously contrasting points of view. Despite all we know and are learning about tests, their purpose, and what's good or bad, we still see some serious misuses of standardized test scores. The public at large does not realize the limitations of test scores alone or that they are a deceptively convenient way of judging quality and making ordinarily difficult decisions. The most disturbing aspect of this phenomenon is the fact that it cannot truly be said that those in charge do not know better. When we read the literature written by testing critics, the major concerns tend to fall into three areas:

1. High stakes decisions—decisions of promotion, retention, funding, and staffing;
2. Classifying students, individual schools, and entire school systems;
3. Using test scores as a basis for curriculum reform.

In reality, the "high stakes" question is talked about far more often than we truly see an effort to make it come to pass. Just as the physicians in the fictional analogy quoted earlier in this chapter knew that thermometer scores alone were not a comprehensive measure of health, educated people likewise know that test scores alone do not provide a clear picture of teaching and learning. Actually, every state that has attempted to implement a high stakes program has seen what is a grossly inflated and deceptive increase in scores that didn't last long (International Reading Association, 1999). Every state that has attempted high stakes programs has abandoned the idea because when gains catch up with reality, they are left with no evidence that such programs increase achievement (Black & Willams, 1998). Additionally, scholars in testing and measurement are quite adamant that making such important decisions as promotion, retention, or funding is a matter that should require long-term data, not one imperfect measure.

It is often threatened that if a school does not present desirable test scores that the school funding will be cut. Reducing much-needed funding to schools with a struggling student population is not going to cause the school to function any better. This idea is seriously flawed and makes about as much sense as keeping food away from those who are starving. Depriving the malnourished of food will not make them healthy. We know the schools that produce the poorest scores are those that serve the poorest population, have the least resources, and have a student population who are at the greatest disadvantage from the start (Berliner, 1993). How can it make sense to cut off the funding where it is obviously needed the most? Donlevy (2000) states:

Perhaps the greatest injustice of the "high" standards movement is the inability or unwillingness of those in state leadership positions to understand that those at the bottom of the system—the poor, the handicapped and the vulnerable—need to be strengthened in their efforts to progress along the educational continuum. They should not be blamed for shortcomings they did not instigate or be consigned to inferior positions as a result of the schools and programs to which they were subjected . . . raising academic requirements, in the absence of basic supports, is a harsh measure by any dispassionate standard. (pp. 335–336)

There is another area in which undesirable test scores lead to threats from leaders and policymakers—school staffing. We have repeatedly seen political publicity stating that low-performing schools will dismiss the entire faculty and administration and start over by recruiting the most experienced and qualified teachers and administrators. While we do know that difficult schools, for various reasons, are often forced to utilize the services of less-experienced or less-qualified teachers, this makes a most flawed assumption and shows the lack of understanding of policymakers who generate such rhetoric. How can it be assumed that because students did not perform well on one test that all the professionals in that one school did their job poorly? Would the general public be so gullible as to believe that because people who live in a geographic area have certain life habits or do a certain job yet continue to experience certain health problems as a result of doctors doing their job poorly? Of course not. The use of test scores to make serious, high stakes decisions is a dangerous thing to do. Just as the epigraph at the beginning of this chapter asserts, those who make decisions by test scores alone will likely be disappointed in the long term.

Another area in which the misuse of test scores borders on unethical, or at least unkind, is the classification, comparison, and ranking of children, schools, and school districts (Kaufhold, 1998). He states:

Faced with all these deterrents, a well-meaning school official could say, "Yes, but if we don't teach to the test, we will be low in comparison with other schools in other locations." A proper response to that might be "Why compare?" When demographics, student abilities, financial capability and community expectations differ from place to place, what valid reasons can there be for comparing schools, counties, states and even countries? What is gained by these comparisons and what do they prove? What is wrong with measuring each school, county or state against itself? (p. 15)

State Departments of Education and the media often publish a listing of schools by test scores alone, ranking schools from the best to the worst. Educated people know that many factors outside of the school bring a far greater influence on test scores than anything that goes on in school. For example, the media reports seldom indicate that the poor school ranking at or near the bottom is serving a student population of 50–60% or more who is living in true poverty. It should stand to reason that using test scores alone as a tool to categorize, separate, or classify children is simply unfair. Alfie Kohn (1999), the author of *The Schools Our Children Deserve* and a vehement opponent to testing, makes an interesting suggestion. Since we have known for years that poor students do not perform as well on standardized tests and since the test scores are being used to classify and categorize, let's make it easier and save a lot of money. At the beginning of each school year, simply ask the children how much money their parents earn and classify them from there. The results would be strikingly similar!

But the most serious misuse of test scores occurs when used to make decisions relative to curriculum reform. The test is not the curriculum but is instead only a sample of the curriculum. Reducing what is taught in order to better reflect on test scores is unethical.

AN ILL-INFORMED PUBLIC

There is much about the testing industry that the general public and many educators do not know. Polite conversation among well-meaning people often finds its way to the topic of test scores. The presumption that high test scores unquestionably indicate success, literacy, and academic standing is so entrenched in our culture that few ever think to question otherwise. Test scores become the badges of pride worn by those who don't know better. There is much to know about tests, test scores, and the testing business that would skew the public perception should such information become part of polite conversation.

First, the educational testing industry is exactly that—an industry. It is a business whose mission is to provide a useful product for a fee and make a profit at the same time. Those who work in the testing business are skilled professionals in the science of measurement. Contrary to the accepted belief, these people are not experts in teaching (Popham, 1999; Weiner, 1999). Although not discussed in polite conversation, there is national competition among testing companies for what is a large, but still finite, market. Every test publisher tries to create a test, or series of tests, that will provide the most comprehensive coverage for the dollars spent. Just like any other product on the open market, each testing company must convince the school systems, or sometimes the states, that their test will far better meet their need than the competition. Every test has to have its own "niche" to grab a share of the market. According to Toch (1991), test companies are under pressure to create tests that are "easy" so that school systems and superintendents "look good" (p. 211).

Popham (2000) describes the phenomenon that causes test makers to behave as they do as the practice of "score spread." In order for a set of test scores to fall within a normal distribution (meaning fit the traditional bell curve) the set of scores must fall across a wide range. If too many scores fall toward the center the distribution is not particularly useful because it is difficult to make relative comparisons between individuals. If too many scores fall toward the bottom it creates the illusion that children don't know anything, that teachers have taught poorly, or that leaders have made some bad decisions. Too many scores at the top would cause all sorts of undesired public attention, bringing about questions of the test being too easy or cheating. In order to ensure that student scores do not create an unusable "cluster" in the top, center, or bottom of the bell curve, test items must be chosen very carefully. Test makers accomplish this by "field testing" certain test items at every test administration. The software programs that score the massive amounts of answer sheets do not calculate those questions into the individual student score but discard questions that too few or too many students missed on subsequent test administrations. This maintains controls and ensures that a reasonable and desirable distribution of scores will occur.

So why is Popham's verbiage of "score spread" so critical? Quite simply, if there are no differences in test scores, there is nothing to compare. With nothing to compare, the testing industry would be lacking something to do. To those individuals who are knowledgeable in the field of testing and measurement, it is most disheartening to see the American public naively place so much faith in one imperfect set of numbers. Haertel (1999) poses some questions about high stakes testing that probably cause discomfort among legislators and policymakers. First, what do we intend to accomplish scholastically as a result of testing? Second, what pattern of test scores would make everyone happy? He states:

> Would we be happy, for example, if all students earned identical scores? My immediate reaction is that, if that happened, testing would cease to be of any value at all. Would we be happy if tests continued to show individual differences in performance, but the score distributions for different schools, different states, or different demographic groups all overlapped perfectly? That sounds to me like it would be an improvement, but there would still be pressure to move all the distributions higher and probably agitation to get everyone above the mean. . . . To paraphrase my colleague, Ray McDermott, I am afraid the answer may be that the only pattern of scores that would please everyone would be a pattern whereby everyone outscored everyone else and that will not happen. (p. 9)

INTERPRETATION OF TEST SCORES

Few things stir the public like the rhetoric that gets reported to support a set of test scores. Test scores can be "interpreted" in so many ways the public often has trouble knowing who or what to believe. In 1987 a West Virginia small town physician, John Jacob Cannell, released a report that embarrassed the education community, greatly annoyed the testing industry, and cause much of thinking America to sit up and ask some very pointed questions. Cannell and his colleagues noticed that all 35 of the 50 states that administered a particular standardized test reported their scores to be above the national average (Cannell, 1988). This phenomenon quickly became known as the "Lake Wobegon Effect" named after the popular radio show and the mythical Lake Wobegon where "all the women are strong, all the men are good looking, and all the children are above average" (Haney, 1988, p. 4). Cannell (1989) suggested several possible explanations for this phenomenon including cheating, unethical testing practices, or deliberately skewed or misleading reporting of data.

Cannell is a physician, not a statistician, and as such, his research methods were vehemently attacked and questioned as irregular, and it was argued that some of his findings could be attributed to things that simply were not explainable (Phillips, 1990; Phillips & Finn, 1988). Some testing authorities argued adamantly that trying to gather a uniform measure every year and make national, state, and local comparisons was futile (Burstein, 1990). Others argued that possibly Cannell and his colleagues just happened to hit upon a year in which scores really were "up" (Linn, Graue, & Sanders, 1990; Shepard, 1990). But the public awareness was heightened by two facts that repeatedly came forth:

1. Norms for standardized tests are typically set every seven to eight years. Setting norms is a huge undertaking, a time-consuming process, and an enormous expense for testing companies.
2. Norms are set based on a representative sample. This is accomplished by administering similar forms of the test nationwide to what is considered a sample representative of the national population. Testing experts are quite adept at these types of statistical maneuvers, but they are only correct in theory. Even those collecting the representative sample data have no way of knowing for sure if they included a correct percentage of minority, poor, disadvantaged, and so forth.

There are certain phenomena and procedures relative to the reporting of test scores, much of what is quite misleading to those lacking formal training in testing and measurement. Percentiles and their misinterpretation were discussed earlier in the chapter. When we compare percentile to percentile ranks, we find they differ considerably. The percentile score ranks the student against a theoretical group of 100 students across the nation. The reported percentile score is not indicative of how the individual actually scored, only how they scored in relation to everyone else. The scores reported as percentile ranks are another matter entirely, first because they are based on a scale in which the intervals are not consistent. Percentile rank scores are small intervals toward the middle and larger at each end (Green, 1987). Second, unlike percentile scores, percentile ranks are relative to one test administration and one sample.

The reporting of grade equivalent is another score reporting mode that is often misunderstood. For example, many people will see a 5th-grade student with a grade equivalent in reading of 8.3 and immediately assume the 5th-grade student is reading at the level of eighth grade, third month. This is clearly incorrect, as the tested material is not at the 8th-grade level; it is at the 5th-grade level. As such, the grade equivalent score actually indicates that the fifth grader scored as well as an eighth grader in the third month of school should have scored. These scores are really of little use in making individual or collective decisions and become less useful as students get older. Green (1987) states:

> An 11th grade student scoring at the 5th percentile in reading comprehension has a grade equivalent score of about 6.6. Does that mean that these students should be instructed with 6th grade basals? Recognizing that these students have probably been exposed to such materials for years by the time they reach the 11th grade may make it clear why this conclusion is not appropriate. . . . It must be concluded that grade equivalent scores have limited use and meaning for interpreting test performance at the high school level. Certainly they should not be used alone; other scores are needed to put them in perspective. (pp. 32–33)

MISTREATING EDUCATORS

There is no question that using tests and tests scores in ways for which they were never intended is not only unethical but harmful to children and our entire system of public education. There is not a professional organization representing the social sciences, pure sciences, or medicine anywhere in this country that supports or advocates the use of educational tests in a high stakes manner. Various professional associations have spoken out against the current use of high stakes testing including the International Reading Association (1999) and the American Educational Research Association (2000). Both of these organizations represent the most scientific and scholarly individuals in the nation relative to teaching, learning, and student achievement. The International Reading Association unequivocally states their opposition to high stakes testing, but not testing in general. Similarly, the American Educational Research Association is opposed to the practice of making any decision on the basis of one score. The International Reading Association (1999) states:

Tests are imperfect. Basing important decisions on limited and imperfect information can lead to bad decisions—decisions that can do harm to students and teachers and that sometimes have unfortunate legal and economic consequences for the schools. Decision makers reduce the chance of making a bad decision by seeking information from multiple sources. However, the information from norm-referenced and criterion-referenced test is inexpensive to collect, easy to aggregate, and usually is highly reliable; for those reasons it is tempting to try to use this information alone to make major decisions. (p. 314)

Perhaps the most vile mistreatment of educators (and children) comes in the publication of test scores to compare schools against schools, districts against districts, and states against states. Those knowledgeable about testing know that test scores were never intended to be used in such a manner. The National Assessment of Educational Progress (NAEP) has for many years been a gauge by which educational leaders and policymakers could make general observations about the status of our schools. NAEP score reports have recently caused some reported dramatic gains at the state level to come into question. According to Koretz (1991), since we find the same positive correlation between state level socioeconomic factors and educational quality, NAEP scores can't really tell us anything we don't already know.

It should be evident to thinking adults that the current unethical and overdependence on test scores is not coming from the social science scholars of society but instead from political factions wanting a simple fix to complex problems that no one wants to correctly address. The use of test scores to "fix" educational problems that are not related to the function of the school is about as logical as using a hammer and nail to fix a flat tire. The continued misuse simply cannot be a matter of ignorance of the facts. Yet educators continue to be mistreated in several ways:

1. Educators, particularly classroom teachers, are run ragged, being forced to reduce any science or art of teaching to those questionable practices that falsely inflate test scores rather than truly educate children (Kohn, 2000).
2. Test scores are consistently reported to the public in such a manner as to unfavorably skew the results, creating an unfair public perception of the work of the schools.
3. In the case of the state where I reside, teachers were run ragged only to have the rules relaxed to meet political pressure. When we create rules that cannot be enforced, they probably won't be.
4. Science and simple logic dictate that misuse of test scores is a bad idea. Just as the physicians in the fictional analogy in this chapter were forced to abandon common sense and good judgment in making health decisions, educators are forced to acquiesce to poor practices for reasons that clearly are not in the best interest of children.

7

✛

Schools, Realities, and Teachers' Work

Knowledge of history is the most powerful tool anyone can have. . . . People don't make intelligent choices by instinct. They are guided by experience.

Ernest R. May, Harvard professor

I have been inspired to write this book partly out of curiosity and partly out of anger. The curiosity aspect asked if I could really do such a thing. The anger aspect because after two decades I am quite weary of how seemingly polite conversation so brutally treats the educators of this society. There have been a number of books written in the past four or five years that addressed much of what is wrong with our schools and give ideas of how they are to be corrected. Most are well written, supported by documentation or extensive anecdotal observation, and do present a realistic picture of what truly does go on in our schools. Common sense dictates that we have many areas that need improvement for whatever reasons, but that same common sense would tell most thinking individuals that, despite the obvious difficulties and lacking areas, the schools do successfully educate far more than they fail to educate. Likewise, the enlightened individual should see that teachers are not the crux of the problem, but instead are used as scapegoats in too many ways that simply are not fair (Ravitch, 1985). It would stand to reason that if polite conversation can only find the bad in our schools and assume there is absolutely nothing good, one would suspect that those engaged in polite conversation are not sure what they're looking for, or at least are not seeing the entire picture. In ordinary adult relationships—friendly, professional, whatever—when we know someone who is entirely negative about most things, we tend to discount their perspective as shallow, uninformed, or self-serving. I have close friends, most of whom are educated people, who truly believe that everything our schools do is wrong, misdirected, mismanaged, and that the entire system is a joke. These same educated friends assume that no particular training is needed to be a teacher, yet will emphatically assert how disappointing it is to see that we don't have a truly academic teaching force. These same educated people likewise assume that any problem or issue faced by the schools can be resolved by applying some particular universal model of problem resolution. Obviously, with these friends, we don't discuss schools too often!

Some time ago I read the book that caused me to say "this is enough" and inspired me to write my own perspective as someone who has spent 20 years successfully doing what is considered wrong, misdirected, mismanaged, and entirely a joke. *The Conspiracy of Ignorance* by Martin Gross (1999) was an unsettling, scathing indictment of our system, the workings and management of the schools, the training and quality of teachers, and essentially everything about public education. I would assume that Gross's perspective is based on his professional experiences and his level of education, and I would never want to discount his ideology just as I would expect the same from him. And while I, and most learned individuals, would agree with some of what he says, I take issue with many, possibly most, of his perspectives not because some major changes are not necessary, but because of his oversimplified recommendations to a very overburdened system battling some very complex problems. Gross is a journalist, not an educator (although he does teach some university classes and apparently is much in demand as a speaker and adjunct instructor), and his writing style is reflective of such. As is typical in journalistic writing, his presentation is noticeably skewed toward the sensational and does not present a fair balance so that a learned reader can draw informed conclusions. Additionally, in a typical journalistic style, he tends to cite one or two isolated, anecdotal examples to support each aspect of his cruel indictment of a system that is doing the best it can with all that is imposed upon and expected of it.

Gross indicts, among other things, that school curricula are weak, that teachers are not educated in their discipline, and that teachers in general are the lowest of the academic ranks. He further asserts that colleges of education are fraudulent and should be totally abolished in favor of a system more in line with what we are seeing in "alternative certification" type programs, specifically that all teacher education should be at the graduate level. He refers to the certification of teachers as a "nationwide sham" and brutally describes the teacher testing fiasco in Massachusetts as the basis for his indictment. In reality, the Massachusetts fiasco is a very poor example of the way to test anything. There were so many discrepancies in the test design and administration that Massachusetts would do best to hang their head in shame and perhaps try again (Fair Test Examiner, 1999). Anyone with any knowledge of testing and measurement knows that when more than half the test takers fail any test, it can mean any number of things, but most likely indicates there is something wrong with the test. It does not take a team of Ph.D.-level psychometricians to figure out that when you create a test after the test preparation has been completed, you might get some disappointing results (Hardy, 2000). It is generally known that about one third of the attorneys taking the bar exam each year do not pass the first time, as is the case with the huge majority (about 90%) of the accountants at the first sitting for the CPA exam. For some reason, law schools and business schools are not cited as being inferior or not having attained their major tasks when large percentages of graduates don't pass.

I would ask where Gross gets the distorted idea that teachers, generally, are so close to illiterate. When discussing the Massachusetts testing fiasco, he cites two or three examples of some very poorly written responses, which were hideous, to say the least, and would cause one to ask how a person with such poor writing skills managed to complete the work required for a university degree. Who could argue that these individuals should not be teaching our children? But I doubt that these hideous examples were typical, and I would not expect Gross to say so lest he undermine his argument. We can all cite anecdotal examples of individuals who were not particularly scholarly in various aspects of their lives. I happen to know physicians and attorneys who do not write particularly well. From a personal perspective, I have several friends who are practicing physicians who frequently bring me their writing work to be edited. These people have earned a university degree in the sciences, graduated from medical school, passed their licensing exam, as well as completed a specialized residency and the subsequent specialty exam. The fact that they aren't secure in their writing does not mean they are fools. By virtue of the fact that most physicians have always been exemplary students and generally exceptional individuals, most do write very well. But scholarly writing is not a critical part of their medical school training because their time is spent in clinical work, not scholarly endeavors.

Gross's perspective is quite typical of how those outside (and sometimes inside) the profession erroneously assume that simplistic, one-shot answers will fix all that is wrong. Polite conversation seldom takes into account that even if it were possible for one massive reform effort to fix everything and make an imperfect system into a perfect one, those things are not instant and the system will have to continue to function in the interim.

The discussion in a previous chapter on the doctor of education degree (Ed.D.) was prompted by Gross's description of the degree as "inferior, lacking in content" and a "false" doctorate (p. 250). As will be the case in any imperfect system, there certainly are individuals who completed the program requirements and were conferred the Ed.D. who probably should not have been. It would be ignorant to assume that such problems have never existed or do not exist in any doctoral program around the country. Researching Dissertation Abstracts International can be an informative experience in regard to what gets written in partial fulfillment of the requirements for the Ph.D. Completing the mechanics of a quantitative study does not necessarily create information that is useful in solving problems or bringing about desired change, nor does it automatically elevate a person to the level of scholar. Cornelia Yarbrough, a brilliant researcher and professor of music at Louisiana State University, once jokingly stated, "One quantitative study doth not a scholar make." I take issue with Gross's perspective and assert that he is absolutely wrong in stating such generalities when he clearly is misinformed on the issue. I hold the Ed.D. and I dearly earned it in the same manner as anyone else earned theirs—by making the commitment to study seriously at that level and by demonstrating the highest degree of scholarly writing. When comparing shallow perspectives to deep, complicated issues, scholarly discussion and polite conversation should not take Martin Gross seriously.

One of the more brilliant books to be written recently that defended the profession and attempted to set the record straight on some complex issues was *The Manufactured Crisis* by David Berliner and Bruce Biddle (1995). In an articulate and scholarly manner, Berliner and Biddle refute many of the popular myths concerning the "mess" in the schools, using the very research that is often quoted and, more often, misquoted in scholarly discussion and polite conversation. The same unsubstantiated myths that have brutalized our system and profession have been around for some 30–40 years. Polite conversation involving the simplistic, prevailing attitude that American schools are at the bottom of everything never seems to take into account that America is the only industrialized nation that even attempts to educate every single child, regardless of handicapping condition, social background, or other impacting factors that the schools cannot control. We have known for many years that a strong correlation exists between poverty and lack of student achievement. America has a much larger student population living in poverty that still attends school than any other nation that would be developed enough to take part in international educational comparison studies. Other industrialized societies only educate the elite who by virtue of their status of birth will likely become leaders in society. Berliner and Biddle seriously call to question many of the highly quoted, highly touted governmental reports that supposedly lend credence to the misguided notions that mistreat educators.

WHAT REALLY GOES ON IN SCHOOLS?

I have learned over the years to dismiss privately the ill-informed remarks that come out of polite conversation about the schools and how terrible everything is. After being in schools and universities for two decades, it is not difficult to tell from conversation who has either not been in a school in some time or who is clueless as to what really goes on there. What does a teacher's work entail? Why is a teacher's work so difficult? Let us look a bit further.

While much has been written that is unfair and unrealistically critical of the teaching profession (Bracey, 1998), others have been fair and present a realistic picture of what really does go on and what should go on. One of the most sympathetic books I've read in recent years concerning teachers, their work, and the real problems in the schools was *Improving Schools from Within* by Roland Barth (1990). Barth's experience as a teacher, school administrator, and university professor refutes many of the current myths about all that is wrong in the schools. By his perspective the schools will never improve until teachers are allowed to improve them. Barth makes a clever comparison of a teacher's daily work when he states:

> A tennis shoe in a laundry dryer. Probably no image captures so fully for me the life of an adult working in an elementary, middle or senior high school. For educators, schoolwork much of the time is turbulent, heated, confused, disoriented, congested and full of recurring bumps. (p. 1)

This is a pretty accurate description of a typical teacher's workday. Every day teachers make hundreds of decisions to hundreds of questions that don't have specific or exact answers. Every day teachers face a classroom full of real, live humans with real, live human needs and a complex collection of experiences. Each day a teacher is expected to bring some continuity to those collective experiences and do so in a manner that makes everyone happy. Polite conversation often makes a very wrong assumption that teaching fifth grade is a matter of managing the average 10-year-old 25 times. Twenty-five children means 25 entirely separate sets of problems, sets of experiences, and untold circumstances that get in the way of providing uniform educational experiences for them all.

As a public schoolteacher I work in an urban school system that polite conversation often describes as the least desirable place to work in the entire state. If we were to walk randomly through the school system and visit schools without any particular order or plan, we would likely note some startling demographic data:

1. The average age of the average school building is 67 years;
2. School buildings that were built 45–70 years ago were not intended to support the student populations or the utilities (electrical, phone, Internet accessibility) needed today;
3. Many of the plumbing systems are so old that they frequently mal-

function, forcing administrators to bring in portable toilets and place commercially ordered water coolers in the classrooms;

4. There are still a number of schools that are not air conditioned;
5. More than 60% of the student population lives in circumstances and environments that fall into the category of "poverty"; at least this percentage lives in single-family, broken homes, or are being raised by grandparents of other relatives;
6. The school system is so desperate for teachers that upwards of 50% of the teaching force is either not certified at all, is certified from another state, or is working toward certification while continuing to teach. Although there are nine universities in the city, the district actively recruits teachers nationwide and abroad;
7. Operating budgets are so tight that teachers are often forced to spend personal money for such generic supplies as copy paper, chalk, stapler and staples, or bulletin board materials to add some color to classroom walls;
8. Band instruments will include brass instruments that no longer have lacquer on the finish, drum heads repaired with duct tape, and drum sticks repaired with electrical tape;
9. Much of the classroom furniture is as old as the buildings with ragged edges, splintered wood, and rickety support for equipment and computers.

But despite the dismal conditions of the facilities and the poor socioeconomic status of most of those served by the schools, if we walk through the average school building we will see business as usual. We would see teachers in charge, doing what teachers are supposed to be doing. We would see students meaningfully engaged in appropriate learning activities. We would see teachers doing exactly what they are supposed to be doing— teaching. But what obstacles might we see causing the teacher's job to be far more difficult than one would imagine?

First, there is never a "down" moment. By the nature of the educator's work, there are certain understood aspects that are accepted as the way things must be. For example, people who work in a business setting, or perhaps own their own business, can have the leisure of occasionally arriving to the work site late. In the private sector, usually a phone call to say "I'm having a bit of a problem—I'll be there shortly" is usually sufficient. This is not the privilege of the educator because when the doors are "open for business" there absolutely must be adults present because children, by law, must be supervised at all times. The legal ramifications of an accident or other trauma to schoolchildren absent of adult supervision are unimaginable. This aspect alone creates a work situation for teachers unlike other professionals in that from the moment one enters the work site until the moment one leaves there is never a "down" moment. A teacher spends his/her entire workday in "high gear," making decisions, motivating others, and pushing forward. The teacher seldom has the luxury of regularly scheduled coffee breaks, restroom breaks, or simply the opportunity to regroup for the continuation of the day. I have friends who will make such naive statements as, "Well—you need to just find a minute and step outside for a break." Obviously, these friends have no clue what the commitment to being a teacher is about. It is the nature of the work that there is absolutely no loose time whereby teachers are not responsible for the behavior and action of children. It should then come as no surprise that the burnout rate in our business is greater than any other, including that of the air traffic controller. During the entire workday the teacher is responsible for 20–30 live adult humans who do not have the legal autonomy, maturity, or social skills to make most decisions for themselves. For the entire duration of each workday, the teacher must maintain order and manage a program of instruction while still seeing to the needs of both the group and the individual. Behavioral studies have indicated that the average teacher makes about 1,000 decisions a day, most of which are of necessity made with little or no time to think through the situation entirely. It is the nature of humans that some decisions are bad ones. If we make 1,000 decisions and get 950 of them right, I would say those odds are pretty good.

As a teacher faces a group of students every day, each of those small, live humans comes from a different home with different backgrounds, different experiences, and different needs not only as a student but also as a person. Each of those 20–30 small, live humans is totally dependent on that adult to see that their day is spent safely sheltered from the traumas of childhood as well as meaningfully engaged in work and activities that contribute to their preparation for life. It is amazing that the perception exists that teachers don't do a great deal.

TEACHER STRESSES/CHILDREN'S BEHAVIORS

The stresses faced by teachers are unlike any other group of professionals. Stress created from the demands of bureaucracy is one set of matters. The stress in the classroom is another that can really be traced to two broad categories—the inadequate backgrounds of the children and the social inadequacies of the children. Overcoming the background inadequacies is relatively easy. Overcoming the social inadequacies is not.

The greatest source of stress in a teacher's day is the inordinate amount of instructional time wasted in dealing with socially inappropriate behaviors. Year after year, the extremes in inappropriate behaviors continue to be seen in younger and younger children. Studies are showing that children are reaching puberty earlier but reaching social maturity later. As a result, children are terribly deficient in simple recovery skills. They are so angry that many assume an imposition on their personal space justifies violent behavior. It is not terribly uncommon any longer to see children as young as five demonstrate violent behaviors at school and even curse their teachers. A few years ago, one of the elementary schools in the district where I taught made the news because a kindergarten child went totally out of control and was taken away by the police. In retrospect, the media probably made a much bigger ordeal of the matter than was warranted. The child was out of control and since there was not a parent or guardian available to pick up the child, out of necessity, the police had to be called. I never imagined I would see the day that the police were called to deal with the behaviors of 5-year-old children. It is the nature of schools, public and private alike, that one child's behavior can and often does disallow anything productive to go on in a classroom.

It is a major complaint among teachers at all levels that student discipline is poorly or inadequately supported by building administration (Bruner, 1982; Taylor & Bogotch, 1993). People who attended school 50 years ago do not report the rampant disciplinary distractions that are commonplace today. Children from that era who, for whatever reason, were unable to behave appropriately in school simply did not attend school. The families kept them home to work and contribute to the family sustenance. But today every child is expected to attend school regardless of background, ability, handicapping condition, or behavior. To attempt to educate every single child is a most noble calling and unquestionably the ethical thing to do. But such democratic ideals are not without certain trade-offs, the most prominent of which are the conglomeration of socially inappropriate behaviors and the differences in children's abilities—all of which must somehow be addressed.

The question of maintaining a social order in the schools often translates to issues of social politics and public perceptions. No organization of children or adults can possibly move in a forward direction if the members are not so focused. It stands to reason that no educational leader will want to be in charge of an organization (school) in which the majority of the members (children) are not focused on common goals (learning outcomes) or where there is not a sense of order (the members are responsible and self-disciplined). Despite all we know of group dynamics and human psychology, the most competent leader charged with leading a difficult organization is soon perceived to be incompetent.

General reputations among educational leaders are a precious commodity not to be marred by the public perception of the inability to create a controlled and ordered organizational environment. Building administrators are certainly accountable to central office personnel for the organizational climate they create in the school that is characterized by the maintenance and order of a disciplined following. District level administrators, however, are so consumed with their work that it is not uncommon for such individuals to visit school buildings only twice or three times in a year. Such anecdotal observations provide only the most superficial perspectives of the day-to-day operations of the school and its decorum. For administrators above the level of the school building, statistics of disciplinary incidents requiring administrative action are far more helpful. As such, building administrators can be notorious for creating leadership directives that create the illusion of order and control but in reality create further problems. Such directives essentially dismiss the more notorious of inappropriate behaviors and often ignore them most toward the end of the school year when the inappropriate incidents tend to escalate.

As an example from my experience, a new vice principal in a school with difficult children and a high suspension rate set forth the goal of lowering the suspension rate. This individual created an addition to the existing district disciplinary plan whereby a teacher was not disallowed but strongly discouraged from completing the required discipline forms (for which administrative action is mandated) until the third infraction. This essentially gave the perpetually disruptive child three free rides when previously they would have had one. This administrator further complicated matters by allowing the child to "start over" just prior to being suspended if they would remain trouble free for four weeks. Children are not dumb, and consequently those who were prone to tying up instructional and administrative time over their choices of behaviors soon learned to "work" the system to their benefit. Knowing how to work the system to the benefit of those determined to disrupt rather than participate caused many very serious behaviors to go on basically unaddressed.

It would be unfair to imply that building-level administrators are not bound by the same human capabilities as anyone else. Unlike the private schools that have the autonomy to expel disruptive children, the public schools are limited in how best to handle such disruptions. Short of expulsion, which is usually a complicated process in the public schools, the most extreme repercussion that can be imposed on a disruptive child is to remove him/her from the setting. Removal does grant a slight reprieve from the behaviors for both teacher and the other children, but is hardly the desired thing to do for three reasons. First, the child certainly doesn't learn anything if he/she is not present. Second, removing the child does not recover the instructional time lost in dealing with the behaviors. And third, removing the child does not fix whatever is causing the disruptive behavior. Everyone loses, particularly the child.

DETERMINING EXCELLENCE

Due to the social science aspect of the work of educators, there will never be a single, infallible manner of determining quality in teaching that is free of personal judgment, individual opinion, an evaluative component, or political influence. This is particularly problematic for the classroom teacher because at this point teaching has not truly surpassed the traditional labor/management hierarchy. Teaching falls into the category of "labor"—or at least "production." When the question of quality is raised, the classroom teacher will forever be, at best, at a disadvantage, or at worst, at the mercy of the system.

There is a body of quantitative and qualitative literature addressing what many for years have attempted to determine as "excellence" in teaching. The argument will forever fall on both sides of the question of product or process (Kysilka, 1989). For many years educational leaders argued that if no learning had taken place, then likewise no teaching had taken place. The flaw in this logic is easily seen, as it is doubtful one would ever assume that because an illness or injury did not heal that the physician provided no treatment. Today scholars of teaching and learning recognize the question to be far more complex than many assumed as recently as 30 years ago. Prybylo (1998) states:

> Teachers, however, do not shape raw materials into finished products that can be counted or assessed for quality and craftsmanship. Nor do they provide a service that can be immediately rated by a consumer. Instead, pedagogy is, for the most part, intangible and somewhat elusive. Given that the fundamental job of teaching is to induce learning, the ultimate result of this work may not become apparent until long after the work is complete and may well depend on a host of external influences over which the teacher has no control. If we accept this purpose of teaching, then, with the exception of those mechanical aspects of teaching such as lesson plans, curricular materials, assessment tools, etc., teaching cannot be objectively quantified, measured, rated or calibrated, and business models of employee evaluation are inadequate tools with which to assess the teacher's work. (pp. 561–562)

Unfortunately, the body of literature that calls for teaching excellence via certain specific teaching behaviors seems to miss the point of the inexactness of it all. The cogent point to be made here is that teaching excellence is virtually always determined by the whims, wants, or opinions of those individuals charged with making the determination of quality. Let us consider two very extreme examples from my experience.

A choral director colleague of mine had for a number of years served as choral director and music teacher for a prestigious private high school in the city. She had long established herself as a capable professional in every regard and was much in demand as a guest conductor, festival judge, and choral critic. Performances by her choirs were much in demand around the city. On more than one occasion her choirs, by invitation, had traveled to Rome to perform at St. Peter's Basilica for the pope. Clearly, we have a choral director and music educator of the highest caliber who should be welcomed as an addition to any faculty.

When this person moved on to teach in the local public schools, her experiences were not nearly so positive. The teacher was assigned to a middle school where there had previously not been a structured choral program. In one year's time she built a program of the caliber that three groups qualified to compete at the state level. But building a quality performance-based program is not without its share of compromises with existing programs and does not happen easily without proper administrative support. This principal, unfortunately, did not want any part of a performance-based vocal music program, insisting instead on the general music-type classes that make convenient electives for disruptive children and don't compete with existing band, athletic, or honors programs. For five years this teacher who had previously been considered the epitome of excellence in a city where music is revered was reduced to a "marginal" status based solely on the whims and perceptions of one unscrupulous principal. After five years the director left to assume the choral director position at a prestigious citywide access magnet school located on the campus of a major research university. Amazingly, this teacher is no longer marginal but excellent again. I have to ask the question of what determined quality. It is doubtful that this teacher arrived at the middle school, forgot what excellence in teaching is about, and simply did everything wrong for five years.

But most unfortunately, the reverse scenario is equally as true. In my experience, a new building principal was forced to confront a 20-year veteran teacher who had for years been evaluated favorably. The sad reality, however, was that this person had for years "taught" primarily with color sheets, word-search puzzles, candies, and was frequently seen sleeping in class. It is doubtful the new principal arbitrarily created a rule against poor teaching and sleeping in class. The simple fact is that someone, or possibly several people, prior had determined this teaching behavior to be at least acceptable. It is truly a sad state of affairs when we can see such nebulous criteria determining excellence. It is equally sad when instructional priorities are skewed as described by Stone and Clements (1998): "Thus good teaching has come to be thought of as teaching that is well received and that incidentally produces some degree of learning" (p. 3).

SUPPORT OF PROFESSIONAL ORGANIZATIONS

Polite conversation often laments the role that professional organizations/teacher unions play in the running of the schools. When one hears talk of teacher unions the perception is that of a very militant organization that runs rough-shod over principals, defends incompetent and lazy teachers, and adamantly fights any reforms that educational leaders and policymakers deem necessary to improve the schools. None of these perceptions are a fair assessment of what teacher unions actually do. Contrary to popular belief, unions neither support nor condone incompetent or lazy teachers. Local organizations of teacher unions are there to protect their members by seeing that due process is observed in maters of personnel, assignment, benefits, working conditions, and instruction. One aspect of union work that polite conversation seems to miss is that unions would have little to do if teachers were always treated fairly.

Local teacher organizations are part of the larger national and state organizations and the work done at each level is representative of the fact that education is a national concern, a state responsibility, and a local function (Webb & Norton, 1999). The primary work of state and national organizations is to lobby for the betterment of the profession. The American Medical Association, the American Dental Association, and the American Bar Association all fight to disallow or overturn frivolous or ill-informed legislation that would prevent these professionals from doing their best work or would create undue and nonbeneficial burdens. So it is with the work of national and state teacher organizations. The local organizations, however, focus on the day-to-day running of the schools and in creating working environments for members that are most conducive to effective education for the youngsters. The local organizations work with locally elected school officials and administrators to achieve these ends via a detailed contract specifying boundaries that each side will observe. Polite conversation seldom includes the fact that every detail of a union contract exists because it was once an issue that created undue and unnecessary hardships on teachers, took advantage of teachers, or created working conditions for teachers that simply were not fair.

It is often told that union contracts with strong seniority clauses undermine the authority of the principal in selecting the most qualified and appropriate staff to implement and support the programs of the school. Unfortunately, this does happen, but what is usually told in polite conversation is generally only a "half-truth." It is a matter of concern, particularly in large districts, that many teaching positions that would ordinarily require the most skilled and qualified are filled by seniority rather than an appropriate match between person, qualifications, and position. Although not the desired, there is a very good reason this scenario exists. We know that every clause in a union contract exists because it was once an issue that was not treated fairly. When such rules are not in place, unscrupulous administrators are free to make capricious and arbitrary personnel decisions on many bases other than qualifications. In school systems where such rules are not in place, it is not uncommon to see teaching positions that would ordinarily require an individual of extensive expertise filled by a novice teacher who may hold the paper credentials but is lacking in experience and professional maturity. Expertise in any discipline or profession comes about far more often from experience and longevity than the mere acquisition of credentials. While longevity and experience do not in and of themselves guarantee quality and commitment, or even that a person is particularly smart, there certainly is a much closer parallel between maturity and expert than novice and expert. Common sense aside, there are data supporting the fact that teachers of more experience are directly related to reduced rates of drop out and the likelihood that students will want to continue their education beyond high school (Berliner, 1993). When administrators are allowed to mask credentials as qualifications or expertise, we find this provision of union contracts doing exactly what it was intended to do—ensuring that decisions are made as closely as possible to qualifications rather than by flagrant favoritism, politics, or personal prejudices. Such a practice is hardly perfect and in the same manner that courts of law and judges make errors, seniority clauses do make errors as well. But seniority clauses do ensure that those who have labored in the system and "paid their dues" and acquired requisite real life experience have a fair shot at what is often the more desirable of situations. Additionally, such clauses serve to ensure that those who work in the system and the children who are educated by the system enjoy the expertise that years of experience brings.

It is difficult to sympathize with critics of seniority clauses when we have seen the reverse work to the detriment of the system so many times. Recently a colleague of mine was in line for a particularly desired secondary position and of all the applicants was clearly the most qualified in terms of credentials, experience, and past performance. The position required the individual to maintain and direct a choral program of national reputation that had been in place for over 30 years. The position was awarded to a novice teacher with no experience in such work. The quality of the program declined significantly within a year.

To an outsider looking in many of the provisions/clauses in a union contract may seem trite and/or exaggerated. To the teacher who has been victim to the excesses imposed by unscrupulous, thoughtless, or ill-spirited administration, such provisions are a blessing. To the elementary music, PE, or art teacher who has repeatedly been required to "keep" in excess of 120 children for two to three hours at a time so that classroom teachers can grade exams, a rule forbidding such treatment is most welcome. As an elementary choral director I knew for several years the disappointment and frustration of the nonteaching portion of my day (planning time) being greatly abused. The time was broken into intervals of 10, 15, and 20 minutes, the last of which was taken by duty and required weekly meetings. These tiny blocks of time were both useless and wasted as it was impossible to accomplish anything relative to planning and program management in those few minutes. The vice principal who created such a terrible situation insisted "it adds up to the same 45 minutes everyone else gets." A contract clause mandating that planning times cannot be broken into increments of less than 30 minutes might seem trivial. But to someone who spent several years without the luxury of a real restroom break and who was forced to do all planning and program management on his/her own time, it is far from trivial. Often one will find contract clauses stating that daily planning time cannot be routinely taken with meetings called by administrators. Many would think it reprehensible that such directives would need to be in writing, but such directives only exist when the issues at one time were, at the least, a problem for all concerned or at the worst, a source of administrative abuse.

Many years ago I taught in a large urban school system with a very strong and active teacher union. During my tenure with that school system some directives came from the union and the superintendent mandating that principals could only call one faculty meeting per month. The principal of my building was an excellent manager of programs, was respectful of people's time, and seldom called a faculty meeting anyway. Unfortunately, there were other building principals who were notorious for calling one or more faculty meetings weekly that would go on for hours. To those teachers victimized by such practices, such a directive was nothing short of relief. Another directive came that disallowed principals to dictate excessive details in lesson planning. Any plan of instruction will include an objective, the activity to meet the objective, the materials to be used, and the mode of evaluation to determine having met the objective. Apparently, there were principals demanding that each component of daily planning be written in a different color ink (and having to handwrite a second copy for the office), thereby exponentially but unnecessarily increasing the time needed to complete plans. The scenario may seem petty, but when what would ordinarily be a two- to three-hour task weekly is needlessly expanded into six to seven hours weekly, the issue is far from petty. Teacher unions only intervene in such matters when they are pushed beyond the scope of what can be considered reasonable, fair, and necessary.

UNFAIR FOCUS

It is often said in polite conversation that the schools are "so political." While this statement is true in one unfortunate aspect, another makes it an advantage. If we research the origins of the word politics, the word people appears. The schools are supposed to be about people. But the unfortunate aspect of the politics of education puts the teacher at a considerable disadvantage. The role of the teacher and other educators is often a very easy political target (Berliner & Biddle, 1995; Wirt & Kirst, 1992). Bracey (2000) (citing Schrag, 1997) states, "good news about schools serves no one's political reform agenda" (p. 3). This is so for several reasons:

1. The teacher's work is so visible to the public and under increasing scrutiny;
2. There is practically no one in society who has not experienced, or even possibly been victim to, the work of many teachers;
3. Only the most ill-informed and devoid of conscience would not want the teachers of society to be the best;
4. There is no air of mysticism or attitude of selectivity in the teaching profession as would be found in the practice of medicine, law, or accounting (Lebaree, 1999);
5. The education business is fully funded by public dollars. This can give the false illusion that education should cater to the wants, needs, and individual desires of every person in society.

This combination of factors causes the teaching profession often to become an easy but very unfair political scapegoat for matters that are far beyond the power base of teachers. It is well known that teachers, schools, and the education profession are frequently blamed for societal problems and failures that have nothing to do with schools and their function. It was the argument of Berliner and Biddle (1995) in their book that many, if not most, of the "problems" in schools today are created by overzealous politicians out of a need to fix something that really isn't broken.

While writing this book such a callous and unfair political maneuver aimed at teachers came to the forefront. The state legislature where I reside was in regular session and a bill was introduced that, if passed, would have ordered the mandatory drug testing of every teacher and school administrator in the state. Needless to say, the bill did not go very far as the knowledgeable people in the legislature could clearly see that it was an unwarranted political attack and not an effort to address a real problem. Consider the following:

1. While there probably are teachers, just like any others in society, who recreationally use drugs, it can hardly be realistically said that drug use among teachers is rampant, out of control, or by any means a problem that should necessitate legislative action;
2. By virtue of the average age of teachers in this state, their level of education, and lifestyle, teachers are far less likely to fall into a category or fit a profile of those likely to abuse drugs;
3. The cost to taxpayers to drug test that many people would have been staggering;
4. If the cost were not an issue, what could possibly have been gained by such a political action and such a potentially huge tax expenditure?

Obviously this house bill was not intended to solve a societal problem because such a problem did not exist. It was meant either to treat educators unkindly or create a pseudopolitical stance for a novice educator. Any political argument will favor one side over another while retaining a common link. The common link is a distracter to the public. Marker (2000) states:

> We need to stop blaming teachers and punishing students for the educational politics of neglect during the last two decades in California and across the nation. If the last twenty-five years are any indicator, politicians do not have the solutions to the education reform. Let's demand that those who are most invested in education—families and teachers—have a voice in determining the course of educational reform. (p. 8)

REAL SCHOOLS, REAL CHILDREN, REAL PROBLEMS

Several years ago I taught fourth grade in a rural school. It was a school year in which I did some serious rethinking about my role as a teacher, my personal and professional expectations, and the realization of what things I can and cannot change. I inherited a class of 26 children, 9 of whom were repeating fourth grade. When about one quarter of the class has failed the previous year, you start with a very unbalanced group, in both age and social maturity. There is a serious controversy in our business on the effectiveness of retaining children. This is a complicated question, but children who are repeating a grade are usually angry at being in the same grade for a second time. These were generally very poor children, many of whom came from home situations that we assume we would only read about in sociology books. Of the 26, only three were not on the free lunch program. At the time I was a 10-year veteran of teaching. I had been quite successful at managing groups of children and had established myself as a very capable disciplinarian. I had several years' experience teaching poor inner-city children, but never poor rural children. I was amazed at the lack of socialization and the simple lack of personal dignity among this group. At the time I was unable to see that their behavior was not an affront to the school, their education, or to me personally, but instead was simple survival skills.

As an example of the stress faced when so many children have so many varied needs, early on in the school year the school nurse came to the school to do the routine annual vision screening. Of my 26 children, 8 of them indicated a need for "preferential seating." This might seem a simple problem to solve, but there were only six front row seats in the classroom. There was a child in the group who had some serious health issues and had to be excused twice a day to take medications. Early into the school year the child's parent decided it was necessary for her to have a midmorning snack. These kinds of interruptions are certainly medically necessary, but add to the "things" a teacher has to remember, keep up, and document. The child was the source of many of the other children's jokes, and I had to constantly come to her aid. During the course of that school year, I would estimate that probably 75% of my life energy simply went into policing behaviors and maintaining order.

There was a young girl in the class, a repeater, whose behavior was such that I had never seen and have not seen since. Except for the days the girl was not in school, not a single day passed that she was not the greatest of disruptions. To this day I have never determined what triggered the child's behavior, but I learned quickly that when the tantrums started my only recourse was to see that other children were not within arms distance of her. By spring, the child had been suspended five times and had to go before a committee for an expulsion hearing.

Then again, there was a young boy, also a repeater, who seemed to have no idea as to boundaries in social behavior. The child would blurt out anything that came to his mind and did so on a number of occasions, the contents of which would be both inappropriate and offensive to repeat in this medium. In retrospect, there were many ways in which I could have better handled that child. He was the oldest of five (the fifth was born that school year), and he was practically raising his siblings. Their home was missing glass in many of the windows, and they frequently went without lights. His mother had some serious drug problems and had sold much of their furniture to support her habits. She would often come home in the middle of the night with a date, wake him, and force him to prepare them something to eat. I can see now that under those circumstances it was futile for me to truly expect that child to sit still at 8:00 a.m. while I teach him to read or expect him to stay awake all day. I learned the hard way that there are many things in a teacher's day that the teacher simply cannot control.

There was another child who was essentially being raised by his grandparents. A very few days into the school year, the grandmother was apparently unhappy with the demands for discipline that I was imposing on these children. She called me at home demanding to know some things such as where I had previously taught, why I was at this school, and so forth. She then verbally attacked me over the fact that I insisted that the students remain seated and reasonably quiet during dismissal and waiting for buses. I had realized by now that I was not dealing with a rational person and intended to end this conversation by telling her that I did not need to justify or explain why I would expect decent behavior and manners from any child. At this point, she yelled at her daughter across the room, but into the phone and my ear. Of course I hung up the phone. While she never yelled at me again, that was the first of several very strained conversations I would have with her during the school year. It still amazes me that the woman assumed it appropriate to call me at my home, on my time, and curse at me because I expected her child, and every other, to behave in an ordered and cooperative manner throughout the school day.

I could write volumes concerning the struggles I encountered during that school year. I taught in that school for another two years before leaving to pursue the doctorate. In my years as a public schoolteacher that year handed me the biggest collection of challenges. But the isolated events that I have described are not extraordinary occurrences and will not be too far outside the scope of experience for any public school teacher. Often those who have taught in the more desirable areas and school systems encounter such behaviors. I can say that my year with those children taught me four critical things:

1. The basic tenet of human psychology that states that one person cannot change the behavior of another is equally true of students and teachers. If a child is determined to yell vulgarities during a math lesson, the teacher is absolutely powerless to stop him/her from doing so.
2. No amount of detailed instructional planning will cause a child to cooperate if his/her intention is to be uncooperative.
3. When proper planning is in place, student misbehavior is not the fault of the teacher and as such, the teacher should not take such behavior personally.
4. Teachers must accept and recognize that there are matters over which they have absolutely no control.

DUAL SCHOOL SYSTEMS: FAILING OR HUMBLE? EXCELLENT OR ARROGANT?

Despite all we know and are continuing to learn, there still exists a phenomenon that some writers and researchers refer to as "dual school systems." This essentially is acknowledging the correlation of successful and failing schools to the schools serving the "haves" and the "have-nots." Social scientists argue that our society is without social class and that we are not a "caste" system. But at the same time polite conversation tells children that one can advance beyond the status of their birth by hard work, study, and "getting a good education." Unfortunately, the schools we see and in which educators must actually work tell an entirely different story. The schools are a reflection and cross section of society at large, and one need only take a few anecdotal glances at our schools to see the duality of what exists.

Schools that are successful are seldom discussed. Schools that are failing make a wonderful topic of polite conversation. But there are reasons for such dualities. Berliner (1993) describes it this way:

> Let me be clear. We have failing schools in this nation. But where they fail we see poverty, inadequate health care, dysfunctional families, and dysfunctional neighborhoods. Where our public schools succeed—in Princeton, New Jersey; in Grosse Pointe, Michigan; in Manhasset, New York—we see well-paying jobs, good health care, functional families, and functional neighborhoods. Families that can live in dignity send the schools children who have hope. Those children we can educate quite well. Families that have lost their dignity function poorly. They send us children with no hope for the future. Those children we cannot easily educate. (p. 40)

We find dual school systems—school systems serving the middle class and affluent, as opposed to serving the minority and the poor—wherever we have schools. We see the dual system in the same city, the same local districts, and even in the same classrooms (Schwebel, 1985). One system is generous, flowing with opportunity, abundantly productive, and generally indicative of a very polite and civilized way of life. On the other side we see a system in which resources are tight (if available at all), choice is virtually nonexistent, the graduates are less capable, and generally indicative of a way of life that is rough and vulgar.

The dual school system brings with it an inherent collection of common attitudes and values. In the more desired school systems we often find a mindset of entitlement. Although not without their share of real human problems, the families are comparatively stable. They hold responsible and well-paying professional positions, they are educated, and they diligently work to hold together the middle-class family values that are found in communities with successful schools. They have followed the rules and worked hard for what they have. Their way of life is not privilege but simply the reward for a job well done. In the less desirable school systems we most often see a mindset of simple survival. Through circumstances that are not necessarily their own fault we see families that are the antithesis of stable. In these school systems it is quite common to see grandparents or aunts raising children, not mothers and fathers. We do not see well-paying jobs supporting the household but instead whatever menial jobs can be found to supplement government entitlements. These households' members are not educated, as they are products of the undesirable school systems. In these households the values to be held in place are far from polite and civilized but are typical of those found with failing schools. Their focus is enough beds and food for everyone and safety in the event that violence erupts outside their doors. These people have not broken any societal rules and in their own day-to-day existence have not worked any less diligently than the middle-class parents of the desired school systems.

Their life and existence is not punishment for a job poorly done. It is simply the consequence of their status of birth.

Each system knows the other exists. Each system knows that their operation supports the status quo and perpetuates the disparities between the systems. Regardless of the unfairness of it all, school must go on and of course will continue to produce the huge discrepancies that everyone knows directly and perfectly correlates to what comes to school, not what is done at school. The educators who must work within the dual system will bear the burden of making it work and the blame when it doesn't.

In my own experience the failing/humble/excellent/arrogant mindset became abundantly clear on a day that test scores that ranked schools were published in the local paper. At the time I was teaching in a suburban school system that was considered a desirable place to live, teach, and send your children to school. This school system had done quite well in producing some impressive test scores, whereas the inner-city district next door presented some most humble scores. An individual walked into the teacher's lounge and made a most callous remark concerning the humble scores of the inner-city schools. I was really saddened to see such ignorance played out before me. I knew that the suburban school system was responsible for teaching a student population in which possibly 5% was living in true poverty. The inner-city schools were responsible for teaching a student population in which 50–60% or more was living in poverty. Common sense tells us we will see some serious differences. I thought to myself, "If this system is so blessed as to be teaching such a small population of poor children, then they better produce some really pretty test scores."

CREATED PROBLEMS

There exists another very real dichotomy between the dual school systems that is seldom discussed in polite conversation or even academic dialogue. In the poor school systems we know the problems that are brought to school contribute to the ineffectiveness of the system. In the poor school systems, the educator's role is quite clear-cut and the problems painfully visible. But the work of the affluent school system is not hampered by such social ineptitude as poverty, hunger, or violence. As such, it is not terribly uncommon to hear educators in the more affluent school systems complain of the "created problems"—problems that influence almost everything from instruction to personnel. These problems translate into little more than the creation of more "things" for the educators to do. Many of these things have little or nothing to do with instruction, are not required by local or state law, do not create a more effective learning environment, and often discourage qualified applicants (Darling-Hammond, 2001). In short, they are simply more "things to do." As an example, a number of years ago I taught in a relatively affluent suburban school system. Toward the end of the school year, when there is ordinarily a massive rush to complete required paperwork, we received directives that epitomized the "more things to do" syndrome. In the upper elementary grades, the children went to a different teacher for each subject, so every teacher taught every child in the grade level. As such, report cards and promotion/retention materials had to be passed among members of the grade-level team. The teachers were directed to pass around photocopies of the end of year reports on each child (which was a remarkable amount of paper) and have each teacher complete their portion of the grades and comments where appropriate. When the records were complete, each teacher would then recopy the entire set of documents for each child so that the final copies of the document would be in the same penmanship. It is hard for me to imagine a group of professionals anywhere in society who would have tolerated such mistreatment. Polite conversation seldom truly realizes the amount of paperwork that is really necessary for educators at the end of each grading period. In my experience, I have found it to be a more common complaint in the affluent districts that paperwork and documentation are taken to such an extreme as to be ridiculous. There is a school system in my experience that went to such extremes as to create an elementary report card that involved four full pages. When students would move to another state the schools would have to call and ask what all the information on the report card meant. The ultimate result was school systems in other states that would sneer at the silly arrogance rather than respect the effort.

The more common complaint from teachers in the well-to-do school systems is the inordinate amount of professional time that is tied up in meetings that are planned and required under the guise of staff development or program maintenance. To keep any organization running smoothly it is always necessary (on occasion) to have all the members in the same place at the same time. Such gatherings should facilitate open communication and allow for the exchange of ideas for improvement and upgrade of services. However, in view of the inexact work done by educators, such meetings are often taken to such an extreme as to become nonproductive, unduly burdensome, and wasteful of time that is so precious to educators in completing the plethora of noninstructional tasks required of them. In my own experience, I have known meetings to be called in which teachers were directed to "meet with grade level groups, discuss the school's mission philosophy, and write a reflective narrative describing how your personal philosophy fits within that of the school." It is not uncommon to have building administrators sit in on such meetings to see that teachers are in compliance. Meetings of this sort are not an inherently bad thing to do were it not for the issue of time. One can scarcely imagine an administrator so lacking in professional demands as to have the luxury of time to sit in on such meetings.

NOT ENOUGH TEACHERS

The political and media rhetoric often bypass and minimize the crucial teacher shortage this country is battling. Some media reports state that there are enough people in society who are credentialed as teachers, they simply are doing other things. This may very well be true since we know that one of three college graduates in teacher education will never teach and of those who do, one in five will leave within three years. This certainly makes for a lot of people in mainstream society who are trained and licensed as teachers but for whatever reason have never entered the profession or didn't stay long.

Other reports claim that there are enough teachers to fill classrooms around the country, they are just not distributed well because everyone wants to teach in the more desirable places. It is no secret that the least desired places with the most challenging children to teach have the worst time recruiting and retaining teachers. As Jonathan Kozol (1991) reported, many teachers may work for a year or so in the least desirable, inner-city schools, but as soon as they have some experience and are a bit more marketable, they move to the suburban districts for more money, better working conditions, and fewer social problems to face. One can hardly fault teachers for wanting to better themselves, but it does contribute to the perpetual problem of the least-experienced teachers working where the most experience is needed.

All their arguments make sense but are flawed in one way. Regardless of how we interpret the statistics of how many credentialed teachers are floating around in society or the demographics of where the current teaching force is located, one fact still remains. In some places as many as 40% of the classrooms in America simply do not have a qualified person to staff them. Further complicating the problem is the lack of persons with credentials in certain areas. For example, various reports indicate that upwards of 60% of those who teach math do not hold a math degree (Scherer, 2001). In my experience, I have frequently seen classrooms that did not have a permanent teacher the entire year but anecdotally, I see this happen less often in the more desired places to teach. This is a relatively common problem in the poor schools where no one wants to work. At the time of this writing I witnessed two classes in separate schools that were of the age to be required to take a high stakes exam that progressed through the school year with a string of substitute teachers. On the days when no substitute was available the children would be divided and distributed among other teachers in the building, regardless of grade level. One can imagine the frustration felt by these principals. Moving a permanent teacher from another class doesn't fix the problem—it simply passes it on to someone else. The percentage of people floating around in mainstream society with teaching credentials did no good for these principals and these children. A society full of credentials does not put teachers in classrooms.

Several years ago I was teaching in a suburban school system that was considered to be a more desirable place to teach mostly because the salaries were slightly higher and working conditions were rumored to be superb. A committee was convened to hire a replacement for a teacher who left early in the school year due to health problems. The committee interviewed four people for the position. We were disillusioned when the first two candidates who were offered the position turned it down. One had chosen to work for the Peace Corp and the other "did not want to teach here." The third accepted with some reservations. It was here that I came to realize the significance of how seriously short of teachers we are. Although we were considered the most desirable place to teach in the state, we still had to offer a classroom teaching position to three people before someone would accept it.

The realization of the need for capable teachers came home to me again a couple of years later. I was in the process of moving from the suburban school system to the inner-city schools to teach music and pursue some other interests. The phone rang one morning and a polite voice asked to speak with Dr. Norris. An elementary school principal enthusiastically offered me a position teaching first grade without ever having met me. I thanked the lady very kindly, explained that I was coming to the system to teach elementary music, but I was curious and asked how she had found me. She replied that she had seen my file on the corner of someone's desk in the personnel department. She saw male, certified teacher, advanced degrees, two decades in public education, experienced in teaching the primary grades, and wanted to "grab" me before someone else did. Before the conversation ended, the lady asked, "Dr. Norris, are you sure I couldn't convince you to come teach with us?" That simple phone conversation was certainly flattering but more humbling by forcing me to look one more problem in the face—one that is a little more water thrown on people who are drowning yet continuing to persevere and do the best they are able against insurmountable odds.

Recently, as teacher shortages have become more and more serious, school systems have begun to utilize recruiting practices similar to what many larger companies, and even churches, have used for many years. We are finding school systems, particularly in remote areas, vigorously recruiting and offering very attractive perks if teachers will choose and commit to work in their system for several years. Such perks include attractive sign-on bonuses (ranging from $1,000 to $20,000 to be paid over several years), moving expenses paid, and even paying closing costs on a home—an indicator the person intends to stay. In my experience I saw a tiny rural school system offer signing bonuses of $1,000 to all teachers, new and returning. It is fair to say that school systems are getting serious about attracting, recruiting, and retaining the best. But the long-term effectiveness of such efforts is still to be seen.

Several years ago I saw an acquaintance of mine use the annual review process to his advantage in a most unique and beneficial way. This individual had recently completed the MBA as well as passing the CPA exam and had already established himself well in the banking industry. When his annual review and performance evaluation came about, he did not negotiate for a higher salary. Instead, he negotiated for more time off. Interestingly, I hear similar arguments among educators quite often. By the time a person has taught for 20 years and earned an advanced degree in the interim, their salary, though nowhere near what it should be, is one you can live with. But when politicians talk of giving teachers a pay raise in exchange for more training, more days on the job, and so forth, I often hear it said, "Don't give me more money. Give me an extra hour each day without having to supervise children so I can complete the multitude of paperwork required of me."

Factoring into the question of too few teachers is an issue that Ingersoll (1999) refers to as unprepared and underqualified teachers. One must recognize that in this context unprepared and underqualified does not refer to incompetent or lazy teachers, but instead to teachers teaching out of their field or yet lacking a full teaching credential. According to Ingersoll, this problem is far more prevalent than polite conversation is aware. He states:

> I found, for example, that about a third of all secondary school teachers who teach *math* [emphasis in original] do not either have a major or a minor in math, math education, or related disciplines like engineering or physics. About one quarter of all secondary school *English* teachers have neither a major nor minor in English or related subjects such as literature, communications, speech, journalism, English education, or reading education. In *science*, slightly lower levels—about one fifth of all secondary school teachers—do not have at least a minor in the sciences or in science education. Finally, about a fifth of *social studies* teachers are without at least a minor in any of the social sciences, public affairs, social studies education, or history. (p. 27)

Ingersoll investigates several typically held opinions as to why so much out-of-field teaching occurs. Contrary to popular belief, it is not poor training on the part of education schools, nor is it unions with seniority clauses that cause such discrepancies. The basis of the problem is simply that there are not enough teachers to go around. We know that regardless of qualifications or certifications, there simply must be an adult at the front of the classroom. Administrators often have no choice but to "hire less-qualified individuals, assign teachers trained in another field or grade level to teach in the understaffed area, and make extensive use of substitute teachers" (p. 32).

Every state has their own laws concerning uncertified school personnel, but because of the absolute need for an adult's presence regardless of credentials, most states have generous loopholes that allow school administrators a great deal of relief in these areas. A choral director in my experience fell victim to such practices several years ago. The individual accepted a choral director position at a high school only to find that the assignment included two thirds of the instructional day teaching a class in which the individual had virtually no formal training. Apparently enrollment surges, coupled with several teachers on leave, created the need for more elective classes. This individual's training and primary purpose for joining the faculty (to direct a choral program) was marginalized by going on record as an "uncertified teacher." Consequently, this individual fell victim to the scenario described by Ingersoll.

It is often discussed that the rather large percentage of beginning teachers who do not stay in the profession contribute to teacher shortages. Croasmun, Hampton, and Hermann (1999) bring forth some useful data relative to teacher shortages. The percentage of new teachers who leave the profession quickly (within the first three years) for reasons of job dissatisfaction rather than marriage or other life changes is alarmingly high. However, the percentage of those leaving the profession decreases with the increase of years of experience. Additionally, there seems to be less likelihood of leaving the profession if they have pursued some level of graduate study in teacher education. The writers theorize that spending additional years or pursuing graduate study creates an "investment" in the profession, lessening the likelihood of leaving permanently.

There are many questions to be considered relative to the shortage of teachers, but one can be answered without reservation. There will continue to be a shortage of teachers until there is adequate support for the novice teacher and the workload is such that it is manageable and considered both reasonable and fair.

CONCLUDING THOUGHTS

The average sector of the American population has no clue what is asked and expected of the professionals comprising the workforce in American education. The arguments in this book have clearly shown that society imposes expectations on educators that would never be expected of similarly educated professionals in the private sector. With the exception of a few mean-spirited individuals, it would not make sense to assume that society makes such impositions in order to be cruel. Society makes such impositions out of a genuine but ill-informed concern for the betterment of our youth and a true desire for the system to work. It is often said that anyone who has been to school considers him- or herself to be an expert on education. Society speaks of supporting teachers and public education, but clearly we are not willing to bear the cost.

The political leaders who tout themselves as "involved in education" have no clue how damaging the "quick-fix" mentality is to the system. The legislators who truly believe that success or even excellence can be determined by one set of standardized test scores clearly do not understand that every day educators like me stand before children who have not eaten since they left school the day before. These political leaders do not see the children who must wear the same clothes for five days in a row because it is all they own. I do not believe these leaders understand that every day I stand before children who spent the night dodging gunfire. These leaders should know the heartbreak of seeing an 8-year-old child return to school and graphically describe for his classmates how his father's body convulsed violently while being struck by one bullet after another.

The shortage of teachers will continue to grow in direct proportion to the professional status, compensation, and treatment of teachers by the society that they serve. It should be an embarrassment to American society that many individuals who have made teaching their career want their own children to consider other career options. The seriousness of the teacher shortage is not a societal problem that can be hidden in the rhetoric. States across the country are all battling for the same pool of trained teachers. State A goes to State B to recruit teachers when State B is already critically short on qualified individuals. Perhaps the wake-up call will resound as more and more states begin to publish institutional report cards showing the percentage of teacher graduates who actually enter teaching and remain within the state where they were trained. The sad reality, however, is that no amount of publicly reported accountability data will make a difference until the cause of the problem is addressed and teaching becomes a more attractive option to the brightest and the best of society. Recently I spoke with a very insightful young man who was about to begin his first year of college intending to become a teacher. In the conversation he stated, "You know—the people who know the least about something will be the first to criticize." I would gather from the conversation that this young man is not entering the profession as blindly as some others.

My argument throughout this book has been that there is not a group of professionals in our society who are more dedicated to their mission yet treated so shabbily by the society they serve. From the perception of what teaching is about to what society demands, teachers and educators at all levels are mistreated by being unfairly held to a separate and virtually unattainable set of standards.

Bibliography

Abbott, J. (1998, January). Turning learning upside down and inside out. *School Administrator, 55,* 17–21.

Abbott, J., & Ryan, T. (1999, November). Constructing knowledge: Reconstructing schools. *Educational Leadership, 57*(3), 66–69.

Allalouf, A., & Ben-Shakhar, G. (1998).The effects of coaching on the predictive validity of scholastic aptitude tests. *Journal of Educational Measurement, 35*(1), 31–47.

American Educational Research Association. (2000). *AERA position statement concerning high-stakes testing in preK-12 education.* Retrieved April 8, 2001, from http://www.ggg-nrw.de/Lager/AERA.Stakes.html

Anderson, J. R., Reder, L. M., & Simon, H. A. (1996). Situated learning and education. *Educational Researcher, 25*(4), 5–11.

Apple, M. (1999, Summer). Why assess teachers? *Rethinking Schools Online, 13*(4), 1–5. Retrieved May 6, 2001, from http://www.rethinkingschools.org/Archives/13_04/assess.htm

Babbie, E. (1999). *The basics of social research.* Boston: Wadsworth.

Banks, C. G., & Murphy, K. R. (1985). Toward narrowing the research-practice gap in performance appraisal. *Personnel Psychology, 38*(2), 335–345.

Barth, R. S. (1990). *Improving schools from within.* San Francisco: Josey-Bass.

Berg, C. A., & Clough, M. (1991). Hunter lesson design: The wrong one for science teaching. *Educational Leadership, 48*(4), 73–78.

Berliner, D. C. (1993, April). Mythology and the American system of education. *Phi Delta Kappan, 74*(8), 632–640.

Berliner, D. C., & Biddle, B. J. (1995). *The manufactured crisis: Myths, fraud, and attack on America's public schools.* New York: Longman.

Black, P., & Williams, D. (1998, October). Inside the black box: Raising standards through classroom assessment. *Phi Delta Kappan, 80*(2), 139–148.

Blair, J. (1999). Teaching prospects show mixed SAT results. *Education Week, 18*(36), 8.

Block, B. (1992, September–October). They murdered the pigeons! The failure of state mandated teacher appraisal systems. *Clearing House, 66*(1), 35–36.

Boljonis, A., & Hinchman, K. (1988). Third graders' perceptions of reading and writing. In J. E. Readence & R. S. Baldwin (Eds.), *Dialogues in reading research: Thirty-seventh yearbook of the national reading conference.* Chicago: National Reading Conference.

Boze, D. (1999, May 25). An examination of class size reduction. *In Brief, 9*(2). Retrieved February 10, 2001, from http://www.effwa.org/website/publications/inbriefs/9–2.htm

Bracey, G. W. (1995, October). The fifth Bracey report on the conditions of public education. *Phi Delta Kappan, 77*(2), 149–160.

Bracey, G. W. (1998, May). TIMMS, rhymes with "dims," as in "witted." *Phi Delta Kappan, 79*(9), 686–687.

Bracey, G. W. (2000). High stakes testing. Center for Educational Research, Analysis and Innovation. University of Wisconsin. Retrieved April 8, 2001, from http://www.uwm.edu/Dept/CERAI/

Brandt, R. S. (1986, October). On the expert teacher: A conversation with David Berliner. *Educational Leadership, 44*(2), 4–9.

Brualdi, A. C. (1996). Multiple intelligences: Gardner's theory. *Eric Digest,* ED 410226.

Bruer, J. T. (1997). Education and the brain: A bridge too far. *Educational Researcher, 26*(8), 4–16.

Bruner, A. L. (1982). Stress producing conditions in the secondary classroom. ERIC No. ED 213699.

Burstein, L. (1990, Fall). Looking behind the "average": How are states reporting test results? *Educational Measurement: Issues and Practice, 9*(3), 23–30.

Bushweller, K. (1997, September). Teach to the test. *American School Board Journal, 184*(9), 20–25.

Bushweller, K. (1998, September). Other voices: Listening to what fellow teachers, parents and students have to say in teacher evaluation. *American School Board Journal, 185*(9), 24–26.

Camilli, G. (1999, Winter). Values and state ratings: An examination of the state-by-state education indicators in quality counts. *Educational Measurement: Issues and Practice, 18*(4), 17–25.

Cannell, J. J. (1988, Summer). Nationally normed elementary achievement testing in American public schools: How all 50 states are above average. *Educational Measurement: Issues and Practice, 7*(2), 5–9.

Cannell, J. J. (1989). How public educators cheat on standardized achievement tests: The Lake Wobegon report. ERIC No. ED 314454.

Chall, J. S. (2000). *The academic achievement challenge: What really works in the classroom?* New York: Guilford.

Chall, J. S., Jacobs, V. A., & Baldwin, L. E. (1990). *The reading crisis: Why poor children fall behind.* Cambridge, MA: Harvard University Press.

Charlesworth, R., Fleege, P. O., & Weitman, C. J. (1994). Research on the effects of group standardized testing on instruction, pupils and teachers: New directions for policy. *Early Childhood Development, 5*(3), 95–212.

Charters, M. (1998, March 9). Testing 1, 2, 3. *Publishers Weekly, 245*(9), 37–39.

Charters, M. (1999, March 1). Hitting the books. *Publishers Weekly, 246*(9), 37–39.

Cohen, P. (1995, September). Understanding the brain: Educators seek to apply brain-based research. *Education Update, 37.* Retrieved May 10, 2001, from http://www.ascd.org/pubs/eu/septu95.htm

Coulombe, G. (1994, July–August). Remembering Madeline Hunter. *Clearing House, 67*(6), 37.

Cremin, L. A. (1964). *The transformation of the school: Progressivism in American education 1876–1957.* New York: Vintage.

Croasmun, J., Hampton, D., & Hermann, S. (1999). Teacher attrition: Is time running out? Retrieved May 11, 2001, from http://horizon.unc.edu/projects/issues/papers/Hampton.asp

Cunningham, G. K. (2001). The culture of progressive education and the culture of the traditionalists. Retrieved May 11, 2001, from http://www.EducationNews.org

Dahl, K. L., & Freppon, P. A. (1995). A comparison of innercity children's interpretation of reading and writing instruction in the early grades in skill-based and whole language classrooms. *Reading Research Quarterly, 30*(1), 50–74.

Darling-Hammond, L. (1985). Mad-hatter tests of good teaching. In B. Gross & R. Gross (Eds.), *The great school debate: Which way for American education*. New York: Simon and Schuster.

Darling-Hammond, L. (1999, January–February). Educating teachers: The academy's greatest failure or its most important future? *Academe, 85*(1), 26–33.

Darling-Hammond, L. (2001, May). The challenge of staffing our schools. *Educational Leadership, 58*(8), 12–17.

Dauwalder, D. P. (2000, Winter). Formulating sound conclusions and recommendations. *Delta Pi Epsilon Journal, 42*(1), 6–13.

Davis, O. L. (2001, Winter). So what? *Journal of Curriculum and Supervision, 16*(2), 91–94.

Davis, S. M. (2000–2001, Winter). Look before you leap: Concerns about "brain-based" products and approaches. *Childhood Education, 77*(2), 100–101.

Donlevy, J. (2000). The dilemma of high stakes testing: What is school for? *International Journal of Instructional Media, 27*(4), 331–337.

Ducharme, E. R., & Agne, R. M. (1982). The education professoriate: A research based perspective. *Journal of Teacher Education, 32*(6), 30–36.

Dufay, F. R. (1966). *Ungrading the elementary school*. West Nyack, NY: Parker Publishing.

Duff, A. B. (1999, November 11). Failure of progressive education: Survey says employers find grads lacking basic skills. *Investor's Business Daily*. Retrieved December 1, 2001 from http://www.cblpolicyinstitute.org/duffy.htm

Dunkin, M. J. (1997). Assessing teachers' effectiveness. *Issues in Educational Research, 7*(1), 37–51. Retrieved May 4, 2001, from http://cleo.murdoch.edu.au/gen/iier/iier7/dunkin.htm

Education Week. (2001, April 5). Phonics and whole language. Retrieved April 17, 2001, from http://www.edweek.org/context/.../issuepage.cfm?id=1

Educational Testing Service. (1998). The latest on teachers: The good news and the bad news. Retrieved April 20, 2001, from http://www.ets.org/aboutets/thelatest.html

Eisner, E. W., & Peshkin, A. (Eds.). (1990). *Qualitative inquiry in education: The continuing debate*. New York: Teacher's College Press.

Fair Text Examiner. (1999, Winter). New Massachusetts teachers' test fails professional standards. Retrieved February 10, 2001 from http://www.fairtest.org.examar.../estestma.htm

Feistritzer, C. E. (1996). *Profile of teachers in the U.S.* Washington, DC: National Center for Educational Information. Retrieved on March 13, 2001 from http://www.ncei.com

Finn, C. E., Petrilli, M. J., & Vanourek, G. (1998, November 11). The state of the standards: Why most don't "cut the mustard." *Education Week, 18*(11), 56.

Fontenot, M. S. (1998, April 19). Don't hold teachers accountable for what they can't control. *Lake Charles American Press*, A11.

Gambrell, L. B. & Palmer, B. M. (1992). Children's metacognitive knowledge about reading and writing in literature based and conventional classrooms. In C. Kinzer & D. Leu (Eds.), *Literacy research, theory and practice: Forty-first yearbook of the National Reading Conference* (pp. 215–223). Chicago: National Reading Conference.

Gardner, E. (1989). Five common misuses of tests. ERIC No. ED 315429.

Gardner, H., & Hatch, T. (1990). Multiple intelligences go to school: Educational implications of the theory of multiple intelligences. *Educational Researcher, 18*(8), 4–9.

Georgia Department of Education. (1999, March 19). *Research and Policy Newsletter, 4*(11).

Gersten, R., Chard, D., & Baker, S. (2000, September–October). Factors enhancing sustained use of research-based practices. *Journal of Learning Disabilities, 33*(5), 445–457.

Gersten, R., & Unok Brengleman, S. (1996, March). The quest to translate research into classroom practice: The emerging knowledge base. *Remedial and Special Education, 17*(3), 67–74.

Gersten, R., Vaughn, S., Deshler, D., & Schiller, E. (1997, September–October). What we know about using research findings: Implications for improving special education practice. *Journal of Learning Disabilities, 30*(5), 466–476.

Gibbony, R. A. (1987, February). A critique of Madeline Hunter's teaching model from Dewey's perspective. *Educational Leadership, 44*(5), 46–50.

Gill, B., & Schlossman, S. (1996, November). A sin against childhood: Progressive education and the crusade to abolish homework. *American Journal of Education, 105*, 27–66.

Gitomer, D., Latham, A. S., & Ziomek, R. (1999). *The academic quality of prospective teachers: The impact of admissions and licensure testing.* Princeton, NJ: Educational Testing Service.

Glatthorn, A. A. (1999, Fall). Curriculum alignment revisited. *Journal of Curriculum and Supervision, 15*(1), 26–31.

Goldenberg, C., & Gillimore, R. (1991). Changing teaching takes more than a one-shot workshop. *Educational Leadership, 49*(3), 69–72.

Goldfien, S. D. (2000, July–August). Address of president-elect Steven D. Goldfien, M.D. to the House of Delegates. *California Society of Anesthesiologists Bulletin, 49*(4). Retrieved March 8, 2001 from http://www.calsocanes.com/bulletin.htm

Gordon, S. P., & Reese, M. (1997, July). High stakes testing: Worth the price? *Journal of School Leadership, 7*(4), 345–368.

Graham, S., & Harris, K. R.(1995). The effects of whole language on children's writing: A review of the literature. *Educational Psychology, 29*, 187–192.

Green, D. R. (1987, February). A guide for interpreting standardized test scores. *NASSP Bulletin, 71*(496), 23–35.

Gross, M. L. (1999). *The conspiracy of ignorance: The failure of American public schools.* New York: HarperCollins.

Grossen, B. (1996). What does it mean to be a research-based profession? University of Oregon. Retrieved November 12, 2000 from http://darkwing.uoregon. edu/bgrossen/resprf.htm

Grossen, B. (1998a). Child-directed teaching methods: A discriminatory practice of western education. University of Oregon. Retrieved on December 10, 2000, from http://darkwing.uoregon.edu/bgrossen.cdp.htm

Grossen, B. (1998b). What is wrong with American education? In W. M. Evers (Ed.), *What's gone wrong in America's classrooms*. Stanford, CA: Hoover Institution Press.

Grossen, B., Coulter, G., & Ruggles, B. (1998). Reading recovery: An evaluation of benefits and costs. University of Oregon. Retrieved December 10, 2000, from http://darkwing.uoregon.edu/bgrossen/rr.htm

Grossman, P. L. (1989, Winter). Learning to teach without teacher education. *Teacher's College Record, 91*(2), 191-208.

Guadagnino, C. (1998, April) Does standardization equal quality? *Physicians News Digest*. Retrieved June 29, 2001, from http://www.physiciansnews.com/ cover/498.htm

Gullatt, D. E., & Bullard, L. M. (1998, March). Choosing the right process for teacher evaluation. *American Secondary Education, 26*(3), 13–17.

Hadderman, M. (2000). Standards: The policy environment. ERIC No. ED 444239.

Haertel, E. H. (1999, Winter). Validity arguments for high stakes testing. *Educational Measurement: Issues and Practices, 18*(4), 5–9.

Hall, D. E. (1998). Class size and demographics: What 3rd grade test results suggest about their impact on achievement in New Hampshire. Report of the New Hampshire Center for Public Policy Studies, University of New Hampshire. Retrieved May 10, 2001, from http://www.unh.edu/ipssr/nhcpps/clsize/ clsize.html

Haney, W. M. (1988, Summer). Editorial. *Educational Measurement: Issues and Practice, 7*(2), 4, 32.

Hanushek, E. A., & Pace, R. R. (1994). Understanding entry into the teaching profession. In R. G. Ehrenberg (Ed.), *Choices and consequences: Contemporary policy issues in education*. Ithaca, NY: ILR Press.

Hardy, L. (2000, September). The trouble with standards. *American School Board Journal, 187*(9), 23–26.

Haug, I. E. (1999, Fall). Boundaries and the use and misuse of power and authority: Ethical complexities for clergy psychotherapists. *Journal of Counseling and Development, 77*(4), 411–417.

Herman, J. L., Abedi, J., & Golan, S. (1994, Summer). Assessing the effects of standardized testing on schools. *Educational and Psychological Measurement, 54*(2), 471–482.

Heynes, B. (1988). Educational defectors: A first look at teacher attrition in the NLS-72. *Educational Researcher, 13*(3), 24–32.

Hirsch, E. D. (1995). *The schools we need and why we don't have them*. New York: Doubleday.

Hirsch, E. D. (1997a, April 10). *Mathematically correct*. Address to the California State Board of Education. Retrieved on April 22, 2001, from http://ourworld. compuserve.com/homepages/mathman/edh2cal.htm

Hirsch, E. D. (1997b). Why traditional education is more progressive. Retrieved May 11, 2001, from http://www.theamericanenterprise.org/ taema97e.htm

Hirsch, E. D. (2000, Spring). "You can always look it up . . ." or can you? *American Educator*, 4–9.

Hirsch, E. D. (2001, Spring). The roots of the education wars. *Education Matters More*. Retrieved April 22, 2001, from http://www.edmattersmore.org/2001/sp/hirsch.html

Hoover, R. L, Farber, K., & Armaline, B. (2000). A brief response to the Youngstown Vindicator editorial of January 14, 2000. Retrieved on April 20, 2001, from http://cc.ysu.edu/~rhoover/ClassConnection/OPT/Vindicator_editorial1rebut.html

Hughes, L. W., & Hooper, D. W. (2000). *Public relations for school leaders*. Boston: Allyn and Bacon.

Hunter, M. (1985). What's wrong with Madeline Hunter? *Educational Leadership*, 42(5), 57–60.

Ingersoll, R. M. (1999, March). The problem of underqualified teachers in American secondary schools. *Educational Researcher*, 28(2), 26–37.

Innerst, C. (1999, May). Method madness: Why are public school teachers so poorly trained? *The Washington Monthly*, 31(5), 1–6. Retrieved May 30, 2001, from http://www.washingtonmonthly.com

International Reading Association. (1999, November). High stakes assessment in reading: A position statement of the International Reading Association. *Journal of Adolescent and Adult Literacy*, 43(3), 305–312.

Jacobs, H. H. (1997). Mapping the big picture: Integrating curriculum and assessment K–12. ASCD. Retrieved April 5, 2001, from http://www.ascd.org/readingroom/b.../jacobs97book.htm

Johnson, J. A., Dupuis, V. L., Musial, D., Hall, G. E., & Gollnick, D. M. (1999). *Introduction to the foundations of American education*. Boston: Allyn and Bacon.

Jones, R. (2000, September). Making standards work. *American School Board Journal*, 187(9), 27–31.

Kaestle, C. F. (1993, January–February). The awful reputation of educational research. *Educational Researcher*, 22(1), 25–31.

Kantrowitz, B., & Wingert, P. (2000, October 2). Teachers wanted. *Newsweek*, 37–42.

Kaufhold, J. (1998, December). What's wrong with teaching for the test? *School Administrator*, 55, 14–16.

Kellaghan, T., Sloane, K., & Alvarez, B. (1993). *The home environment and school learning: Promoting parental involvement in the education of children*. San Francisco: Josey-Bass.

Killian, L. J. (1992, Winter). A school district perspective on appropriate test-preparation practices: A reaction to Popham's proposals. *Educational Measurement: Issues and Practice*, 11(4), 13–15, 26.

Klinger, J. K., Vaughn, S., Tejero Hughes, M., & Arguelles, M. E. (1999, September–October). Sustaining research-based practices in reading: A 3 year follow-up. *Remedial and Special Education*, 20(5), 263–274, 287.

Knoll, M. (1996). Faking a dissertation: Ellsworth Collings, William H. Kilpatrick, and the "Project Curriculum." *Journal of Curriculum Studies*, 28(2), 193–222.

Kohn, A. (1999). *The schools our children deserve: Moving beyond traditional classrooms and "tougher standards."* Boston: Houghton Mifflin.

Kohn, A. (2000, December). High-stakes testing as ethnic cleansing. *Education Digest, 66*(4), 13–18.

Koretz, D. (1991). State comparisons using NAEP: Large costs, disappointing benefits. *Educational Researcher, 20*(3), 19–21.

Kovalik, S., & Olsen, K. D. (1998, May). How emotions run us, our students and our classrooms. *NASSP Bulletin, 82*(598), 29–37.

Kozol, J. (1991). *Savage inequalities: Children in America's schools.* New York: Harper-Collins.

Kramer, R. (1997, Winter). Inside the teachers' culture. *The Public Interest, 126,* 67–74.

Kysilka, M. L. (1989). Product or process: What is effective learning? University of Central Florida. Retrieved May 12, 2001, from http://reach.ucf.edu/~edg7221/product_V_process.html

Lamb, D. H. (1999, September 11). Addressing impairment and its relationship to professional boundary issues: A response to Forrest, Elman, Gizara and Vacha-Haase. *Counseling Psychologist, 27*(5), 702–711.

Languis, M. (1998, May). Using knowledge of the brain in educational practice. *NASSP Bulletin, 82*(598), 38–47.

Latham, A. S., Gitomer, D., & Ziomek, R. (1999, May). Supporting beginning teachers: What the tests tell us about new teachers. *Educational Leadership, 56*(8). Retrieved February 16, 2001 from http://www.teachingandlearning.org/rschnews/research/edtstnew.html

Lebaree, D. F. (1999, January–February). Too easy a target: The trouble with ed schools and the implications for the university. *Academe, 85*(1), 34–39.

Lemann, N. (1999). *The big test: The secret history of the American meritocracy.* New York: Farrar, Straus and Giroux.

Linn, R. L. (1993, Spring). Educational assessment: Expanded expectations and challenges. *Educational Evaluation and Policy Analysis, 15*(1), 1–16.

Linn, R. L., Graue, M. E., & Sanders, N. M. (1990, Fall). Comparing state and district test results to national norms: The validity claims that "everyone is above average." *Educational Measurement: Issues and Practice, 9*(3), 5–14.

Lorenzen, M. (2000). Education schools and library schools: A comparison of their perceptions by academia. Michigan State University. Retrieved October 21, 2000, from http://www.lib.msu.edu/lorenz1/libschool.htm

Madaus, G. F. (1985, Winter). Public policy and the testing profession: You've never had it so good. *Educational Measurement: Issues and Practice, 4*(4), 5–11.

Magestro, P. (1994, April). Tribute to Madeline Hunter. *Educational Leadership, 51*(7), 83.

Mangan, K. S. (1997, December 19). Some medical and nursing schools declare a truce and start to work together. *Chronicle of Higher Education, 44*(17), A10–A11.

Marker, P. (2000). Standards and high stakes testing: The dark side of a generation of political, economic and social neglect of public education. Retrieved December 21, 2000, from http://www.pipeline.com/.../MarkerOrlando.ht

Marsh, M. (1992, November 25). Twelve difficulties encountered when attempting to start a revolution in education. *Education Week, 12*(13). Retrieved December 1, 2001 from http://www.edweek.org/ew/ew_printstory.cfm?slug=12marsh.h12

Marshall, K. (1996, January). How I confronted HSPS (hyperactive superficial principal syndrome) and began to deal with the heart of the matter. *Phi Delta Kappan,* *71*(5), 336–345.

Mayo, R. Weidner. (1997, May–June). Trends in teacher evaluation. *Clearing House,* *70*(5), 269–271.

McGill-Franzen, A., & Allington, R. L. (1993, January–February). Flunk 'em or get them classified: The contamination of primary grade accountability data. *Educational Researcher, 22*(1), 19–22.

McGrath, H. (2001). The multiple intelligences model and years 5 to 8. *Victorian Curriculum and Assessment Authority.* Retrieved April 28, 2001, from http:// www.bos.vic.edu.au/csf/midyears/multintl.htm

McLaughlin, M. W. "Enabling Professional Development: What Have We Learned?" In A. Liberman and L. Miller (eds.) *Staff development for education in the 90's: New demands, new realities, new perspectives.* New York: Teachers College Press, 1991.

McNeil, L. M. (2000, June). Creating new inequalities: Contradictions of reform. *Phi Delta Kappan, 81*(10), 728–734.

Miller, D. W. (2001, March 2). Scholars say high-stakes tests deserve a failing grade. *Chronicle of Higher Education,* A14.

Murray, C. E., & Grant, G. (1998, Summer). Teacher peer review: Possibility or pipedream? *Contemporary Education, 69*(4), 202–204.

Nelli, E. (1984). A research-based response to allegations that education students are academically inferior. *Action in Teacher Education, 6*(3), 73–80.

Nelson, M. (1997). Are teachers stupid? Setting and meeting standards in social studies. ERIC No. ED 426035

Norris, J. (1996). Maybe the problem isn't whole language. *Journal of Children's Communication Development, 17*(2), 67–71.

Norris, N. D. (2001). *Practitioner perspectives on staff development experiences.* Manuscript submitted for publication.

Northeast Educational Foundation for Children (NEFC). (2000). http://www. responsiveclassroom.org/aboutus.htm

Olson, L. (1999, April 21). Tugging at tradition. *Education Week, 18*(32), 25.

O'Sullivan, R. G., & Page, B. (2000). Collaborative evaluation of schools attuned. ERIC No. ED 441824.

Oyler, C., & Becker, J. (1997). Teaching beyond the progressive-traditional dichotomy: sharing authority and sharing vulnerability. *Curriculum Inquiry, 27*(4), 453–467.

Palmaffy, T. (1997, November–December). See Dick Flunk. *Policy Review, 86.* Retrieved April 17, 2001, from http://www.policyreview.com/nov97/ flunk. html

Peterson, K. D. (1995). *Teacher evaluation: A comprehensive guide to new direction and practices.* Thousand Oaks, CA: Corwin Press.

Phelps, R. P. (1997, Fall). Are U.S. students the most heavily tested on earth? *Educational Measurement: Issues and Practice, 15*(3), 19–27.

Phelps, R. P. (1998, Fall). The demand for standardized student testing. *Educational Measurement: Issues and Practice, 17*(3), 5–23.

Phelps, R. P. (1999). Why testing experts hate testing. Fordham Report. Retrieved December 21, 2000, from http://www.edexcellence.net/library/ phelps.htm

Phillips, G. W. (1990, Fall). The Lake Wobegon effect. *Educational Measurement: Issues and Practice, 9*(3), 3, 14.

Phillips, G. W., & Finn, C. E. (1988, Summer). The Lake Wobegon effect: A skeleton in the testing closet. *Educational Measurement: Issues and Practice, 7*(2), 10–24.

Popham. W. J. (1987, February). Can high-stakes tests be developed at the local level? *NASSP Bulletin, 71*(496), 77–84.

Popham. W. J. (1993). *Educational evaluation.* Boston: Allyn and Bacon.

Popham. W. J. (1999, Fall). Where large scale educational assessment is heading and why it shouldn't. *Educational Measurement: Issues and Practice, 18*(3), 13–17.

Popham. W. J. (2000). *Testing! Testing! What every parent should know about school tests.* Boston: Allyn and Bacon.

Pressley, M., & Rankin, J. (1994). More about whole language methods of reading instruction for students at risk for early reading failure. *Learning Disabilities: Research and Practice, 9*(3), 157–168.

Prybylo, D. (1998, November). Beyond a positivistic approach to teacher evaluation. *Journal of School Leadership, 8,* 558–583.

Raebeck, B. (1994, June). The school as a humane business: Organizing problems out; designing productivity in. *Phi Delta Kappan, 75,* 761–765.

Ramos, D. (1996, April 3). St. Charles, St. John teachers lag in degree tally. *The Times-Picayune,* B1, B2.

Rasinski, T. V., & DeFord, D. E. (1985). Learning within a classroom context: First graders conception of literacy. ERIC No. 262 393.

Ravitch, D. (1985). *The schools we deserve: Reflections on the educational crises of our time.* New York: Basic Books.

Ravitch, D. (1998, December 16). What if research really mattered? *Education Week, 18*(16), 33–34.

Ravitch, D. (2000). *Left back: A century of failed school reform.* New York: Simon and Schuster.

Reducing class size: What do we know? Retrieved October 10, 2000, from http://www.ed.gov/pubs/ReducingClass/Class_size.html

Robelen, E. W. (2000, May 24). Louisiana set to retain 4th, 8th graders on state exam. *Education Week, 19*(37), 24.

Roberts, R. B. (1991) Writing abilities of first graders: Whole language and skills-based classrooms. ERIC No. ED 341 981.

Rothstein, R. (1993, March 21). The myth of public school failure. *The American Prospect, 4*(13). Retrieved April 19, 2001, from http://www.prospect.org

Rothstein, R. (1999, December 6). Blaming teachers. *The American Prospect, 11*(2). Retrieved April 19, 2001, from http://www.prospect.org

Sacks, P. (1999). *Standardized minds: The high price of America's testing culture and what you can do about it.* Cambridge, MA: Perseus Books.

Savage, D. (1989, August). The press and education research: Why one ignores the other. ERIC No. 311464.

Scheirer, M. A., & Kraut, R. E. (1979, Winter). Increasing educational achievement via self-concept change. *Review of Educational Research, 49*(1), 131–150.

Scherer, M. (2001, May). Improving the quality of the teaching force: A conversation with David C. Berliner. *Educational Leadership, 58*(8), 6–10.

Schmoker, M. (1992, May 13). What schools can learn from Toyota of America. *Edu-*

cation Week, 11(35). Retrieved December 1, 2001 from http://www.edweek.org/ew/ew_printstory.cfm?slug=34schm.h11

Schrag, P. (1997, October). The near-myth of our failing schools. *Atlantic Monthly, 280*(4), 72–80.

Schwebel, M. (1985). The other school system. In B. Gross & R. Gross (Eds.), *The great school debate: Which way for American education?* New York: Simon and Schuster.

Searfoss, L. W., & Eng, B. J. (1996, March). Can teacher evaluation reflect holistic instruction? *Educational Leadership, 53*(6), 38–41.

Sewall, G. T. (2000, Summer). Lost in action: Are time consuming trivializing activities displacing the cultivation of active minds? *American Educator,* 4–9, 42–43.

Shea, C. (2000, May–June). It's come to this. *Teacher,* 32–41.

Shepard, L. A. (1990, Fall). Inflated test score gains: Is the problem old norms or teaching the test? *Educational Measurement: Issues and Practices, 9*(3), 15–22.

Singley, M. K., & Anderson, J. R. (1989). *Transfer of cognitive skills.* Cambridge, MA: Harvard University Press.

Skinner, B. F. (1968). *The technology of teaching.* New York: Appleton-Century-Crofts.

Slavin, R. E. (1987a, April). The Hunterization of America's schools. *Instructor,* 56–58.

Slavin, R. E. (1987b). The PET and the pendulum: Faddism in education and how to stop it. *Phi Delta Kappan, 70*(10), 752–758.

Slavin, R. E. (2001, March). Show me the evidence. *American School Board Journal, 188*(3), 26–29.

Sousa, D. A. (1998a, January). The ramifications of brain research. *School Administrator, 55,* 22–25.

Sousa, D. A. (1998b, December 16). Is all the fuss about brain research justified? *Education Week, 18*(16), 52.

Stahl, S. A., McKenna, M. C., & Pagnucco, J. R. (1994). The effects of whole language instruction: An update and a reappraisal. *Educational Psychologist, 29,* 175–186.

Steinberg, L., Bradford Brown, B., & Dornbusch, S. M. (1996). *Beyond the classroom: Why school reform has failed and what parents need to do.* New York: Simon and Schuster.

Sternberg, R. J., Grigorenko, E. L., & Jarvin, L. (2001, March). Improving reading instruction: The triarchic model. *Educational Leadership, 58*(6), 48–51.

Stone, J. E. (2000a). Aligning teacher training with public policy. *The State Education Standard, 1*(1), 35–38.

Stone, J. E. (2000b, December 7). *Teacher training and Texas education reform.* Speech presented to Public Education Reform in Texas, Austin.

Stone, J. E., & Clements, A. (1998). Research and innovation: Let the buyer beware. In R. R. Spillane & P. Regnier (Eds.), *The superintendent of the future.* Gaithersburg, MD: Aspen Publishing.

Stout, M. (2000). *The feel-good curriculum: The dumbing down of America's kids in the name of self-esteem.* San Francisco: Perseus Books.

Sylwester, R. (1998, January). The brain revolution. *School Administrator, 55,* 6–10.

Tanner, D. (1998, January). The social consequences of bad research. *Phi Delta Kappan, 79*(5), 344–349.

Tanner, D. E. (1995). The competency test's impact on teachers' abilities. *The Urban Review, 27*(4), 347–351.

Taylor, D. L., & Bogotch, I. E. (1993). Teacher working conditions and school reform. ERIC No. ED 357473.

Taylor, J. A., & Baker, R. A. (2001). High stakes testing and the essential curriculum. CBE, BE Online Edition. Retrieved May 25, 2001, from http://www.c-b-e.org/be/iss0101/a3taylor.htm

Thomas B. Fordham Foundation. (1995–1996). *Standards: Much talk, not much action.* Part II. Retrieved April 10, 2001 from http://www.edexcellence.net/library/epcn.html

Toch, T. (1991). *In the name of excellence: The struggle to reform the nation's schools, why it's failing, and what should be done.* New York: Oxford University Press.

Varble, M. E. (1990, May–June). Analysis of writing samples of students taught by teachers using whole language and traditional approaches. *Journal of Educational Research, 83*(5), 245–251.

Vaughn, S., Klinger, J., & Hughes, M. (2000). Sustainability of research-based practices. *Exceptional Children, 66*(2), 163–171.

Von Blum, P. (1986). *Stillborn education: A critique of the American research university.* Lanham, MD: University Press of America.

Walker, M. H. (1996). What research really says. *Principal, 74*(4), 41, 43.

Webb, L. D., & Norton, M. S. (1999). *Human resources administration: Personnel issues and needs in education.* Columbus, OH: Prentice-Hall.

Weiner, H. (1999, Winter). Comparing the incomparable: An essay on the importance of big assumptions and scant evidence. *Educational Measurement: Issues and Practice, 18*(4), 10–16.

Wheeler, D. L. (1998, September 11). Neurologists take stock of brain research studies. *Chronicle of Higher Education, 45*(3), A20–A21.

White, W. F., Burke, C. M., & Hodges, C. A. (1994, September). Can Texas teacher certification be predicted from SAT scores and grade point averages? *Journal of Instructional Psychology, 21,* 298–299.

Willie, C. V. (1985, May). The problem of standardized testing in a free and pluralistic society. *Phi Delta Kappan, 66*(19), 626–628.

Wirt, F. M., & Kirst, M. W. (1992). *Schools in conflict: The politics of education.* Berkeley, CA: McCutchen Publishing.

Wood, C. J. (1992, March). Toward more effective teacher evaluation: Lessons from naturalistic inquiry. *NASSP Bulletin, 76,* 52–59.

Worthen, B. R., Sanders, J. R., & Fitzpatrick, J. L. (1997). *Program evaluation: Alternative approaches and practical guidelines.* New York: Longman.

Wraga, W. G. (1999, Fall). The educational and political implication of curriculum alignment and standards based reform. *Journal of Curriculum and Supervision, 15*(1), 4–25.

Wu, H.-H. (1999, Fall). Basic skills versus conceptual understanding: A bogus dichotomy in mathematics education. *American Educator,* 1–7.

Yekovitch, F. R. (1994, April). Current issues in research on intelligence. *Eric Digest,* ED385605.

Zakutansky, T. J., & Sirles, E. A. (1993, Fall). Ethical and legal issues in field education: Shared responsibility and risk. *Journal of Social Work Education, 29*(3), 338–346.

Index

About the Author

Norman Dale Norris, Ed.D., has worked in public education for 20 years with experience as a choral director at all levels, classroom teacher, teacher trainer, and university instructor. As an advocate for the development of choral performing programs for children's voices, his performing groups have consistently been ranked as superior at the regional and state levels. Dr. Norris holds undergraduate and master's degrees in music education and piano and a doctorate in school management and instructional leadership.

Dr. Norris is in demand as a speaker, lecturer, teacher trainer, and university teacher. He has published articles on staff development and often lectures on staff development and other professional issues. He is frequently requested to teach graduate courses in educational administration, supervision, foundations, and research.

A resident of New Orleans, Louisiana, Dr. Norris is the father of a teenage daughter and enjoys historical home restoration. This publication is his first book.